INTELLIGENCE for EARTH

Clarity, Diversity, Integrity, & Sustainability

Robert David Steele

Companion and Sequel to
COLLECTIVE INTELLIGENCE: Creating a Prosperous World at Peace

Earth Intelligence Network
Oakton, Virginia

Available by Box of 20 at 50% Retail
Facsimile Orders at 80% Retail: (703) 281-0888

Published by Earth Intelligence Network   February 2010
Post Office Box 369, Oakton, Virginia 22124
www.earth-intelligence.net

Cover graphic combines two photographs from the National Aeronautical and Space
Administration (NASA). The Earth by itself is available in a round color sticker as Item
Apollo 17(E) from EarthSeals, POB 8000, Berkeley, CA 94707.

Jacket design and interior layout by Deb Tremper, www.sixpennygraphics.com

Printed and bound in the United States of America

9 8 7 6 5 4 3 2

LIBRARY OF CONGRESS CATALOGING-IN-PUBLICATION DATA

STEELE Vivas, Robert David, 1952-
    INTELLIGENCE for EARTH: Clarity, Diversity, Integrity, & Sustainability/by
Robert STEELE Vivas (Author)
    p. cm.
Includes bibliographical references and free online searchable "virtual" index.
ISBN 13: 978-097-15661-7-0 (alk. paper)
ISBN-10: 0-971-5661-7-8 (alk. paper)
1. Collective intelligence. 2. Cognitive science. 3. Mass collaboration. 4. Distributed
cognition. 5. Macrocognition. 6. Open source. 7. Peer production. 8. Internet.
9. Decision-support. 10. Public intelligence. 11. Organizational intelligence.
12. Commercial intelligence. 13. Peace intelligence. 18. Information science—social
aspects. 19. Collaboration. 20. Cognitive bias. 21. Distributed problem solving.
I   Title
JK-468-16574 2010 1
327.1273—dc21   00-029284

Table of Contents

An index is not provided because this is a hybrid book with all notes and many key persons or ideas hyper-linked to their original source. The easily searched digital book is free online at http://www.phibetaiota.net/?p=19357.

Figures

IV TECHNICAL INTELLIGENCE—CLARITY   207

Preface

The truth at any cost reduces all other costs. I am a recovering spy who in 1988 discovered that virtually all of our very expensive secret sources and methods were largely worthless in terms of decision-support to policy-makers, acquisition managers, and operational field commanders. Today the US taxpayer funds a $75 billion a year intelligence-industrial-congressional complex (alongside a $750 billion a year military-industrial-congressional complex), and the verdict is in: the secret world provides, "at best" 4% of a top commander's knowledge; and in my own findings and those of the US Army Strategic Studies Institute (SSI) and others, the Pentagon is optimized for 10% of the threat—state on state high-intensity conflict. Today in both Afghanistan and Iraq, our earnest warriors are turning to open sources of information, and striving to create human capabilities that yield no profit to the beltway bandits but actually accomplish the mission. We wage war badly while the Chinese and others wage peace very effectively.

This week (of 23 February 2010) the Secretary of Defense Dr. Robert Gates has lambasted the Europeans, and The Netherlands in particular, for being averse to war, calling their demilitarization and their "mood" a "danger to peace." I am not making this up—this is how insane a world power without responsible intelligence (decision-support) can get. Dr. Gates, like all professional civil servants and most senior political appointees, is a good person trapped in a bad system—a badly broken system that cannot connect means (revenue), ways (force structure), and ends (desired outcomes) because it has become so corrupt, so vested in the special interests who receive the taxpayer funds rather than in the public interests of those who pay the taxes, that it is an abomination—an outrage, a scandal, a crime against humanity, not just the US taxpayer, but against all humans who suffer the ignorant, ideological decisions of the American political and policy apparatus acting "in our name" but not in our best interests. This book is my personal effort to offer an alternative paradigm, vastly updated since I first did so in an article, E3i: Ethics, Ecology, Evolution, and Intelligence (An Alternative Paradigm for National Security), published in the *Whole Earth Review* (Fall 1992). Sandra Cruzman, my former boss and then the senior female for the entire Central Intelligence Agency (CIA) is reported by Ross Stapleton-Gray, our mutual colleague, to have said "This confirms Steele's place on the lunatic fringe."

I cite that ignorant and arrogant condemnation of my work then because I and others like me continue to be ignored by the "establishment" that is so deeply rooted in its bad practices and its corrupt feed-back loops that from their point of view, I remain on the lunatic fringe, at best a crank and at worst a traitor. Such views shame the Republic—America the Beautiful.

There is something terribly wrong when those in power are so insulated from reality that they can send to war hundreds of thousands of the citizen-soldiers who are supposed to be sovereign over the administrative government; kill with impunity across many sovereign borders, murdering civilians at a 10 to 1 ratio for every ostensible but generally unconfirmed terrorist "target" they hit with very expensive drone munitions—and they can continue to do this without regard to which party of the two-party tyranny is in power. America is committing suicide by allowing the two-party tyranny and Wall Street to continue to dictate how taxpayer revenue is spent. ENOUGH!

I do not favor a violent over-through of the administrative government, and am troubled by the hanging of census workers by vigilante mobs, the crashing of an airplane into an Internal Revenue Service (IRS) office, and many other signs of deep anger that I first began to understand when I read *Harvest of Rage* followed by *Deer Hunting With Jesus*

My proposed solution for creating a prosperous world at peace is to actualize the vision and understanding of so many others, creating the World Brain with an embedded Global Game; creating an informed public and as quickly as possible among the five billion poor, a connected public armed with cell phones and able to access education and information "one call at a time."

Five sentences summarize my knowledge as of today:

1. There is PLENTY of wealth—money, knowledge, everything—with which to create a prosperous world at peace.

2. We know all we need to know, but the knowledge is fragmented while the wealth is concentrated, and those are the two obstacles to achieving human consciousness and a prosperous world at peace.

3. Confiscating ill-gotten gains is *not* the answer for it will not meet the need. Only the creation of infinite revolutionary wealth will create a prosperous world at peace.

4. The *only* means by which we can create infinite revolutionary wealth is by leveraging the one inexhaustible resource we have, the human mind, spirit, and imagination.

5. The *only* means by which we can actualize the full consciousness of humanity is by connecting the five billion poor to knowledge "one cell call at a time" because in the aggregate, we only achieve our Collective Intelligence when we are Whole.

My path to the above simple ideas is in the pages that follow.

I beg of the reader patience. I read in 98 non-fiction categories, and this book is a hybrid book that instead of endnotes offers active links throughout the book. While sold at cost and recommended for reading first in hard-copy, the book is also free online with all links active, and is the best offering I can give to humanity—a portal into over 1,500 non-fiction works that in the aggregate make it clear that the only thing standing between us and a prosperous world at peace is our own ignorance, our own lethargy, and our remarkable tolerance for corruption across all governments, corporations, and non-governmental organizations. By withdrawing our financial support from political parties, governments and corporations, we can restore the commons.

There are four books, one of them a United Nations report, which changed my life, each of them in isolation at first, and most recently, in the aggregate, as Tom Atlee's latest book introduced me to the fourth book, which brought to closure my two year struggle to define this book

Of course I have been influenced by the many others books I have reviewed at Amazon and at Phi Beta Iota, the Public Intelligence Blog, but these four are rather special, and there is no finer way to introduce this book than by giving credit where it is due, to three individual minds and one group that have inspired me to become intelligence officer to the public.

2003 *The Tao of Democracy–Using Co-Intelligence to Create a World That Works for All*

My review of 30 November 2003 described this book as **Utterly Sensational— Basic Book for Humanity.** My full review need not be repeated, I will just say that it was this book that opened my eyes to how the Internet has opened the door for a cross-fertilization of knowledge and emotion and concern across all boundaries such as the world has never seen before, and it has made possible a new form of structured collective intelligence.

It was *also* this book that made it clear to me that the Internet was nothing more than a means of connecting human minds, it is not now and never will be a substitute for humanity coming together face to face and as a community of spirit and imagination. In addition to this book was Tom's gentle outreach in the form of his DVD *Group Wisdom: Making Magic*, (still available for a donation of $110 to the Co-Intelligence Institute, mention the DVD) that introduced me to what surely must be the diametric opposite to the world of spies, the world of Open Everything.

Most recently Tom has been called to publish *Reflections of Evolutionary Activism*, a capstone work to which my own book now is intended to be a companion.

2004 _A More Secure World—Our Shared Responsibility—Report of the Secretary-General's High-level Panel on Threats, Challenges and Change_

Although I read this report when it first came out in 2004 free online (I sent it to be printed), it was not until 2008 that I reviewed the for sale version at Amazon, entitling my review of 8 May 2008 **Seminal Work that Redirected My Life.** I meant it then and I mean it now. This report is a world-changing one.

This book literally blew my mind into smithereens in part because LtGen Dr. Brent Scowcroft, USAF (Ret) was the American representative, and in part because for the first time in modern history, the high-level threats to humanity were placed in priority order:

01 Poverty	06 Genocide
02 Infectious Disease	07 Other Atrocities
03 Environmental Degradation	08 Proliferation
04 Inter-State Conflict	09 Terrorism
05 Civil War	10 Transnational Crime

I cannot over-state the force with which this list hit me. I suddenly realized that the Panel had delivered one side of a strategic matrix for creating a prosperous world at peace—I and the other 23 co-founders of EIN went on to identify the twelve core policies (more on all this later) that must be harmonized among nations, corporations, organizations, and communities.

Despite the existence of other superb books, such as _High Noon 20 Global Problems, 20 Years to Solve Them; The Future of Life_; and _Plan B 3.0: Mobilizing to Save Civilization, Third Edition_, no one—no one—had created a list in priority order that calls into question every national security budget on the planet, but especially that of the USA.

2005 *The Fortune at the Bottom of the Pyramid–Eradicating Poverty Through Profits*

Writing on 9 December 2005, I summarized: **Nobel Prize Material–Could Transform the Planet.** Here's the math that I was surprised to not see in the book: the top billion people that global businesses focus on are worth less than a trillion a year in potential sales. The bottom four billion, with less than $1000 a year in disposable income, are worth four trillion a year in potential sales.

Driving the point home the author observes that the top billion can afford disposable sub-zero refrigerators, while the bottom four billion need a two-dollar ceramic refrigerator consisting of two long-necked containers with an air gap between them; buried in the ground it will keep meat fresh for five days.

As the US Department of Defense is now discovering, its $750 billion a year budget is being spent on a heavy metal military useful only 10% of the time. Stabilization and Reconstruction are a much more constructive form of national defense, because if we do not address poverty and instability globally, it will inevitably impact on the home front. This author has presented the most common sense case for turning business upside down. He can be credited with a paradigm shift, those shifts that Thomas Kuhn tells us in *The Structure of Scientific Revolutions* come all too infrequently, but when they come, they change the world. It may take years to see this genius implemented in the real world, but he has, without question, changed the world for the better with this book, and made global prosperity a possibility.

See also *The Bottom Billion–Why the Poorest Countries are Failing and What Can Be Done About It*; *Creating a World Without Poverty–Social Business and the Future of Capitalism;* and *Capitalism at the Crossroads–The Unlimited Business Opportunities in Solving the World's Most Difficult Problems.*

Finally in 2009, and here I again credit Tom Atlee and his most recent book, I was introduced to the concepts of cultural and non-zero evolution.

2009 *Nonzero–The Logic of Human Destiny*

Published in 2001, I read and reviewed this book 28 November 2009, summing it up as **Beyond 6 Stars–Nobel Prize (Of Old, Before Devalued).**

QUOTE: "Non-zero-sumness is a kind of potential–a potential for overall gain, or for overall loss, depending on how the game is played."

This book is one of the most sophisticated, deep, documented, and influential I have ever read, right up there with *Consilience: The Unity of Knowledge*. Published in 2000, this book has NOT received the marketing promotion or the public attention it merits. *This book has substantially altered my perception.*

Historically rooted, this book takes a very long view, and discerns patterns in history that I find credible. In brief, cultural evolution is the advance in social complexity and the means of dealing with complex challenges facing dense complex social systems. It is rooted in the advance of technology with particular respect to the technologies of communication, transportation, and energy, but culture is itself a "technology" that is "at bottom a way of learning from the learning of others without having to pay the dues they paid."

The author teaches me a new understanding of war and conflict and a new appreciation for "barbarians" that are not barbarians at all, merely different cultures that sense weakness or injustice in "our" culture and exercise a cleansing aspect. Bin Laden, with his opposition to the pathologically criminal "royal" family in Saudi Arabia, and the US military presence in Saudi Arabia–and the many others who oppose the US Government's bi-partisan affection for 42 of the 44 dictators willing to do rendition and torture at our behest, can easily be perceived by those who are ideologically-blinded to be such a "barbarian," while billions of others see him as a "freedom fighter."

See my much longer review at Phi Beta Iota, and also *Holistic Darwinism: Synergy, Cybernetics, and the Bioeconomics of Evolution*.

Although I had understood the concepts of *Infinite Wealth* (Barry Carter), *Wealth of Networks* (Yochai Benkler), *Wealth of Knowledge* (Thomas Stewart), and *Revolutionary Wealth* (Alvin Toffler, who also gave us *Powershift—Knowledge, Wealth, and Violence at the Edge of the 21st Century*) prior to reading *Non-Zero*, this last book was the book that finally made my own new book possible. This was the book that persuaded me I must stop wasting my time trying to educate governments, and instead go directly to the people.

Industrial-Era organizations—governments, corporations, foundations, non-profits—are replete with fraud, waste, and abuse. They are ignorant, inefficient, and more often than not they are operating on behalf of special interests rather than in the public interest.

It's time We the People got back in touch with *The Compassionate Instinct—The Science of Human Goodness*—and created a prosperous world at peace.

Lest this book be considered too idealistic, I respectfully recommend that it be read together with the first book organized by EIN, *COLLECTIVE INTELLIGENCE: Creating a Prosperous World at Peace*. The 55 authors represent the clarity, diversity, integrity, and sustainability that I believe is imminently achievable.

Free Online Copy of This Book

Http://www.phibetaiota.net/?p=19357

with all links active therein...

Part I

STRATEGIC INTELLIGENCE— SUSTAINABILITY

Creating a Prosperous World at Peace

Part I consists of seven chapters addressing the United Nations (UN) as the interim foundation for creating the World Brain originally envisioned by H. G. Wells in 1936 and also explored in the *Encyclopédie française* in 1937. Prior to the imagining of the World Brain Pierre Tielhard de Chardin introduced the concept of *noosphere* as the essence of his Law of Complexity/Consciousness in which social networks evolved toward the Omega Point of perfect integration and harmonization.

In more recent times, the idea has been developed further, both in the sense of a total construct such as *Global Mind* or *Global Brain*, and in the sense of *One from Many*, *Conscious Evolution*, *Collective Intelligence*, and *Evolutionary Activism*.

A virtual flood of books inspired by the potential of human minds working together in the aggregate is also emerging, along two lines: those books exploring *The Fortune at the Bottom of the Pyramid* and the potential wealth creation associated with empowering the five billion poor with Information and Communication Technologies (ICT); and those examining the *Wealth of Networks* and the role that social production divorced from traditional money might play in creating *Revolutionary Wealth* or *Infinite Wealth*.

At the same time, the long-standing literature on the power of the public such as *A Power Government Cannot Suppress* and *The Power of the Powerless* has been followed by a new form of emphasis on collective intelligence or the

1

aggregate capacity of humanity, addressed in such books as _Smart Mobs_, _Army of Davids_, _Wisdom of the Crowds_, _Smart Nations_, and _Public Intelligence_ as well as _Here Comes Everybody–The Power of Organizing Without Organizations_, _Mobilizing Generation 2.0–A Practical Guide to Using Web2.0 Technologies to Recruit, Organize and Engage Youth_; and _Groundswell–Winning in a World Transformed by Social Technologies_.

Nothing about this book is intended to suggest that the UN is now or ever should be any kind of World Government. Rather, the proposal is put forward that the UN, as the most global and multi-functional of the Industrial-Era enterprises, is well-suited to being an intermediate enabler of the transformation from a past in which organizations sought to control information for selfish advantage, to a future in which we actually achieve the visions of Pierre Tielhard de Chardin and H. G. Wells, among others, and find that the Omega Point connects all humans with all information in all languages all the time, and furthermore makes it possible for _Panarchy_ instead of Anarchy to be the condition of humanity.

The purpose of this book is set forth the means, ways, and ends for creating a World Brain Institute with an embedded Global Game such that governments and corporations become—over time—largely disembodied, replaced by an infinite number of self-organizing human social networks that are characterized by clarity of purpose, diversity of view, integrity of exchange, and sustainability of process. J. F. Rischard, at the time Vice President of the World Bank for Europe, inspired me with his concept of Global Issue Networks as set forth in _HIGH NOON: 20 Global Problems, 20 Years to Solve Them_.

Chapter 1, Strategic Intelligence and the Ten High-Level Threats to Humanity, summarizes the findings of the UN High-Level Panel on Threat, Challenges, and Change, discusses the eight tribes of intelligence now separated by the iron curtains of bureaucracy, and outlines a strategy for achieving Mahatma Gandhi's vision of a prosperous world at peace.

Chapter 2, The United Nations (UN) System—A Starting Point, provides a concise and blunt description of the UN "System" that is not a system at all as the Secretary General has virtually no authority over most of the pieces. The chapter concludes with a depiction of the global multinational engagements that the UN is failing to address adequately for lack of intelligence (decision-support) as well as lack of resources (both direct and indirect), and a summary of the nine pillars of peace engagement that this book strives to support.

Chapter 3, The Brahimi Report: Panel on United Nations Peace Operations, summarizes the general findings of this vitally important and very critical review of how the UN is not able to be effective for lack of an information and intelligence (decision-support) infrastructure. A major premise of this book is brought forward here, to wit, the UN would be more effective if it focused on becoming a truly global information-sharing and sense-making network, *instead of* seeking to acquire physical and other resources from Member states. I believe the UN should leverage open public information and intelligence (decision-support) to influence how all others—not just governments but corporations, foundations, non-governmental organizations, and individuals— plan, program, budget, and spend trillions of dollars. We call this *Information Peacekeeping* and address the idea in more detail in Chapter 6.

Chapter 4, First Steps: Joint Centers for Operations and Analysis, provides a summary of the very good efforts of various UN elements, notably the Department of Peacekeeping Operations (DPKO) and with a major personal contribution from MajGen Patrick Cammaert, RN NL, then the Military Advisor to the Secretary General and later the Force Commander for Eastern Congo, in the creation of Joint Operations Centres (JOC) and Joint Military Analysis Centres (JMAC). While still in their infancy and lacking the robust global information collection, processing, analysis, and decision-support capabilities so desperately-needed, one important step has been taken: intelligence is no longer a "dirty word" associated with espionage, but is now more properly understood as decision-support such as the UN needs to get the mandate right (strategic intelligence); devise the correct force structure (operational intelligence); manage the mixed civilian-military forces in the field to good effect (tactical intelligence); and pursue such modern initiatives in persistent monitoring and peace enforcement as are needed (technical intelligence).

Chapter 5, The Fragmentation of Knowledge Among Eight Intelligence Tribes, presents the problem that underlies the ineffectiveness of the Member states themselves. Completely apart from the politicization of intelligence and the excessive reliance on secret sources and methods among Member states, such that the UN, like the North Atlantic Treaty Organization (NATO) and regional organizations such as the African Union (AU) can be easily deceived, mis-led, and lied to by Member states, the larger problem is that of the fragmentation of knowledge generally.

Chapter 6, An Alternative Construct: UN Open-Source Decision-Support Information Network (UNODIN), brings together ideas that have been under discussion with selected UN officials for over a decade, but only now are finding a broader receptive audience among Member states realizing that the only affordable means of achieving multinational and multifunctional information-sharing and sense-making is by embracing the proposition, now 21 years in gestation, that Open Source Intelligence (OSINT) should be the source of first resort and allow for 80%-90% of all decision-support needs to be met inexpensively, legally, and ethically.

Chapter 7, Conclusions and Recommendations, provides a synopsis of what needs to be done at the strategic level in order to create a prosperous world at peace. Brazil, China, India, Indonesia, Iran, Russia, Venezuela, and Wild Cards— the eight demographic powers of the future—have a special role to play, as do the regional organizations. The United States of America (USA), willfully deaf, dumb, and blind these past fifty years, could—if it were to choose the path of truth & reconciliation—play a vital role in funding, training, equipping, and organizing the World Brain. Assistance from the USA should be accepted on one condition: Open Everything.

Chapter 1
Strategic Intelligence and the Ten High-Level Threats to Humanity

Secretary-General Kofi Annan named Anand Panyarachun, former Prime Minister of Thailand, to chair a high-level panel on global security threats and reform of the international system, on 3 November 2003.

A more secure world: our shared responsibility (United Nations, 2004) is freely available online in multiple forms including with and without footnotes, and as stated in the Preface, is one of four works that literally changed my life.

Below are the ten threats in priority order, followed by a very concise summary of each.

01 Poverty
    02 Infectious Disease
        03 Environmental Degradation
            04 Inter-State Conflict
                05 Civil War
                    06 Genocide
                        07 Other Atrocities
                            08 Proliferation
                              09 Terrorism
                                10 Transnational Crime

Figure 01. Ten High-Level Threats to Humanity

I provide a list of all of the distinguished members of the High-Level Panel at the end of this chapter because in combination with the Brahimi Report, addressed in Chapter 3, this newer report, published in 2004, is without question the single most authoritative, well-intentioned, actionable guide for mobilizing the distributed intelligence of the Whole Earth. It is not sufficient of itself, but when used as the foundation for all that follows in this book of four parts, twenty-eight chapters, it serves as a catalyst for creating the World Brain with embedded Global Game, which will in turn allow us to achieve a prosperous world at peace by connecting all human minds with all relevant information. Only Member states can suggest new initiatives to the General Assembly, the purpose of this book is to inspire many Members to do so.

Below are "snapshots" of the ten high-level threats from my perspective, not from the reference source, which should be consulted directly. In every instance, corruption and fraud (with attendant enabling secrecy and deception of the public) play a major role in nurturing any given threat. Everything here is either fact or common sense, yet none of this is being discussed by any of the world leaders, who would prefer to talk about carbon trades, a form of phantom wealth that is merely a scam at the highest levels, not something actually intended to help the five billion poor.

1. **Poverty** is pandemic, 5 billion globally, (1 billion extreme, increasing in the USA), foundation for all else—we cannot buy or give our way out of poverty, we must empower the poor to create infinite wealth by connecting them to one another and to information.

2. **Infectious Disease** without borders, kills leaders and wealthy, prevention critical, low-cost medicine works—USA pays $600 a unit for something that sells for $6 overseas.

3. **Environmental Degradation** is poisoning air, water, and land while also accelerating—changes that took 10,000 years, now take 3 years—it is not just Global Warming—fresh water vanishing, earth toxifying. When an aquifer (dropping a meter a year) takes in salt water it is lost forever.

4. **Inter-State Conflict** is made possible by UN Security Council members who sell the guns instead of banning exports. We should create regional peace networks, use planned giving to negotiate peace terms, and invest in peace at one third the cost of war.

5. **Civil War** is a manifestation of corruption—USA supports 42 of 44 dictators looting their respective commonwealths, a story most ably documented by Ambassador Mark Palmer in _Breaking the Real Axis of Evil–How to Oust the World's Last Dictators by 2025_ (Rowman & Littlefield, 2003).

6. **Genocide** coincides with resource scarcity and lifetimes of shared hatreds—it can be anticipated and prevented. Israel must adapt, instead of arming Arabs and Israel the USA should invest in a fifty-year education & prosperity regime that raises an entire new generation in peace.

7. **Other Atrocities** include child and adult slavery and prostitution, "by name" kidnapping of movie starlets and girls that catch a wealthy foreign predator's eye, and murder for body parts.

8. **Proliferation** defined as Nuclear, Radiological, Biological, & Chemical (NRBC), should also include cluster bombs and small arms while continuing the campaign to not only eliminate landmines, but clear all existing landmines that continue to maim indigenous populations. UN Security Council members are the proliferators!

9. **Terrorism** is a tactic, not a threat, but included by the Panel to recognize the potential for catastrophic consequences, e.g. radiological poisoning of an entire city. Law enforcement can and should resolve this _providing_ that USA and others wage peace instead of war.

10. **Transnational Crime** is seriously under-estimated. It is at least $2 trillion a year. The Mafia, the Vatican, Wall Street, and elements of the US Government are entwined. Drug cash is Wall Street's liquidity.

The High-Level Panel report makes the following general comments:

A threat to one is a threat to all. Globalization, complexity, our relatively unsophisticated mechanisms for sharing information and making sense out of changes that we barely perceive, much less understand, all assure that any major threat—and especially non-state threats such as infectious disease—will cross borders with impunity.

We must get serious about prevention. I encourage one and all to read General Al Gray, USMC, "Global Intelligence Challenges of the 1990's," *American Intelligence Journal* (Winter 1989-1990) in which he calls for a redirection from the Soviet Union to the Third World; a massive investment in Open Source Intelligence (OSINT); and the use of OSINT to justify and guide what he called "peaceful preventive measures. No one wanted to listen then, and they still do not wish to take this recommendation seriously.

The report exaggerates the threat to humanity from nuclear, biological, and chemical *weapons*, while completely ignoring the much more pervasive and more deeply harmful effects of the Industrial Era with its many poisons, toxins, and other loosely-managed nuclear, biological, and chemical *materials*.

The report also speaks to the importance of being more pro-active in the future, which I take to mean being less about prevention and more about fostering opportunity for the five billion poor. Finally, the report calls for much enhanced post-conflict peacebuilding such as has not been seen in Iraq and Afghanistan in the aftermath of the two US invasions and occupations.

KEY POINT: Every objective of this superb report requires a strategic intelligence (decision-support) capability that does not exist. At the strategic level, it is very important to have a realistic understanding of who the major players are with respect to the collection, processing, and analysis of major flows of information. We are in the Information Era, yet most governments and corporations and foundations and non-profit organizations are extraordinarily out of touch with reality. The UN *needs* a World Brain with embedded Global Game.

My second graduate thesis examined three Country Teams (the inter-agency combination of personnel working out of any given Embassy) and both their access to, and ability to collect and transfer home all relevant information. My conclusion: the average Embassy collects at best 20% of the relevant information, and in sending most it back in hard-copy, spills 80% of that 20%— hence Washington is running on 2% of the relevant information.

Ben Gilad, a top commercial intelligence scholar-practitioner, reaches a similar conclusion in his book *Business Blindspots*: *Top manager's information is invariably either biased, subjective, filtered, or late.*

These eight tribes (originally seven) are not being harnessed by the UN.

Figure 02. The UN and the Eight Tribes of Intelligence

I first discussed the eight tribes (at the time seven) in my briefing to the Swedish conference on peacekeeping intelligence in December 2004, later published as 2006 IJIC 19/3 Peacekeeping Intelligence & Information Peacekeeping.

I will discuss specifics of engaging all eight tribes in any information challenge throughout the book. It is not possible to achieve a holistic view without leveraging all eight tribes, in all possible languages, all of the time.

It is essential that the UN and its Member states also recognize that 80% or more of the useful information needed to make good decisions about global to local governance—decisions intended to eradicate the ten high-level threats to humanity by harmonizing behavior and budgets across the twelve core policies (itemized and discussed in Chapter 12)—is owned by non-governmental tribes, and is also not secret. It can be shared, but first there must be a global architecture for constructive multinational information-sharing and sense-making. The Internet is tool for that endeavor, not a substitute for human and organizational and national agreements.

In Chapter 5 I discuss the fragmentation of knowledge among and within the eight tribes, here below I simply itemize and describe them:

Academic. Includes all schools and continuing education by all organizations.

Civil Society. Citizen advocates, labor unions, and religions are included.

Commercial. Sharing between small businesses and multinationals is needed.

Government. We can ignore the spies (10%), focus on the open Ministries.

Law Enforcement. Intelligence-led policing and prevention growing fast.

Media. Niche journalism on every topic, and citizen journalism, are growing.

Military. They are a disciplined force, under-utilized for stabilization missions.

Non-Governmental. A great deal of fraud and waste needs to be eliminated.

At the strategic level we need make only one other high-level observation most easily understood by examining the illustration below. Climb the steps from the bottom. Meet Mahatma Gandhi at the top.

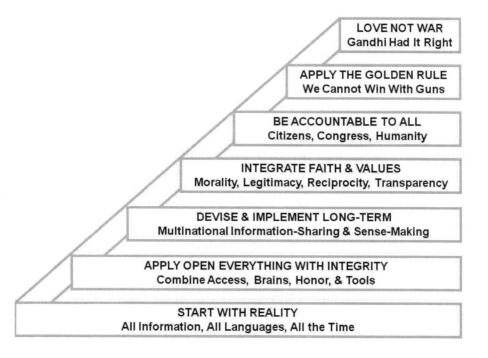

Figure 03. Strategy for Creating a Prosperous World at Peace

The heart of this book, repeated from the Preface:

The truth at any cost reduces all other costs

NOTE: The other 15 members of the Panel were, in alphabetical order Robert Badinter (France), Member of the French Senate and former Minister of Justice of France; João Clemente Baena Soares (Brazil), former Secretary-General of the Organization of American States; Gro Harlem Brundtland (Norway), former Prime Minister of Norway and former Director-General of the World Health Organization; Mary Chinery-Hesse (Ghana), Vice-Chairman, National Development Planning Commission of Ghana and former Deputy Director-General, International Labour Organization; Gareth Evans (Australia), President of the International Crisis Group and former Minister for Foreign Affairs of Australia; David Hannay (United Kingdom), former Permanent Representative of the United Kingdom to the United Nations and United Kingdom Special Envoy to Cyprus; Enrique Iglesias (Uruguay), President of the Inter-American Development Bank; Amre Moussa (Egypt), Secretary-General of the League of Arab States; Satish Nambiar (India), former Lt. General in the Indian Army and Force Commander of the United Nations Protection Force (UNPROFOR); Sadako Ogata (Japan), former United Nations High Commissioner for Refugees; Yevgeny Primakov (Russia), former Prime Minister of the Russian Federation; Qian Qichen (China), former Vice Prime Minister and Minister for Foreign Affairs of the People's Republic of China; Nafis Sadik (Pakistan), former Executive Director of the United Nations Population Fund (UNFPA); Salim Ahmed Salim (United Republic of Tanzania), former Secretary-General of the Organization of African Unity; and Brent Scowcroft (United States), former Lt. General in the United States Air Force and former United States National Security Adviser.

.

Chapter 2
The United Nations (UN) System —A Starting Point

According to the Global Policy Forum, "The United Nations and all its agencies and funds spend about $30 billion each year, or about $4 for each of the world's inhabitants. This is a very small sum compared to most government budgets and it is less than three percent of the world's military spending. "

The UN System is not really a "system" as much as an archipelago of largely independent elements within five large constructs: the Security Council, the General Assembly, the Economic and Social Council, Specialized Agencies (SA), and Peacekeeping Operations (PKO). Below is a graph that extrapolated from the known 2007 numbers to 2009 using known regular and peace budgets in the latter, then assuming similar percentage increases for the other elements (in billions of dollars)—A stands for assessments, V for voluntary contributions.

	REG	PKO	SA (A)	SA (V)	Programs	TOTAL
2007	2.054	5.148	2.198	3.281	12.289	24.970
2009	2.424	7.750	2.594	3.872	14.501	31.141

Known   18% increase in regular and agencies (assessed)
Known   33% increase in peacekeeping operations
Assumed   18% for agencies (volunteered) and programs

Figure 04: UN System Funding

13

On the next several pages the varied UN elements are itemized (with links in the online version of the book) for two reasons: first, to show both the diversity of the elements and also the inconsistency of the elements in relation to the ten high-level threats to humanity and the twelve core policies; and second—taking into account all the other regional and specialized organizations around the world—to suggest the magnitude of both the information failures of the UN and all other organizations, and the opportunities inherent in creating global digital multinational information-sharing and sense-making network.

1. Secretary General (SG) & Major Functional Departments

- Executive Office of the Secretary-General (EOSG)
- Department of Political Affairs (DPA)
- Office for Disarmament Affairs (ODA)
- Department of Peacekeeping Operations (DPKO)
- Department of Field Support (DFS
- Office for the Coordination of Humanitarian Affairs (OCHA)
- Department of Economic and Social Affairs (DESA)
- Department for General Assembly and Conference Management (DGACM)
- Department of Public Information (DPI)
- Department of Safety and Security (DSS)
- Department of Management (DM)

In addition the Secretary General has direct oversight of four internal justice elements; two international criminal tribunals; five special representatives or envoys; five regional economic commissions; three "away" offices (Geneva, Nairobi, Vienna); and other odds and ends.

2. The General Assembly oversees—and hence the Secretary General does not directly control—committees, commissions, boards, councils, and working groups, the United Nations Peacebuilding Commission and the following:

General Assembly Programmes and Funds:

- International Trade Centre (ITC)
- Office of the United Nations High Commissioner for Refugees (UNHCR)

- UN Children's Fund (UNICEF)
- UN Conference on Trade and Development (UNCTAD)
- UN Development Programme (UNDP)
- UN Capital Development Fund (UNCDF)
- UN Development Fund for Women (UNIFEM)
- UN Volunteers (UNV)
- UN Drug Control Programme (UNDCP)
- UN Environment Programme (UNEP)
- UN Human Settlements Programme (UN-HABITAT)
- UN Population Fund (UNFPA)
- UN Relief and Works Agency for Palestine Refugees in the Near East (UNRWA)
- UN World Food Programme (WFP)

General Assembly Research and Training Institutes

- UN Institute for Disarmament Research (UNIDIR)
- UN Institute for Training and Research (UNITAR)
- UN Interregional Crime and Justice Research Institute (UNICRI)
- UN International Research and Training Institute for the Advancement of Women (UN-INSTRAW)
- UN Research Institute for Social Development (UNRISD)

General Assembly Other UN Entities)

- International Computing Centre (ICC)
- Joint United Nations Programme on HIV/AIDS (UNAIDS)
- United Nations Office for Project Services (UNOPS)
- United Nations System Staff College (UNSSC)
- United Nations University (UNU)

3. The Security Council, arguably the real power within the UN, is primarily a decision power rather than an action or administrative power. However, it bears mention that the decisions reached by both the Security Council and the General Assembly are largely uninformed, subject to both the tendency of the Member nations to withhold information or actively misrepresent information (as the US did when Secretary of State Colin Powell briefed known falsehoods

seeking to justify the elective war on Iraq); and the absolute lack of any organic decision-support capability within the UN, the major shortcoming that was highlighted by the Brahimi Report.

4. The Economic and Social Council is the fourth major element, with the following bodies reporting to it.

Functional Commissions: Commission on Crime Prevention and Criminal Justice; Commission on Narcotic Drugs; Commission on Population and Development; Commission on Science and Technology for Development; Commission for Social Development; Commission on the Status of Women; Commission on Sustainable Development; Statistical Commission; United Nations Forum on Forests.

Regional Commissions: Economic Commission for Africa (ECA); Economic Commission for Europe (ECE); Economic Commission for Latin America and the Caribbean (ECLAC); Economic and Social Commission for Asia and the Pacific (ESCAP); Economic and Social Commission for Western Asia (ESCWA).

Standing Committees: Committee on Negotiations with Intergovernmental Agencies; Committee on Non-Governmental Organizations; Committee for Programme and Coordination.

Ad hoc bodies: Ad hoc Open-ended Working Group on Informatics.

Expert Bodies composed of governmental experts: Committee of Experts on the Transport of Dangerous Goods and on the Globally Harmonized System of Classification and Labelling of Chemicals; United Nations Group of Experts on Geographical Names; Intergovernmental Working Group of Experts on International Standards of Accounting and Reporting.

Expert Bodies composed of members serving in their personal capacity: Committee for Development Policy; Committee on Economic, Social and Cultural Rights; Committee of Experts on International Cooperation in Tax Matters; Committee of Experts on Public Administration; Permanent Forum on Indigenous Issues.

Other related Bodies: Executive Board of the International Research and Training Institute for the Advancement of Women; International Narcotics Control Board; Committee for the United Nations Population Award; Programme Coordinating Board of the Joint United Nations Programme on HIV/AIDS.

5. And now, the final part, the **Trusteeship Council, International Court of Justice; Secretariat; and Specialized Agencies, Related Organizations, Funds, and other UN Entities**, all of them relatively autonomous from the Secretary General and his staff.

Specialized Agencies: Food and Agriculture Organization of the United Nations (FAO); International Civil Aviation Organization (ICAO); International Fund for Agricultural Development (IFAD); International Labour Organization (ILO); International Maritime Organization (IMO); International Monetary Fund (IMF); International Telecommunication Union (ITU); United Nations Educational, Scientific and Cultural Organization (UNESCO); United Nations Industrial Development Organization (UNIDO); Universal Postal Union (UPU); World Bank Group [includes International Bank for Reconstruction and Development (IBRD); International Centre for Settlement of Investment Disputes (ICSID); International Development Association (IDA); International Finance Corporation (IFC); Multilateral Investment Guarantee Agency (MIGA)]; World Health Organization (WHO); World Intellectual Property Organization (WIPO); World Meteorological Organization (WMO); World Tourism Organization (UNWTO).

Related Organizations: International Atomic Energy Agency (IAEA); Preparatory Commission for the Nuclear-Test-Ban Treaty Organization (CTBTO) ; Organisation for the Prohibition of Chemical Weapons (OPCW); World Trade Organization (WTO).

Secretariats of Conventions: Convention on the Rights of Persons with Disabilities; United Nations Convention to Combat Desertification (UNCCD); United Nations Framework Convention on Climate Change (UNFCCC).

UN Trust Funds: United Nations Democracy Fund (UNDEF); United Nations Fund for International Partnerships (UNFIP).

6. Finally, administratively overseen by the Secretary General and the Department of Peacekeeping Operations, we have UN force deployments in the field in this instance with precise authorized budgets:

Mission	Amount
MINURCAT (Mission in **Central African Republic and Chad**)	$690.75 million
MINURSO (Mission for Referendum in **Western Sahara**)	$53.53 million
MINUSTAH (Stabilization Mission in Haiti)	$611.75 million
MONUC (Organization Mission in **Dem. Repub. of the Congo**)	$1.35 billion
UNAMID (Hybrid Operation in **Darfur**)	$1.6 billion
UNDOF (Disengagement Observer Force)	$45.03 million
UNFICYP (Peacekeeping Force in **Cyprus**)	$54.41 million
UNIFIL (Interim Force in **Lebanon**)	$589.8 million
UNMIK (Mission in **Kosovo**)	$46.81 million
UNMIL (Mission in **Liberia**)	$561 million
UNMIS (Mission in **Sudan**)	$958.35 million
UNMIT (Integrated Mission in **Timor-Leste**)	$205.94 million
UNOCI (Operation in **Côte d'Ivoire**)	$491.77 million
UNOMIG (Observer Mission in **Georgia**)	$15 million
Support of AMISOM	$138.8 million
Brindisi	$57.95 million
Support Account	$294.03 million
Total	**$7.75 billion**

Figure 05: UN Peacekeeping Deployment Budgets

It is not possible in the context of this brief book to look at all the other organizations around the world, both military (e.g. North Atlantic Treaty Organization) and regional (e.g. African Union) or non-governmental (e.g. International Committee of the Red Cross), but the reader can just imagine, if the UN has a budget of $30 billion a year, multiply this times 100—or 300—and it is easy to see that we are spending perhaps up to a trillion dollars a year on various organizations intended to solve the problems of the world, at the same time that we spend $1.3 trillion a year waging war. In short, there is plenty of money for peace and prosperity, it is simply not well managed.

18

Looking at the UN functionally, using its <u>Thematic Index</u>, below is a list of the UN-defined domains in which they see themselves as active.

Aging	Intellectual Property
Agriculture	International Finance
Atomic Energy	International Law
Children	International Trade
Climate Change	Labour
Culture	Law of the Sea and Antarctica
Decolonization	Least Developed Countries
Demining	Organizational Questions
Development Corporation	Outer Space
Disarmament	**Peace and Security**
Drug Control & Crime Prevention	Persons with Disabilities
Education	Population & Reproductive Health
Elections	Project Services
Energy	Refugees
Environment	Regional Commissions
Family	Science & Technology
Food	Social Development
Governance	Statistics
Habitat	Sustainable Development
Health	Telecommunications
Human Rights	Trade & development
Human Settlements	Transport & Communications
Humanitarian Affairs, Aid, & Relief	Volunteerism
Indigenous People	Women
Industry	Youth

Figure 06: UN Thematic Index

What is utterly fascinating about the above thematic index, copied from the UN's own website, is how far removed it is from the ten high-level threats depicted in Figure 01 on page 5. The five items in bold correspond to core policies that will be addressed in Part II, Chapter 8, "Operational Intelligence and Regional Policy Harmonization." The above UN list is *incoherent and incomplete.*

To conclude our very concise overview, below are briefly discussed what UN employees call the **"Nine Pillars of Peace."** These are as developed with my UN host in slides 60-68 of the UN "Class Before One" as taught in Beirut in August 2007. They are heavily biased toward the concerns of the Department of Safety and Security (DSS) which is not only responsible for the *security* of the entire UN System, but also for its *efficiency*. Everything below has very strong information and intelligence (decision-support) implications, as well as larger Information Operations (IO) implications.

Political Compromise. Implications for safety and security; forget about "national" analysis; focus on regions, tribes, clans, families; grasp history as a foundation; visualize competing equities; value transparency and integrity; the UN System must always be perceived as moral and free of bias.

Media Management. Media is not just the broadcast "main" media but also the Internet, sermons, and other forms of narrowcast; monitoring the media is an essential aspect of situational awareness; "spin" is misunderstood as manipulation; the UN System must focus on getting its message into all forms of media, this is a vital aspect of "intangible" security.

Mandate & Mission. The UN mandates and mission are inherently flawed for lack of adequate decision-support, inclusive of a grasp of history and a nuanced understanding of all regional actors; security comes from accuracy of understanding, before and during the mission.

Posture & Perception. Posture defines perception. A lack of clear communication to every actor of relevance to the UN System is a death wish. Posture is a message. Perception is the mission. Every action the UN System takes to communicate its goodness, its good works, is one less bullet, one less bomb.

Information Management. The UN System is operating at less than 20% of capacity for two simple reasons: Lack of 100MB Internet access for every UN employee at work and at rest and lack of access to the 80% of the open source information needed to be effective at the strategic, operational (regional), tactical, and technical levels. Information is security. Information is efficiency.

20

Information will define the UN System of the future and intelligence (decision-support) will determine the sustainability and efficacy of the UN System.

Operational Procedures. In my opinion, the threat to the UN System is as follows, with the observation that proper information management can resolve all of these deficiencies at very low cost:

- Internal bureaucracy and big egos/small minds
- Lack of full access to all relevant information
- Recalcitrant Member Nations
- Organized opposition groups
- Internal espionage from Member Nations
- Lack of employee training and situational awareness
- Lack of focus by managers at all levels
- Lack of funding for intelligence (decision-support)

Physical Security. Physical security of fixed installations is the most tangible mission of DSS, and also the least important. Virtual security is much more important and demands total situational awareness and total efficiency. Morality, and the perception of the UN System as unbiased and totally for the good of the community being served, is the ultimate security.

Technical Security. Defensive surveillance detection, and especially alert human intelligence able to observe and detect hostile surveillance of UN System sites and individuals, is the single most essential function of DSS. Technical surveillance detection requires both constant audio-visual coverage, and constant human and technical review of the captured images and sounds.

Human Intelligence. DSS is best served by having the most intelligent, dedicated, and intuitive humans on the planet. There is no higher moral duty than to serve the UN System by protecting its missions, facilities, movements, and individuals. Security is not about guns. *Security is about minds in constant action.*

The balance of this book will focus on how best to create a World Brain, using the UN as a starting point, with the intent of ultimately being able to eradicate all ten high-level threats to humanity by harmonizing all policies and spending with clarity and integrity, appreciating diversity to achieve sustainability.

We can indeed use our Collective Intelligence to create a prosperous world at peace, we just need to create Intelligence for Earth.

Chapter 3

The Brahimi Report:
Panel on United Nations Peace Operations

Dag Hammarskjöld, although the second Secretary General (1953-1961) of the UN rather than the first, is widely perceived as the true pioneer in part because his first order of business was the creation of a 4,000 person Secretariat intended to place the UN on a proper management and business footing. He is also the only Secretary General to have died in office, in an aircraft crash while on a mission in Africa.

He was succeeded by U Thant (1961-1971), Kurt Waldheim (1972-1981), Javier Pérez de Cuéllar (1982-1991), Boutros Boutros-Ghali (1992-1996), Kofi Annan (1997-2006), and the now serving Ban Ki-moon (2007-)

While all of the above are credited with many accomplishments—and a fair share of scandals—the next "towering figure" in UN history is, in my view, Lakhdar Brahimi because like Dag Hammarskjold, when given the opportunity he focused on the shortcomings of the existing system of peacekeeping and made specific recommendations for change, focusing on politics, strategy and operational and organizational areas of need.

The Brahimi Report, produced in 2000 by a panel chaired by Brahimi in his capacity as Under-Secretary-General for Special Assignments in Support of the Secretary-General's Preventive and Peacemaking efforts, marks the definition of the UN as a 20th Century organization badly in need of modernization in the area of decision-making at all levels, and consequently in the area of decision-support, the two together being *organizational intelligence*.

Easily accessible online are the Executive Summary, a Summary of Recommendations, the Full Report, Panel Member Biographies, Media Coverage, and Fact Sheets. For the purposes of Intelligence for Earth, what is important about the Brahimi Report is that three of the five areas of concern are directly addressable by creating permanent and rapid-response strategic, operational, tactical, and technical intelligence capabilities that are organic to the UN and not *ad hoc* kludges of Member nation "contributions" of mixed value and reliability.

The Brahimi Report was the underlying foundation for the initiatives undertaken by MajGen Patrick Cammaert, RN NL, addressed in the next chapter. The book, *PEACEKEEPING INTELLIGENCE: Emerging Concepts for the Future* (OSS, 2003) was published to support the initiatives by General Cammaert, and was honored from its day of publication by being on display in the lobby of 1 UN Plaza, and on sale in the UN Bookstore. Phi Beta Iota the Public Intelligence Blog provides short online biographies and links to the individual chapters in the Who's Who section on Peace Intelligence (28).

Speaking to the international conference on open source solutions in 2003, and then to the Swedish Conference on Peacekeeping Intelligence in December 2004, General Cammaert pointed out that every UN Mission, whether a peacekeeping mission or a development mission or a fact-finding mission, was largely dependent for its success on:

- Strategic Mandate
- Operational Force Structure
- Tactical Situational Awareness
- Technical Competence in Communications and Intelligence

Each of these, however talented the individuals making the determination, is substantially dependent on the availability of intelligence—decision-support. In the absence of a full understanding such as can only be achieved by an integrated and "full spectrum" intelligence network, the mandate will be flawed, the force structure will be wrong, the tactical forces will be deaf and blind, and modern technologies will not be brought to bear. These presentations augmented his earlier provision, based on his extensive field experience commanding peacekeeping operations, of the core chapter **Intelligence in Peacekeeping Operations: Lessons for the Future.**

Others have made signal contributions—Deputy Secretary General of the UN Louise Frechette (former Canadian Deputy Minister of Defence and Dr. Patricia Lewis, then Director of the United Nations Institute for Disarmament Research (UNIDIR)—come to mind, but between them, Brahimi and Cammaert are the true pioneers for modern UN Information Operations (IO) and Intelligence (Decision-Support).

Below are listed the strategic recommendations (severely truncated with their original numbering) that bear on this book's vision for a central UN role in creating a World Brain with an embedded Global Game. A full reading of the various elements of the Brahimi Report is recommended.

1. **Preventive action**—more fact-finding missions.

2. **Peace-building strategy**—quick interventions, post-conflict integration.

3. **Peacekeeping doctrine and strategy**—professionalization.

4. **Clear, credible and achievable mandates**—The Secretariat must tell the Security Council what it needs to know, not what it wants to hear.

5. **Information and strategic analysis**—The Secretary-General should establish an entity, which would support information and analysis needs of all.

16. **Other structural adjustments in DPKO**—The current Military and Civilian Police Division should be restructured, moving the Civilian Police Unit out of the military reporting chain; upgrading the rank and level of the Civilian Police Adviser; The Military Adviser's Office in DPKO should be restructured to correspond to the way in which the military field headquarters in United Nations peacekeeping operations are structured; Increasing Assistant Secretaries-General in DPKO from two to three.

18. **Peace-building support in the Department of Political Affairs**

Figure 07. Strategic Recommendations

Below are the operational and tactical recommendations.

6. Transitional civil administration— evaluate the feasibility and utility of developing an interim criminal code.

7. Determining deployment timelines—the ability to fully deploy traditional peacekeeping operations within 30 days after the adoption of a Security Council resolution [90 days for complex operations].

8. Mission leadership—systematize the method of selecting mission leaders.

9. Military personnel—ready for effective deployment within 30 days; a revolving "on-call list" of about 100 military officers be created in UNSAS to be available on seven days' notice to augment nuclei of DPKO planners.

10. Civilian police personnel—national pools of civilian police officers; regional training partnerships for civilian police; single point of contact; evolving on-call list of about 100 police officers and related experts be created in UNSAS to be available on seven days' notice.

11. Civilian specialists—a central Internet/Intranet-based roster of pre-selected civilian candidates; attract the most highly qualified candidates; formulate a comprehensive staffing strategy for peace operations, outlining, among other issues, the use of United Nations Volunteers, standby arrangements for the provision of civilian personnel on 72 hours' notice to facilitate mission start-up.

13. Logistics support and expenditure management—prepare a global logistics support strategy; maintain at least five mission start-up kits; review of the entire procurement policies and procedures; draw up to $50M per mission; authorize missions up to $1M in local procurement.

14. Funding Headquarters support for peacekeeping operations— Headquarters support for peacekeeping should be treated as a core activity of the United Nations, funded through the mechanism of the regular budget.

15. Integrated mission planning and support—Integrated Mission Task Forces (IMTFs).

17. Operational support for public information—unit for operational planning and support of public information in peace operations.

19. Peace operations support in OHCHR **(Human Rights)—create an office**

Figure 08. Operational & Tactical Recommendations

12. Rapidly deployable capacity for public information—Additional resources should be devoted in mission budgets to public information and the associated personnel and information technology required to get an operation's message out and build effective internal communications links.

20. Peace operations and the information age:

(a) Headquarters peace and security departments need a responsibility centre to devise and oversee the implementation of *common information technology strategy and training for peace operations*, residing in EISAS. Mission counterparts to the responsibility centre should also be appointed to serve in the offices of the special representatives of the Secretary-General in complex peace operations to oversee the implementation of that strategy;

(b) EISAS, in cooperation with the Information Technology Services Division (ITSD), should implement an enhanced peace operations element on the current United Nations Intranet and link it to the missions through a *Peace Operations Extranet* (POE);

(c) Peace operations could benefit greatly from more extensive use of *geographic information systems* (GIS) technology, which quickly integrates operational information with electronic maps of the mission area, for applications as diverse as demobilization, civilian policing, voter registration, human rights monitoring and reconstruction;

(d) The *IT needs of mission components with unique information technology needs, such as civilian police and human rights*, should be anticipated and met more consistently in mission planning and implementation;

(e) The Panel encourages the development of *web site* co-management by Headquarters and the field missions, in which Headquarters would maintain oversight but individual missions would have staff authorized to produce and post *web content* that conforms to basic presentational standards and policy.

Figure 09. Technical Recommendations

The Brahimi Report did not seek to address the organic intelligence collection, processing, and analysis needs of the deployed forces, these will be discussed in the next chapter in general terms.

The Brahimi Report recommendations have not been implemented to the fullest extent possible. This report continues to demand more attention.

A concise but supplementary treatment of selected Brahimi Report recommendations from an intelligence (decision-support) perspective is provided at The Brahimi Report: Extracts from the Executive Summary, in *PEACEKEEPING INTELLIGENCE: Emerging Concepts for the Future*.

Here are some conclusions that draw on the earlier and the large body of works by others summarized at Phi Beta Iota under Reviews:

1. **UNRESPONSIVE.** The larger parts of the UN—as little as two thirds, as much as four fifths, are not really responsive to direction from the Secretary General or any of the bodies (General Assembly, Security Council, Economic and Social Council) except in the remote sense of budgetary approvals and generic mandate.

2. **UNINFORMED.** The information collected by most if not all of the UN has no centralized place where it can be made sense of or shared across the UN System, with other organizations, or with the Member governments.

3. **DISENGAGED.** The UN appears to be operating on automatic pilot right now, with Members—and among them, a tiny handful of the larger nations—controlling what issues and concerns are placed before the body. The UN and its elements, despite relationships with various stakeholders, are in no sense of the word "connected" to the Eight Tribes or the Internet or Humanity at large.

4. **INCOHERENT.** Between too many spies filling jobs they are not qualified for, and too much cronyism, on top of a complete absence of a coherent decision-support infrastructure such as the Brahimi Report recommends, the UN is incoherent at the strategic, operational, tactical, and technical levels.

Now, having said all that, I still consider the UN the single best starting point for seeking to create what H. G. Wells described in 1936 as a *World Brain*; what Quincy Wright called for in 1957, a World Intelligence Center; and what we have provided to the Secretary General for discussion among Members, a World Brain Institute with an embedded Global Game.

Chapter 4

First Steps:

Joint Centers for Operations and Analysis

The strategic aims of peace operations have changed fundamentally in recent years, and UN Security Council mandates are increasingly multi-dimensional in purpose. This challenges all stakeholders to respond in kind. It has become ever clearer that the complex range of approaches and instruments that are employed in peace operations require some form of integration if lasting peace is to be secured. Although the UN has taken important steps by adopting innovative policies, mechanisms and programmes, significant challenges remain in relation to improving the integration and coordination of both multilateral and bilateral efforts in countries affected by war.

The above statement is copied from the <u>Norwegian Ministry of Foreign Affairs</u>, typically a leader with the other Nordic countries, in the peace arena. The post goes on to describe how integrated peace operations can

- Improve the coherence and impact of the UN response in conflicts;
- Be improved with the conception, planning and implementation of a multidimensional and integrated peace operation;
- Improve the alignment of mandates, resources and practices;
- Enhance effective protection of civilians, while safeguarding the independence and impartiality of humanitarian efforts; and
- Augment a demographically and gender sensitive approach.

The point of opening this chapter with the above innovation that is emergent— it is by no means past elementary—is to stress that while the emergence of the Joint Operations Centre (JOC) such as found in Beirut, where all UN elements have representation; and the emergence of the Joint Military Analysis Centre (JMAC) such as best executed in Haiti by the United Nations Stabilization Mission In Haiti (*Mission des Nations Unies pour la stabilisation en Haïti*), also known as MINUSTAH) is a good thing, it is not nearly enough in the way of intelligence (decision-support) innovation to meet the needs for multi-dimensional peace operations, i.e. those that have substantive Disaster Relief, Humanitarian Assistance, or Stabilization & Reconstruction elements.

Bassey Ekpe's contribution, The Intelligence Assets of the United Nations: Sources, Methods, and Implications, in the *International Journal of Intelligence and Counterintelligence* (20/3 Fall 2007) continues to be the most current overview of UN information and intelligence capabilities. He makes the following points:

1. UN Headquarters incapacity is often the root cause of all subsequent failures of intelligence at the operational and tactical levels.

2. Despite a multiplicity of information units across all the major departments, internal audits have reported deliberate reluctance to share, mistrust, lack of understanding of one another's needs, and a lack of a consolidated list of indicators (or Essential Elements of Information—EEI) needed to establish a multinational multifunctional peace operation.

3. Among the bright spots that do suggest the UN could yet become a platform for multinational multifunctional information-sharing and sense-making:

   a. Arria Formula (AF) brings Non-Governmental Organizations (NGO) to brief off the record, this often brings forth information Member states have held back or misrepresented.

   b. Past efforts such as the Office for Research and the Collection of Information (ORCI) and the Strategic Planning Unit (SPU) as well as fact-finding missions represent inadequate but important appreciation for the role of information at the strategic level.

c. DPKO has the Military Planning Service (MPS) and roughly 100 desk officers.

d. Office for the Coordination of Humanitarian Affairs (OCHA) has a number of remarkable units that bear specific itemization:

   (1) Humanitarian Early Warning System (HEWS)

   (2) Emergency Relief Coordinator (ERC)

   (3) Early Warning and Contingency Planning Units (EWCP)

   (4) Field Information Unit (FIU)

   (5) Humanitarian Information Capability (HIC), essentially an FIU in a deployable box.

The Situation Centre continues to be a very small element, just a handful of individuals, while replicated across the UN System are country and region desk officers who mix functional expertise with area monitoring.

Summing up, at the strategic level the UN is excessively dependent on Member states, on information briefings from NGOs, and on a wide variety of desk officers across multiple functionalities. The UN does not have a professional intelligence (decision-support) cadre in any sense of the word, nor does it have a table of organization for assuring that all relevant information is collected, processed, analyzed, and disseminated to all those who have a need for both focused information and tailored intelligence (decision-support). A 2006 summary from a DPKO perspective is online.

The Swedish military and I speak of Multinational, Multiagency, Multidisciplinary, Multidomain Information-Sharing and Sense-Making (M4IS2). The Nordic countries have long practiced fully-integrated Nordic (four country) operational and intelligence centers, and in recent years both Belgium, the Netherlands, and Luxembourg (BENELUX) and some of the Central American countries have given thought to redirecting their training, equipping, and organizing in a multinational direction. In the USA, which is the most over-extended nation around the world, there was discussion in 2008 about the need to rebalance the instruments of national power, and much has been made of the fact that the military cannot do

31

everything alone, but no substantive action or decision has been forthcoming from within Congress or the White House. The reality is that none of the civilian agencies less the US Agency for International Development (AID) are designed to "surge" overseas, none of them receive proper intelligence support from the US Intelligence Community, and hence we must in one breath acknowledge *both* the need for multinational multidimensional peace operations *and* the complete absence of any suitable table of organization, equipment, training, and funding.

The seminal public document on the origin of the JMAC is online, and is the text as planned for the remarks of MajGen Patrick Cammaert, RN NL, then the Military Advisor to the Secretary General, speaking to the international conference on peacekeeping intelligence at the Swedish Military Academy in December 2004. A number of related documents are available in the working folder for a work in progress, *INTELLIGENCE FOR PEACE: Multinational, Multifunctional Information-Sharing and Sense-Making*.

The first reference we can find to JOC/JMAC being briefed to the General Assembly is within the remarks by Mr. Jean-Marie Guehenno, Under-Secretary-General for Peacekeeping Operations, on 20 October 2005. He says: "In response to a request by the Special Committee for Peacekeeping Operations, a comprehensive policy on Joint Operations and Joint Mission Analysis Centres (JOC/JMAC) - is being developed, building on best practices from the field and in coordination with the new Department for Safety and Security."

The best available public reference on a JMAC in operation as intended is Dr. Walter Dorn's Intelligence-led Peacekeeping: The United Nations Stabilization Mission in Haiti (MINUSTAH), 2006-07, as published in *Intelligence and National Security* (24/6, December 2009).

The below appears as Figure 1 in that work. Dr. Dorn has confirmed that "Cell" (in the original) was an editing oversight, all JMACs are Centres.

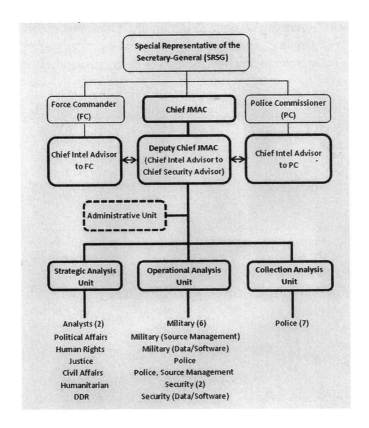

Figure 10. UN Joint Military Operational Centre in Haiti

The distinction between JOC and JMAC is emergent, the first being common to those information-coordination units that serve a UN Mission comprised predominantly of specialized agencies, while the latter is more often associated with predominantly military peacekeeping operations such as in the Congo and Haiti. Earlier experiments, such as the Civil-Military Operations Center (CMOC), also in Haiti, should also be studied. Dr. Dorn has confirmed they are "standard" for all UN missions, and the police are well integrated.

A JOC or JMAC is nothing without collection and processing capabilities, solid multi-lingual and multi-cultural analytic talent, and insightful leadership able to assure the timely creation and presentation of decision-support.

Permitted	**Questionable**	**Prohibited**
(White)	(Grey)	(Black)
Visual observation:		
– From fixed posts	– Observers concealed	
– From vehicles	– Observers camouflaged	
– From aircraft		– Observation using unauthorized entry
	– Observers out of mission area	– Using sting operations
Sensors:		
– Visible (video)	– Thermal (IR), X-ray, radar, metal and explosives detection	
– Satellite	– Hidden devices	– Covert tracking devices
– Ground sensors (acoustic/seismic)		– Using captured devices
Human Communications:		
UN personnel: – Clearly identified	– Unidentified	– Undercover/disguised
Informants: – Unpaid	– Rewarded	– Paid (agents)
Listening devices:	– Message interception (SIGINT)	– Warrantless wiretaps
	* Unencrypted messages * Encrypted messages	
	* Tactical level * Strategic level	
Documents		
– Open source (public)	– Private	– Classified (non-UN) – Stolen

← increasingly overt   increasingly covert →

Figure 11. Information-Gathering from Permitted to Prohibited

The above first appeared in The Cloak and the Blue Beret: Limitations on Intelligence in UN Peacekeeping, chapter 19 in *PEACEKEEPING INTELLIGENCE: Emerging Concepts for the Future*. His earlier article **Intelligence and Peacekeeping: The UN Operation in the Congo, 1960-1964** remains the best exposition of how to use intelligence as the foundation for successful peacekeeping. Dr. Dorn updated the above for the forthcoming Oxford *Handbook on National Security Intelligence* (Loch Johnson, Ed., March 2010 release) and shared the updated version above via electronic mail. Before moving on to address the larger strategic challenge (the fragmentation of knowledge among the eight intelligence tribes) and the proposed solution (a UN Open-Source Decision-Support Information Network or UNODIN), I want to emphasize the role that Requirements Definition plays in assuring early warning that enables peaceful preventive measures, and 360 degree situational awareness that optimizes the application of both stabilization & reconstruction assistance, and peace enforcement at the neighborhood level of granularity.

Requirements Definition is easily one-third of the process and formula for getting it right in the intelligence (decision-support) arena. The other two-thirds are Collection & Processing Management, and the integration of Analysis & Decision-Support as human-to-human *engagement.*

We are wasting $75 billion dollars a year in the USA—money that could be used to much greater effect creating UNODIN and harmonizing how the West and North offer one trillion a year in aid to the five billion poor at the item level of granularity—because the US secret world does not do requirements definition, is not held accountable for its ignorance, and is being allowed to get away with spending inputs rather than providing outputs.

Requirements Definition is fundamental at every level of analysis, as is integrity. The starkest example of this in recent memory is the juxtaposition of the Bush-Cheney White House and the <u>neo-conservative ideologues not understanding</u> the Sunni-Shi'ite divide in Iraq, or the regional implications of the Pakistani nuclear Sunni combined with the Saudi Arabian Wahhabi Sunni being against the Iranian Shi'ites; with their total lack of integrity in telling <u>935 documented lies</u> to the public, Congress, the UN, and the world in their march to an elective war and long-term occupation of Iraq.

Perhaps more to the point—and a major reason why the world needs a public intelligence capability—is to be able to muster the combination of public ethics and public knowledge to put a complete stop to this madness that has cost over <u>three trillion dollars.</u> Stopping war and waging peace starts with requirements definition.

Below are the major domains included in the Expeditionary Analysis Model developed by the Marine Corps Intelligence Center (MCIC) when the Marine Corps found that it could not get what it needed from either the national intelligence community or the other military service intelligence centers.

Environment: 5 Fathom Line	Threat: Air
Environment: Culture	Threat: CNBC
Environment: Key Facilities	Threat: Drugs
Environment: Maps & Charts	Threat: Gray Arms
Environment: NEO Range	Threat: Ground
Environment: Terrain	Threat: Naval
Environment: Weather	Threat: Terrorism

Figure 12: Expeditionary Requirements Definition

All of this is easily understood in the documentation, and in two articles that explore what *reality* means to the Marine Corps and to the US Navy. What is worth noting above, as simple as this model was, is that fully half of the requirements had nothing to do with the "threat" but instead focused on the environment—on actually understanding the *totality* of the challenge.

Although we included Culture and used Language and Religion as sub-sets, we did not focus on History nor did we do what I and others learned later was vitally important, which is to map the Tribes in time (history) and space.

A recurrent theme throughout this book is the urgency of clarity, diversity, and integrity if we are to achieve sustainability.

We must aspire to clarity rather than obscurity and the lies that kill our own; we must revel in—deeply, earnestly appreciate—diversity of view and form; and we must aspire to integrity in all things—not just integrity of honor but integrity of attention to detail and every aspect of assuring that the Whole System feedback loops are running clean—all of them, all of the time.

Chapter 5

The Fragmentation of Knowledge Among Eight Intelligence Tribes

We will begin with a short overview of System Dynamics, the essential foundation for interacting with any Whole System such as the Whole Earth.

First Order Systems are "root" for the Whole System. The first challenge is to identify the discrete first order system; the second challenge is to analyze it in terms of time, energy, consumption, and reactions.

First Order Systems consume and react—what Buckminster Fuller called the **time-energy calculation** or *Critical Path*. How long it takes for a First Order System reaction to begin, peak, and complete is very important, as is the matter of how much energy it consumes or creates.

Second Order Systems are the simplest systems that exhibit oscillations and overshoot. Second order behavior is part of the behavior of higher order systems and understanding second order systems helps you to understand higher order systems. At this point the system element is not isolated.

System Models are the means by which we relate observed and deliberately collected data to assumptions and hypotheses about the system. The purpose of modeling is to be able to convert a mix of data inputs and contrived relationships so as to predict **transformations among systems**.

To be effective stewards of anything, we must understand all systems in relation to one another, all of the time.

The simplest Whole Earth model that is both understandable and useful is that provided by Donella Meadows, Jorgen Randers, and Dennis Meadows in _Limits to Growth_.

The variables they examined were world population, industrialization, pollution, food production and resource depletion.

It is important to emphasize that their focus was on the sustainability of humanity within the larger Whole Earth complex that we still do not understand. _The Resilient Earth_ does not need us, but the Cosmos might appreciate our coming of age with _Integral Consciousness_ achieved through _Conscious Evolution_ aided by _Revolutionary Activism_.

This book accepts as a premise that humanity is intended to evolve along cultural lines so as to achieve _Non-Zero_ "win-win" solutions, that we inhabit a _Living Universe_, and that there is a marvelous emergence one author describes as _Holistic Darwinism: Synergy, Cybernetics, and the Bioeconomics of Evolution_.

More recently—and our final preliminary before getting into the fragmentation of knowledge and why it matters—two seminal works have been published that are of the most extraordinary import to our future precisely because they provide the beginning of a Strategic Analytic Model that will allow us to "get a grip."

The first, discussed in Chapter 1, is the 2004 contribution of the UN High-Level Panel on Threats, Challenges, and Change, and their report, _A more secure world: our shared responsibility_.

The second, a personal effort by a gifted internationalist, J. F. Rischard, is _HIGH NOON: 20 Global Problems, 20 Years to Solve Them_. Published in 2002, it emphasizes six issues related to our planet; six related to humanity's survival and sustainability; and eight issues surrounding how we create a shared rule book or governance system—he recommends global issue networks.

With that preamble, we will now examine the fragmentation of knowledge that has made it impossible for humanity to achieve its full potential.

Below is a map created by Dick Klavens and Brad Ashton, also authors of _Keeping Abreast of Science and Technology: Technical Intelligence for Business_.

In 2002 they addressed the how (Technology Mapping) and the future (Hotspots). The below illustration was provided in personal communications. Their website, Maps of Science, is well worth visiting.

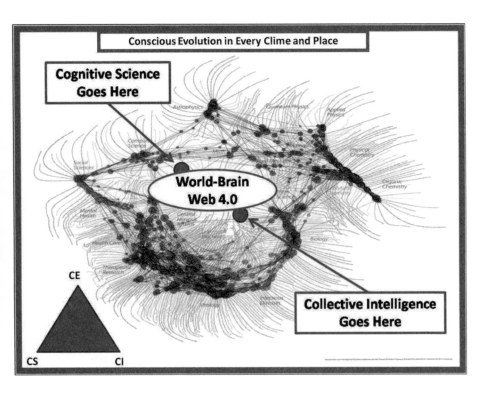

Figure 13. Web of Fragmented Knowledge

The above includes the Humanities. This rendition was created for a lecture in British Columbia. Completely apart from the fragmentation of knowledge due to the constant demand for differentiation that drives micro-specialization, there is also the politicization of science and the politicization of religion.

Cultural Intelligence is in its infancy, in part because science buried the humanities and social science remained an intellectual runt in the litter of academia. While the West has studied its core "great ideas," the West has not studied those same ideas in the East, and has no idea what the cultural identity is of the thousands of tribes that cross artificial boundaries with ease.

Below is an Information Operations (IO) cube constructed for use in the classroom. Whole Systems cannot be understood by science alone, humanities alone, or religion alone.

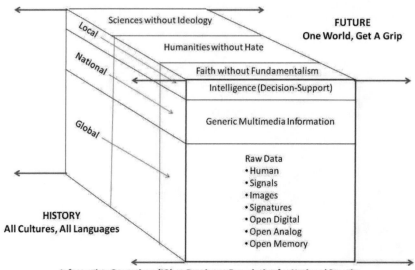

Information Operations (IO) as Dominant Foundation for National Security
Multinational, Multiagency, Mustidisciplinary Multidomain Information Sharing

Figure 14. Information Operations Cube

It merits emphasis that today, despite spending $75 billion a year on all that it does, the US Intelligence Community(US IC) is incapable of processing more than 5% of what it collects, and incapable of collecting the 85% or so that is not secret, not expensive, not online, and not in English but rather in 183 languages we do not speak.

The fragmentation of knowledge is one obstacle, while another is the isolation of the eight tribes of intelligence, depicted in the figure below. This was created by the author in discussion with Alvin Toffler while driving away from a lunch with Defense Intelligence Agency (DIA) senior officers. Starting with the realization that the DIA "leaders" wanted to stay rooted inside their little olive drab green box, we then added the other pieces to illustrate *fragmentation*.

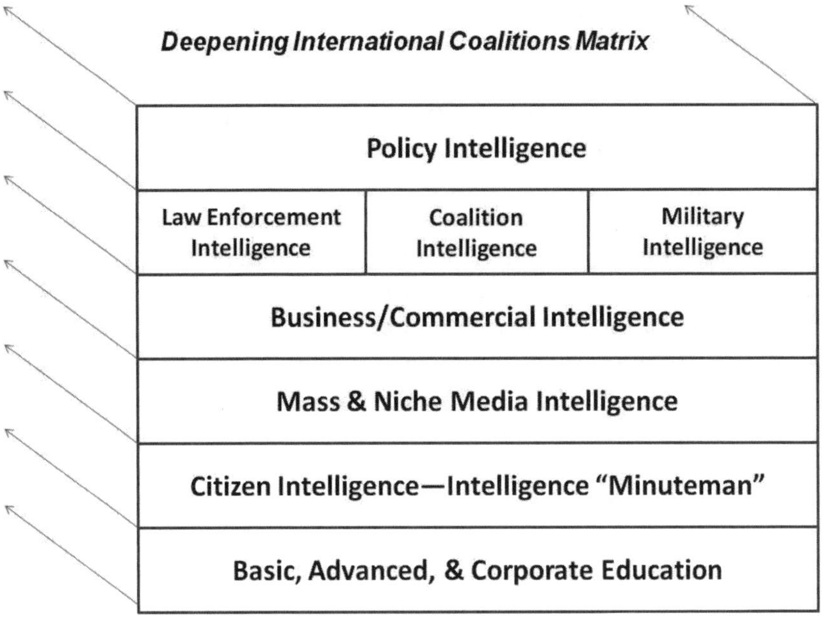

Deepening International Coalitions Matrix

Policy Intelligence		
Law Enforcement Intelligence	Coalition Intelligence	Military Intelligence
Business/Commercial Intelligence		
Mass & Niche Media Intelligence		
Citizen Intelligence—Intelligence "Minuteman"		
Basic, Advanced, & Corporate Education		

Figure 15. Original Toffler-Steele Reaction to DIA Lunch

It is my view that the UN can and should aspire to be the service of common concern for multinational multifunctional information-sharing and sense-making across all boundaries.

The fragmentation of knowledge, and the gap between people with power and people with knowledge, is the root cause of our universal failure to deal responsibly with the ten high-level threats to humanity.

I said this in 1997, writing for the US Institute of Peace Conference on Virtual Diplomacy, in *Virtual Intelligence: Conflict Avoidance and Resolution through Information Peacekeeping*

In an age characterized by distributed information, where the majority of the expertise is in the private sector, the concept of "central intelligence " is an oxymoron, and its attendant concentration on secrets is an obstacle to both national defense, and global peace. The underlying threat to peace and prosperity—the cause of causes—is the ever-widening chasm between policymakers with power, and private sector experts and participants with knowledge. Neither classified information nor information technology alone can bridge this gap—but both can make a positive contribution if they are managed within a larger information strategy which focuses on content as well as connectivity, and enables policymakers to draw upon the expertise available in the private sector. We thus require a strategy to create a "virtual intelligence community" able to both inform governance, and also carry out a new kind of virtual diplomacy, "information peacekeeping". Information peacekeeping can help avoid and resolve conflict, and represents the conceptual, technical, and practical foundation for successful virtual diplomacy—virtual intelligence "is" virtual diplomacy.

The next chapter addresses my strategic vision of how the UN can leverage information as a substitute for wealth, violence, capital, labor, space, and time, an understanding inspired by Alvin Toffler's book, *Powershift–Knowledge, Wealth, and Violence at the Edge of the 21st Century* (Bantam, 1991).

42

Chapter 6

An Alternative Construct: UN Open-Source Decision-Support Information Network (UNODIN)

At the strategic level the single most important concept to understand—one that J. F. Rischard clearly articulated in his discussion of Global Issue Networks within *HIGH NOON: 20 Global Problems, 20 Years to Solve Them*—is the termination of top-down command & control (C2) as the predominant mode of organizing human activity.

The two concepts of organization that replace Industrial-Era or Weberian "bureaucracy" are Epoch B Leadership, a concept devised by Jonas Salk in his book, *World Population and Human Values—A New Reality*; and Open Space Technology (OST), a concept devised by Harrison Owen.

The third concept is that of Open Source Intelligence (OSINT).

The first two above came together for me in the context of reading Tom Atlee's *The Tao of Democracy—Using Co-Intelligence to Create a World That Works for All* and then exploring a wide range of book on Collective Intelligence. Tom has been the single most important influence in my evolution away from trying to help spies make better use of open sources of information, and toward focusing instead on helping the public create public intelligence in the public interest. It was Tom who helped me understand that our Native American forbearers practiced what they called "Seventh Generation" decision-making—to wit, actively considering how any decision might impact seven generations into the future. The book *COLLECTIVE INTELLIGENCE: Creating a Prosperous World at Peace* laid the foundation for *this* book, along with my earlier works, both published in 2006, *THE SMART NATION ACT: Public Intelligence in the Public Interest* (2006); and *INFORMATION OPERATIONS: All Information, All Languages, All the Time*.

Below is my own construct created in the 1990's as I studied what might be the opposite of the dysfunctional system now used by most countries, corporations, international organizations (IO), and non-governmental organizations (NGO).

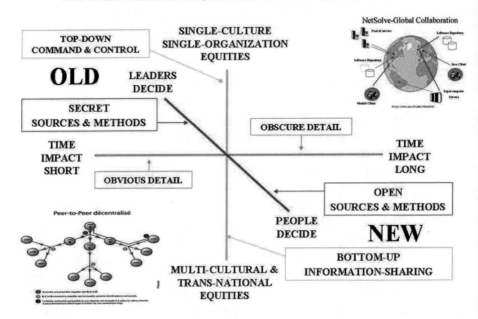

A Revolution is Underway
Peer-to-Peer Distributed Ubiquitous Collective Intelligence Now Possible

Figure 16. Revolution in Human Affairs & Human Leadership

A concept that I have encountered only recently is that of *Panarchy–Understanding Transformations in Human and Natural Systems*, which boils down to everyone representing themselves all the time, and being a full participant in an infinite number of local to global information-sharing and sense-making networks. Imagine a human mosaic in which all humans have access to all information all the time, and comprise, in the aggregate, a World Brain.

The essence of the preceding is that of bottom-up consensual leadership, i.e. instead of top-down command & control we substitute universal suffrage, universal participatory budgeting (more on that in Chapter 23), and completely transparent access to all relevant information all the time. This not only allows for *informed* decisions, but for *sustainable* decisions as well.

There is urgent need for a new means of self-governance that can fully and continuously harness the diversity of human interests and capabilities. We are in the Information Era, but the UN and its Member States are still "dumb" and unable to harness the distributed intelligence of the Whole Earth. Humanity urgently needs some form of global unified archive system without the current "top down" partitioning and access restrictions, such that all organizations and individuals can contribute their knowledge to a creative commons that leaves no knowledge sidelines, and no fraud undiscovered.

World Information Summits and Global Knowledge Summits have not addressed the core need: to connect all human minds with one another and with all information in all languages. The UN and its Members cannot be effective in this new era without creating a **United Nations Open-Source Decision-Support Information Network (UNODIN)** that is "Open" in every possible sense of the word (using open source software and open spectrum, creating open source intelligence), and that allows the harmonization of what the public knows, does, and funds.

Despite the passionate desire of some to turn the UN into a "World Government" the reality is that Copenhagen was a fatal stake in the heart of both the concept of the UN as a manager of anything, and the concept of UN science as anything other than an oxymoron.

Recognizing much of this in the 2006 timeframe, I funded the creation of the Earth Intelligence Network (EIN), today a certified 501c3 Public Charity. At the same time, building on legislative concepts discussed with both Congressman Rob Simmons (R-CT-02) and the US Special Operations Forces and most especially the Civil Affairs element of Special Forces, a Smart Nation – Safe Nation Act outline was developed, and a book built around it, THE SMART NATION : Public Intelligence in the Public Interest

The intent of the draft legislation is to facilitate the emergence of UNODIN.

Twenty-three others joined me refining my earlier reflections and devising implementation ideas that I present in this book. We have already offered this information to the Secretary General (SG) of the UN in the form of a letter and two-page memorandum.

A single World Brain Institute with an infinitely-scalable online Global Game (actually a Participatory Planning and Budgeting System at all levels of governance) can be implemented immediately at a cost of under Euro $12 million a year, with the almost certain prospect of being self-funded within three years by selling very low-cost subscriptions to the one billion rich, enabling free access to the five billion poor. The World Brain and a Global Game are not new ideas—what is new is the combination of the desperate need for reliable "whole systems" analytics, and the immediate availability of information and communication technologies (ICT) to meet that need.

This program, under UN auspices, would encourage regions to establish Regional Information-Sharing and Sense-Making Networks, and Members to create national call centers harnessing the eight tribes of intelligence in each country (academic, civil society, commerce, government, law enforcement, media, military, and non-governmental or non-profit) and able to educate the poor "one cell call at a time."

46

The UN could ask for US funding of an Office of the Assistant Secretary for Decision-Support, and create an Office of Information-Sharing Treaties and Agreements at the same time. A Strategic Analytic Model has been devised along with a concept for extending the proven concept of Participatory Budgeting while harnessing all interested humans to digitize "true cost" information on all products, services, and behaviors.

This is a self-healing self-learning system with an open ethic that guarantees integrity with transparency. Within the Global Game, a Global Range of Needs Table can connect the one billion rich with the item-level needs of the five billion poor, to include free cells phones connecting the poor to knowledge.

A (UN) World Intelligence Centre was first proposed by Quincy Wright in 1957, this now-achievable program will ride the emergent wave of evolutionary activism that can potentially bypass blocking industrial-era bureaucracies and enable the poor to create infinite stabilizing wealth. The UN can become the administrator of the World Brain and Global Game, and in this way harness the distributed intelligence of the Whole Earth while helping all achieve global learning.

ClimateGate and Iraq are the two most recent examples where the lack of world access to public intelligence embarrassed the UN leadership and Members. In the first case a small minority of scientists, roughly 50 in number, hijacked the issue, manipulated the data, suppressed dissenting opinion, and helped create a fraudulent marketplace for Carbon trades.

It is helpful at this point to outline in concise terms the nature of OSINT and the difference between OSINT and the much broader playing field, Open Source Information (OSIF) that most mis-represent at OSINT.

OSINT is decision-support: tailored intelligence relevant to a specific decision by a specific decision-maker or decision-making body. OSIF is everything else, broadcast, broadly shared, generic in nature.

OSIF is any information that can be obtained legally and ethically. It is not limited to published information, indeed a great deal of the historical, cultural, and contextual knowledge that we need to access must be elicited from humans, both direct observers and subject-matter experts.

There are a number of core references on OSINT and OSIF that capture the essence for managers and leaders, I list them here.

- The Future of OSINT [is M4IS2-Multinational]
- 2008 Open Source Intelligence (Strategic)
- 2008 Open Source Intelligence (Operational)
- 2004 Special Operations Forces OSINT Handbook (Strawman)
- 2000-2002 NATO OSINT Handbooks

If a World Brain Institute with an embedded Global Game existed, the SG would be able to see on a large display a visualization of all scientists as well as public leaders and their relative position—a single institution would not be able to mislead the SG. At the same time the SG and Members would have two other benefits:

Climate Change would be presented in relation to ALL ten threats to humanity and in relation to all twelve core policies (Agriculture, Diplomacy, Economy, Education, Energy, Family, Health, Immigration, Justice, Security, Society, Water). It would be understood, in this context, that the social harm to the UN goals of eradicating poverty and infectious disease is greater than the benefit of reducing carbon emission in the poorest of countries, and the misrepresented data could be seen.

In the second instance, it is now clear that the US and UK decisions to invade both IQ and AF were based on ideologically-defined policy preferences, and completely refuted by both secret and public decision-support. In the US those of us prepared to pay $100,000 for full-page information advertisements against the war saw our money refused by a captive press. Within the UN, there was no competing voice armed with public information to refute the lies presented to the UN by the US Administration.

If a World Brain Institute with an embedded Global Game existed, the SG would be able to see on a large display a visualization of all leaders (not just political but religious, economic, and academic) and their relative position—a single government would not be able to mislead the SG. At the same time the SG and Members would have two other benefits:

1. The "true cost" of both the Iraq and the Afghanistan invasions could be properly presented to all Members and their publics, and a rich harvest of multi-cultural perspectives factored in—the US leaders for example, were unaware of the Sunni-Shi'ite split in Iraq, or the implications of the Pakistan Sunni nuclear bomb in relation to the Iranian effort to create a nuclear deterrent against Sunnis, not the US or Israel.

2. The legitimate planning concerns of the diplomats and the commercial specialists, as well as the US military officers such as the Chief of Staff of the Army who knew full well the instability that can occur from going in "light," could have been properly acknowledged, and a multi-national multi-cultural campaign plan developed to leverage the Golden Hour so as not to lose the peace.

The World Brain Institute and Global Game are the means by which the SG leverages the moral and practical value of Open Everything, making it possible to hear all voices, to nurture appreciative inquiry and deliberative dialog at all levels, and to achieve truth & reconciliation across failed states whose poor can be empowered with cell phone connectivity and education "on cell call at a time," so as to create infinite stabilizing wealth *in situ*.

Here we outline the three elements that the UN can inspire—if the USA will not pay for it by passing the Smart Nation – Safe Nation Act—we as a group believe that Brazil, China, India, Indonesia, Russia, Venezuela, and Wild Cards such as

Malaysia, South Africa, and Turkey—could be engaged in the one initiative likely to assure their future prosperity as well as general peace.

The World Brain Institute (WBI) is envisioned as a single international non-governmental organization that is responsible for promulgating standards, sources, and methods nurturing of *Conscious Evolution*, *Integral Consciousness*, *Holistic Darwinism*, and *Non-Zero* Development. Below are elements of a proposed PhD program with the intention of achieving what E. O. Wilson calls *Consilience—the Unity of Knowledge*.

- Accounting, Statistics, & True Cost Forensics
- Administration & Organizational Design
- Anthropology & Sociology
- Co-Creation & Co-Intelligence Methods & Tools
- Collective Intelligence & Cognitive Science
- Commercial Intelligence Sources & Methods
- Cultural Intelligence Sources & Methods
- Decision-Support Sources & Methods
- Global Game & Serious Games for Change
- Earth Sciences & Economics
- Emerging Markets & Bottom-Up Capitalism
- Ethnobiology & Foreign Studies
- Faith-Based Diplomacy
- Geospatial Design, Science, & Technologies
- Global Gift Intelligence Sources & Methods
- Health Intelligence Sources & Methods
- Human Cognition & Evolutionary Psychology
- Information Operations
- Innovation & Applied Technologies
- Peace Intelligence Sources & Methods
- Theory of Change, Paradigms, & Revolution

The World Brain Institute serves as a means of achieving voluntary generic competency among all individuals, organizations, and Member States that wish to participate in striving to achieve a prosperous world at peace.

The second element of our alternative construct is a Multinational Decision-Support Centre (MDSC), ideally embedded within what I hope will one day be a national Open Source Agency (OSA) such as recommended on pages 23 and 413 of the 9-11 Commission Report.

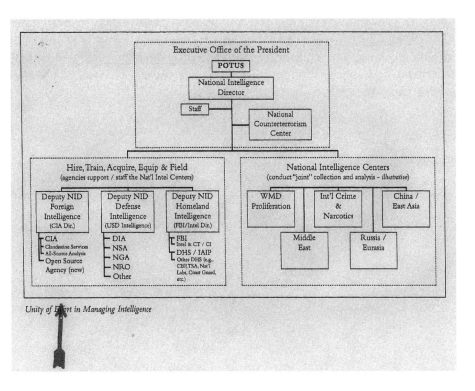

Figure 17. Open Source Agency (OSA) Documented as a Need

Under diplomatic and civil affairs auspices instead of within the secret world, the OSA is an essential foundation for the practice of M4IS2.

The Nordic Community (Denmark, Finland, Norway, Sweden) has displaced the Canadians as the thirty party of choice for direct support to UN peacekeeping intelligence. This may be in part because the Canadians are too dependent on US secret intelligence and have no global capability of their own; and in part because the Nordics combine two essential perceptions: first, a deep appreciation for OSINT, and second, a deep appreciation and long-standing practice of participating in multinational operations and intelligence centers.

The USA lost a major opportunity when it allowed the Coalition Coordination Center (CCC) within the US Central Command (USCENTCOM) to evaporate. Although <u>all were briefed</u> on the opportunity to convert this logistics coordination center into an M4IS2 facility, the <u>US chain of command</u> did not at the time have an appreciation for <u>the possibilities</u>. Below is a depiction of how an MDSC would support the UN and all others.

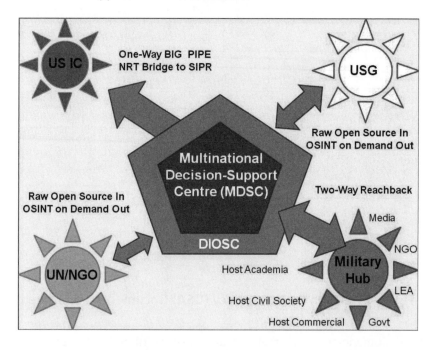

Figure 18: Multinational Decision-Support Centre (MDSC)

The Centre, leveraging both the financial and the global reach capabilities of the OSA, whose funding is anticipated to be between US$2 billion and US$4 billion a year, allows the Centre to address, in one holistic capability, the needs of four important constituencies, three of whom offer *quid pro quo* possibilities:

US (Secret) Intelligence Community. Seven "rules" have been set forth, the most important two of which are 1) the secret world gets everything from the open source world instantly; and 2) in return for which, the secret world has no authority over what we do with the original open source information.

US Government. Although "Whole of Government," "Rebalancing the Instruments of National Power," and "soft power" have come into vogue since 2008, no one is actually providing the unclassified intelligence (decision-support) needed to realize these concepts in practice. Although the non-militarized elements of the US Government would receive priority from the OSA, by extension this would also support all other governments participating in each multinational planning, programming, and budgeting domain.

National Hubs. Both because the funding would be redirected from the US military, and because the military in most nations, including the USA, is the most organized, disciplined, and responsive element of the government, EIN has proposed that the MDSC fund a military-centered "hub" in each country with the intent of establishing two-way reach-back that embraces the eight intelligence tribes in each country—the military and academia, civil society, commerce, government, law enforcement, media, and NGOs.

UN/NGO. Finally, and addressing the now established needs for creating a robust global capability to do Stabilization & Reconstruction (S&R) Operations with a multiplicity of organizations, many not military and most not at all able to receive classified intelligence (decision-support), the MDSC would become the global multinational operations and intelligence center for providing on-demand strategic, operational, tactical, and technical intelligence to any S&R mission anywhere. This would both increase the chances of success for such endeavors, and dramatically reduce the need for direct US intervention.

Finally we come to the idea of a Center for Public Intelligence (CPI) dedicated to creating public intelligence in the public interest. Whereas there would only be one WBI, there can be an infinite number of centers for public intelligence.

The operational, tactical, and technical details are discussed throughout the balance of this book. Here we only need to say that the concept of UNODIN is explicitly universal, seeking to embrace and exploit the distributed intelligence of the Whole Earth, with a particular appreciation for diversity so as to achieve holistic appreciations that are sustainable.

The human brain is the one infinite resource we have and therefore UNODIN via the WBI will promulgate Free/Open Source Software (F/OSS); Open Source Intelligence (OSINT) training, standards, and help desk facilities; and enable Open Spectrum exploitation such that local communications and local information-sharing and sense-making can be infrastructure independent, thus assuring resilience of the whole.

Within the UN "System" there would be no change in personnel, procedures, or funding until UNODIN is fully established and all of the UN System elements are both full participants in the information-sharing aspects of UNODIN, and also fully satisfied beneficiaries of the UNODIN offerings

Hence, each of the UN elements, such as the DPKO and OCHA as well as the varied specialized agencies, would retain their varied country or thematic action officers, but over time, as the intelligence (decision-support) created by UNODIN is absorbed and leveraged, those active officers would spend less time collecting and analyzing information, and more time engaging in pro-active multinational coordination of plans, programs, budgets, and behavior.

Chapter 7
Conclusions & Recommendations

Conclusions

For the first time in history, a High-Level Panel of truly expert individuals has identified, in priority order, the ten high-level threats to humanity.

The UN has the potential to harness the distributed intelligence of the Eight Tribes and it has the potential to create a universal strategy that uses multinational information-sharing and sense-making to create a prosperous world at peace.

The United Nations (UN) System is not a system at all, but it is the one universally-acknowledged global network.

The UN lacks a Strategic Analytic Model; it lacks a strategy for information-sharing and sense-making, and it has no intelligence (decision-support) capabilities.

Recommendations

We should all adopt this specific set of findings for universal action.

The UN needs to create the Office of the Assistant Secretary General for Intelligence (Decision-Support) as soon as possible, even if only one person, to provide a focal point for pursuing this book's suggestions.

We cannot rely on the UN to lead us, but we can support the UN and treat it, with respect, as a starting point.

There are easily correctable deficiencies provided that the emphasis is on open sources and methods, not on secret sources and methods.

The UN has recognized—but not resolved—its intelligence (decision-support) deficiencies. The Brahmi Report, in combination with the JOC and JMAC indicatives in recent years, bode well for the future.

If the UN fails to address its intelligence (decision-support) deficiencies, it will continue to be ineffective at devising strategic mandates, forces structures, and all other programs of interest.

The reality is that knowledge is desperately fragmented across multiple disciplinary and domain boundaries, while at the same time there are eight tribes of intelligence (decision-support) that do not share information with one another.

A revolution in global leadership is underway, one that displaces the top-down "command & control" structures of the past.

A revolution in intelligence affairs has been emergent for twenty-one years. The 9-11 Commission recommendation of an Open Source Agency (OSA) is the culmination of 21 years of effort—but OSA must be diplomatic, not part of the secret world.

The UN should convene a planning forum to discuss how best to implement all of the Brahimi Report recommendations in combination with the recommendations in this book.

The UN leadership should invite all Members States and UN elements to convene planning forums to discuss how best to create a UN Open-Source Decision-Support Information Network (UNODIN)

The UN must acquire an understanding of the information terrain, appreciate the fragmentation of knowledge, and devise a plan to unite the eight tribes of intelligence so as to create a commonwealth of information.

The UN should strive to understand and then adapt to the 2.0, 3.0, and 4.0 social change networks that are emergent and growing.

The UN—and its Member States— would do well to understand the undercurrents in US intelligence— an enormous advantage for peace and prosperity can be achieved if UNODIN and the OSA proceed side by side to create public intelligence in the public interest.

Part II

OPERATIONAL INTELLIGENCE—INTEGRITY

Multinational Multifunctional Regional Centers & Networks

Part II consists of seven chapters addressing the global operational context within which I propose that the UN and its Member States—and all Eight Tribes of intelligence—creating regional networks within which to share information and contribute the diversity of view that is essential to getting a grasp on the truth at any cost—doing so reduces all other costs *and* creates a prosperous world at peace.

This part of the book emphasizes INTEGRITY in the sense that Buckminster Fuller intended—the purity of information feed-back loops among all elements so that we can avoid overshoot and over-reaction (a typical problem within Industrial-Era stove-piped organizations where the chief executive officers are buffered from reality by special interests and sycophants around them).

In my view, regional information-sharing integrity is easier to achieve that global information-sharing integrity, and logically, national internal information-sharing integrity is easier to achieve than regional. Hence, while the stratgic construct or architecture is that of UNODIN, the *substance* of information-sharing is "bottom-up." The first country to become a "Smart Nation" will be a "spike" whose immediate increased internal peace and prosperity will be noticed by and spur on all others.

While the top ten high-level threats to humanity have been identified, no one other than EIN has taken the trouble to blend from among a number of presidential-level endeavors the twelve core policies that must be harmonized, or to devise in detail the information-sharing and sense-making constructs that

57

allow all stakeholders in any given region to "get a grip" on reality and work together to eliminate corruption, waste, and fraud.

In this portion of the book we examine operational-level concepts intended to facilitate appreciative inquiry and deliberative dialog among all stakeholders.

Secrets are a fact of life, sometimes they are needed, and as Figure 2 on page 9 of Chapter 1 illustrates, I anticipate the need for the UN, the regional associations, and others to focus as little as 5% and as much as 20% of their time, attention, and resources on secret sources and methods. However, the default is Open Everything, and a reliance on open sources and methods to the fullest extent possible—and so this book concludes in the final chapter.

Chapter 8. Operational Intelligence and Regional Policy Harmonization, in keeping with the over-all theme of this book, that the World Brain must be an Epoch B or bottom-up convergence, discusses how the existing regional organizations can harmonize their policies and spending with a completely voluntary approach to multinational information-sharing and sense-making.

Chapter 9. State of the Regional Unions, focuses on three of the most important regional organizations, the African Union (AU); the Shanghai Cooperation Organisation (SCO); and the Union of South American Countries (UNASUR).

Chapter 10. Cultures of Catastrophe, Cheating, Conflict, & Conspiracy, addresses the significant obstacle to progress, our pathological cultures.

Chapter 11 Information Asymmetries and Data Pathologies, discusses a second major obstacle to progress, but one that is immediately addressable.

Chapter 12. Revitalizing the Instruments of National Power, examines how we must move from excessive unilateral investments in war to collaborative investments in peace and prosperity, peace costing one third the cost of war.

Chapter 13. An Alternative Construct: Regional Centers & Networks, outlines the specifics of needed regional networks, with an emphasis on Africa, Central Asia, and South America.

Chapter 14. Conclusions and Recommendations, sums up this part.

Chapter 8

Operational Intelligence and Regional Policy Harmonization

This book recognizes the reality of the enormous divides that exist. In Part III we will address Tactical Intelligence and particularly Diversity. This part of the book focuses on the middle ground between strategic recognition that We must be One if we are to prosper within the closed circle called Earth; and the tactical reality of imperfect understanding and imperfect motives in conflict. Here we seek to understand the art and science of the possible at the intersection of regions, culture, information, and instruments of national power.

Apart from the UN and major global international organizations such as the International Committee of the Red Cross (ICRC), the next significant unit of both operations and analysis is the regional political organization. Our objective is to put forward three simple concepts that can be actualized at the national level, at the regional or sub-regional level (e.g. North Africa), and at the trans-regional level (e.g. South America and Africa, Central Asia and Caucasia or the Caucasus, as well as bi-laterally—the Turkey-Iran axis looks enormously interesting in the near-term, and has not been properly studied by the West.

The essence of our approach to the operational challenge of harmonizing regional policies is to begin with an analytic model that is neutral—nothing more than a framework within which to associate data; with a concept for accessing all relevant information and being able to share it and make sense of it; and finally, with a voluntary regional financial information framework for optimizing spending, reducing waste, and enhancing regional peace and prosperity.

The contribution made by the UN High-Level Panel on Threats, Challenges, and Change in identifying and prioritizing the ten high-level threats to all of humanity cannot be over-stated. Without that as a starting point, nothing else in this book would have been possible.

Inspired by the High-Level Panel's contribution, I funded EIN's start-up and with 23 others created the analytic model that is depicted below.

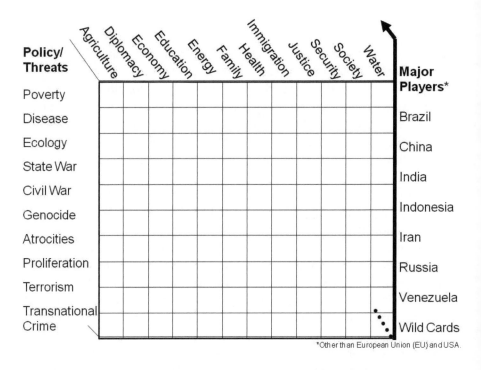

Figure 19. Analytic Matrix for Regional Policy Harmonization

On the next page I explain how we arrived at the twelve policies and eight major players that will determine the future of humanity on Earth.

With the threats established, in theory the wise men and women of the entity responsible for protecting the given commonwealth would devise a "strategy" that in theory takes into account the means (revenues), then orchestrates the ways (or defines new ways that must be devised at cost over time), and finally directs a "campaign" in which all the instruments of national power—and allied power—are used to achieve the ends being sought.

With considerable influence from the Strategic Studies Institute (SSI) of the US Army, which holds an annual US Army Strategy Conference, I realized that no one is doing strategy properly, in part because they simply do not have an analytic model or an information-sharing and sense-making capacity. I realized we had to create that, starting with the identification of "core" policy domains. We used the "Mandate for Change" volumes, both published and online, from the past five presidential transitions to make our selection. Put clearly, isolating core policy domains comes *before* strategy development.

Twelve Core Policy Domains

There are *twelve policies* that must be managed *together*. It makes no sense to allow landowners to sell water aquifers that are part of our national commonwealth, or to use water we don't have to grow grain we don't need to create fuel when we have natural gas right here, right now. Below are snapshots of each of the twelve policies and why they matter, but first we must emphasize that the debt, not just the devaluation of the currency and the total loss of all quality of life gains from the middle class down to the very poor, but the huge $8 trillion dollar debt and the $40 trillion and up known future unfunded obligations, is a "policy" decision that is irresponsible and must be overturned. While couched in terms specific to the USA (this information appears in the chapter on "The Substance of Governance" in *ELECTION 2008: Lipstick on the Pig*), it is inherently internationalist in nature.

01 Agriculture is historically the most Jeffersonian foundation for our communities and our society. We need to return to local and organic, family and community owned farming, and we must learn from our ancestors across the Americas and practice deep root farming without pesticides. It merits comment that only two sustainable agricultural models exist today: the Amish model, and the Cuban model, both without pesticides.

61

02 Diplomacy in the past sixteen years has disappeared as a profession. Between politically-appointed Ambassadors (our Ambassador to Sweden under President Bill Clinton paid a mere $15,000 for the job), and the conversion of our professionals into timid messengers rather than skilled observers and interpreters of foreign history, culture, and reality, we have lost our ability to understand, much less influence, the rest of the world. We need to restore diplomacy, restore the US Information Agency (USIA), and create a global information-sharing and sense-making network that is multinational and competent in all languages.

03 Economy is in severe distress from a combination of Chief Executive Officer (CEO) greed; irresponsible trading in derivatives; financial managers skimming a fifth of the value from the stock market; and the destruction of unions and export of jobs. We must demand full employment of citizens, local supply chains, disclosure of true costs, and higher or "living" wages.

04 Education is both dysfunctional, and insufficient. The Chinese graduate more honor students than our total high school graduation population. Generation 2.0 is the first that is not like us, with "digital native" understanding we lack. We need team learning, learning to learn, self-paced online, and apprenticeships in the trades and professions.

05 Energy is central. We've known this since the 1970's, but Congress—and our Senators in particular—chose to ignore both Peak Oil warnings, and the ready availability of alternative energies including wind, solar, hydrogen, sap ethanol and more recently, amoeba, bacteria and termites. A two-way grid, natural capitalism, biomimicry, and zero waste are all achievable now. Citizens need to demand, however, that energy policy not be created in isolation from all ten threats and the other eleven policies. As we shall see in the next section, we must, as a Nation and as a planet, make policy that respects the massive demographic influence of the Eight Challengers.

06 Family is the foundation for any society of faith. We have killed the family in our Republic by allowing the industrial era to destroy cottage industry, family farms, and small shops—a Wal-Mart anywhere destroys all small shops for 100 to 200 miles around. That's simply not right. Our family policy should enable one job (or two half-time jobs) to support a family, and we should do vastly more to build family-friendly neighborhoods with community centers. Like energy, family should demand a rigorous evaluation of every threat and every policy in relation to its impact on the family now and seven generations into the future. Family is central to the neighborhood, the community, the church, and and the country. It is a non-negotiable first plank that impacts on population policy, health policy, all of our infrastructure and energy arrangements, and so on. As goes the family, so goes the Republic, and the Earth.

07 Health is a public good and along with Family, the core foundation for a strong polity that can nurture and sustain a strong population that is balanced across age and capacity. In my view, and tightly connected to the collapse of education and the media as well as the family as a healthy unit, the health of our population has collapsed. Not only is it now demonstrated that 50% of our expenditures on health go to waste, but the cost to society, to the family, and to the individual of poor health is well-neigh astronomical. Health is a 4-part endeavor: healthy lifestyle; healthy environment; natural or alternative medicine; and *last*, remedial hospitalization and pharmaceuticals. At a minimum, government can mandate the publication of true costs to society and true costs to heal, and impose taxation while also offering or mandating insurance incentives. I will not argue here for either universal health coverage or universal service, but do want to mention three facts:

a) Medicare future unfunded obligations as well as current costs can be reduced to one percent (1%) of the existing tariffs because we can legally buy all of the drugs wholesale overseas for 1% of what we are paying now (at best—10% of what we pay now is a worst case).

b) Evidence-based medicine is coming to the fore at the same time that our society is beginning to appreciate the sensibility of Traditional Chinese Medicine (TCM) and its India-based counterpart.

c) Universal service, for both natural-born citizens and immigrants of any age, is a superb means of baselining the health of the population in multiple ways. At a minimum, it will ensure that the poor receive a complete physical examination

63

including blood work that they would not normally have access to; and it puts all adults at a condition of physical fitness that cannot be achieved efficiently in other ways. The cultural bonding, civic duty, and social responsibility outcomes are naturally very valuable also. In my view, everybody should do boot camp together both after high school or college, and at mid-career, followed by a voluntarily chosen path into the Armed Forces, the Peace Corps, or the America Corps. Two years of universal service after high school or four years after college, and a mid-career fully-funded "sabbatical", will bring us all back together.

08 Immigration is a problem today for two reasons:

a) first, our federal government refused to follow its own prescriptions with respect to the urgent need for a population policy as outlined in Stephen D. Mumford, *The Life and Death of NSSM 200: How the Destruction of Political Will Doomed a US Population Policy* (Center for Research on Population & Security, 1994); and

b) second, our federal government is incompetent at both border control and at the enforcement of visa stay limits. Latinos (and I am a Latino on my mother's side) are not the problem. By accepting "free trade" and ignoring the true costs of exporting jobs and importing twice as much oil as most realize (half to use here, half to get Wal-Mart crap here), we have hurt our earnest blue collar and lower middle class workers twice—first sending their jobs overseas, and then making it possible for non-citizens to fill lower-paying jobs here in the USA, immune to either employer responsibility or government intervention.

09 Justice cannot be addressed without understanding that we have three major failures embedded into our economy: we need to release all marijuana offenders to time served and balance in national service with a full paycheck; wind down the prison-slave complex; and eliminate corporate avoidance of liability through the personality clause.

10 Security is now a global, total, and permanent challenge—there is no hiding from disease, or toxic fumes or poisoned water or food. The USA needs to sharply redirect funding away from waging war and creating monstrously expensive technical systems (both military and for secret intelligence) and instead move back toward the Common Security paradigm that wages peace, funds preventive measures, and empowers the 5 billion poor with access to free education and cell phones. Such a paradigm would only be successful if all nations and organizations agree to:

a) Share information—96% of what we need to know is not secret, not online, not in English, and not known to the federal government as it is now trained, equipped, and organized (for Rule by Secrecy & Cold War)

b) Share the sense-making burden (including historical and cultural) in partnership with all nations and all organizations from all eight tribes that I have been writing about since the 1990's: government, military, law enforcement, academia, business, media, non-profit, and civil society including labor unions and religions;

c) Harmonize policies and investments on a transparent basis—this means BOTH the policies and investments that are made on our behalf with our taxes, AND the policies and investments of all other stakeholders—foreign governments, corporations, international and non-governmental organizations, and foundations: we do this with shared information and the Global Range of Needs Table discussed in Chapter 26.

11 Society in the USA has fragmented. We the People, regardless of who is elected to high office, must demand English as the common language; federally-funded high-quality education across the Nation; universal service with common fitness training and then three choices: Armed Forces, Peace Corps, or America Corps.; and an end to religious incursions into secular governance matters.

12 Water! Most of Earth's water is sea water, and most of the fraction that is fresh water is locked up in ice. Less than 0.1% of Earth's water is available for human use. The primary obstacle to water desalination, apart from expense, has been energy, but with new sources of renewable energy, including deep water thermals and cost-effective wind and solar, it becomes possible to address this as a global project. Think about what $100 million can buy: it can buy a Navy battleship with ammunition and crew; it can buy an Army brigade with tanks and artillery; it can buy 1,000 diplomats or 10,000 Peace Corps workers;

it can buy one day of war over water....or....it can buy a <u>water desalination</u> plant able to produce 100 million cubic meters of potable water a year from the sea, preventing war.

Eight Major Players—Demographic Challengers

Identifying the major players for the future was simple—in the 21st Century demographic power rules for two reasons:

1. There are not enough guns on the planet to overwhelm a resistant population that finds its Collective Intelligence; and

2. The human brain is the one renewable infinite resource we have to work with.

As much as the USA and the European Union (EU) may wish to keep their heads in the sand and allow ideology to shape decisions completely removed from reality, I believe that reality cannot be ignored.

The hard reality is that Brazil, China, India, Indonesia, Iran, Russia, Venezuela, and Wild Cards such as the Chile, the Congo, Malaysia, South Africa, and Turkey enjoy such overwhelming demographic power—and in most cases such large geographic territories all but one adjacent to the sea—that they are going to be the prime determinants of the future of humanity.

This is real simple: NOTHING the USA does in the next ten years is going to be relevant to the future of our children and grandchildren UNLESS we create a compelling story, model, or process that the eight demographic challengers can adopt as their own to prosper without making our Industrial Era mistakes.

Here are snapshots of each of these major powers.

01 Brazil is a major demographic power that is energy independent and has a growing connection to China that is being managed out of Macau at the same time that the Chinese are pressing very aggressively to embrace all former Portuguese colonies.

02 China is deep into two major crises that will be sustained time bombs; the first is Energy and the second is Water. All investments there are at risk, and if China has a plague break out such as is common in India, it could spread like wildfire. The Chinese are doing well at combating poverty, and they are exporting their surplus men—Argentina will be majority Chinese by 2025. They are waging peace across Africa and South America—between the Chinese and Russians, between Brazil and Venezuela (number seven on this list)—the USA could find itself shut out of the Southern Hemisphere as a major player, in large part because the USA has been inept, predatory, and inattentive, taking both Africa and South America for granted.

03 India, like China, has a major water crisis, and in any given year can see 2,000 poor farmers commit suicide due to draught and debt. It represents the most complex, diverse, and potentially conflict-ridden mix of languages, tribes, ethnicity, and religions, most of them very very poor, with the "rich" information technology (IT) sector being a very small segment of the economy. It merits comment that India's IT wealth stems from government investments in regional universities whose goal was to produce the most versatile and skilled IT engineers and programmers on the planet, all of them fluent in English. India, with the Indian Ocean, will be a relative equal to China, Europe, and the USA in Asian affairs specifically, and global affairs generally.

04 Indonesia could become a major power beyond its own territorial waters. It is proving resilient to internal turmoil, and its secular government, with the Chinese business Diaspora lurking in the background, is not only continuing to educate women apace, but with the help of the secularized women, dealing effectively with religious zealots and home-grown terrorists. They are the key to the anti-piracy program in the Malacca Straits, a critical passageway for international ships bearing energy as well as other critical cargoes.

05 Iran is what is left of Persia. We overturned their democratic election, restoring the Shah and his secret police to power. They are an extremely sophisticated nation-state, and feel besieged because they are the Shi'ite minority nation in an overwhelming Sunni world that is funded by Saudi Arabia. Iran is also paranoid about Pakistan, a Sunni nation, having the Sunni nuclear bomb. Important note: The Pakistani nuclear program owes its health to both the deliberate overturning of US proliferation controls by Dr. Zbigniew Brzezinski, then National Security Advisor for President Jimmy Carter, and to the flood of money—billions and billions of dollars—from the US secret agencies to the Pakistani Inter-Services Intelligence (ISI) that most of us believe appropriated at least half if not two thirds of all funds for themselves and selective investments in the Pakistani nuclear program, including the acquisition of French submarines capable for firing nuclear missiles. Iran is afraid of Pakistan and Saudi Arabia, not the USA.

06 Russia is on the rebound. They are energy independent, and as their recent foray into Georgia (and the less publicized simultaneous attack on the southern end of the pipeline in the Middle East) makes clear, they can cut European energy supplies whenever they wish. Russia has enormous potential and merits complete respect—the USA has made a very serious mistake these past sixteen years in not understanding the vital importance of Russia as both a European ally, and a Caucasian bulwark against Chinese movement north into eastern Russia (Siberia, which, like the Empty Quarter in Canada, will be prime real estate as Global Warming progresses).

07 Venezuela is under the rule of its President Hugo Chavez, who strives—with some substantive success—to recreate the vision of Simon Bolivar. With its oil wealth and other natural resources including a significant share of the Amazonia region, Venezuela must be taken very seriously. Chavez has succeeded in creating the South American Union, and enjoys a populist popularity, aided by Cuban intelligence and its extraordinary competence at regional covert operations including media influence and agents of influence.

08 Wild Cards are many, my personal favorites are Chile, Denmark, the Congo, Greenland, Malaysia, South Africa, and Turkey, but virtually any country that commits to becoming a <u>Smart Nation</u> can be its own Wild Card.

Global and Regional Information Exploitation Architecture

The 24 co-founders of EIN (Winston Maike now deceased, replaced by Robert Horn of Information Mapping renown) spent the first six months thinking and in dialog with one another. While the original ten-page mission summary remains online and useful, below is the core concept relevant to this book's goal of inspiring regional as well as global information-sharing and sense-making for universal open exploitation.

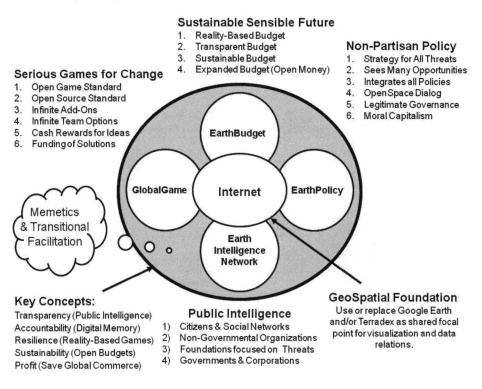

Sustainable Sensible Future
1. Reality-Based Budget
2. Transparent Budget
3. Sustainable Budget
4. Expanded Budget (Open Money)

Non-Partisan Policy
1. Strategy for All Threats
2. Sees Many Opportunities
3. Integrates all Policies
4. Open Space Dialog
5. Legitimate Governance
6. Moral Capitalism

Serious Games for Change
1. Open Game Standard
2. Open Source Standard
3. Infinite Add-Ons
4. Infinite Team Options
5. Cash Rewards for Ideas
6. Funding of Solutions

Memetics & Transitional Facilitation

EarthBudget

GlobalGame   Internet   EarthPolicy

Earth Intelligence Network

Key Concepts:
Transparency (Public Intelligence)
Accountability (Digital Memory)
Resilience (Reality-Based Games)
Sustainability (Open Budgets)
Profit (Save Global Commerce)

Public Intelligence
1) Citizens & Social Networks
2) Non-Governmental Organizations
3) Foundations focused on Threats
4) Governments & Corporations

GeoSpatial Foundation:
Use or replace Google Earth and/or Terradex as shared focal point for visualization and data relations.

Figure 20. Six Circles of Information-Sharing & Sense-Making

Each of these circles merits deeper discussion among those who would implement the ideas that this book summarizes for others to actualize.

Further on in the book I discuss tactical and technical implementation concepts. The illustration below is the culmination of over a decade of thinking about Information Peacekeeping as inspired by Alvin Toffler's conclusion in *Powershift–Knowledge, Wealth, and Violence at the Edge of the 21st Century* (1991) to wit, that information is a substitute for violence and wealth as well as time, space, labor, and capital.

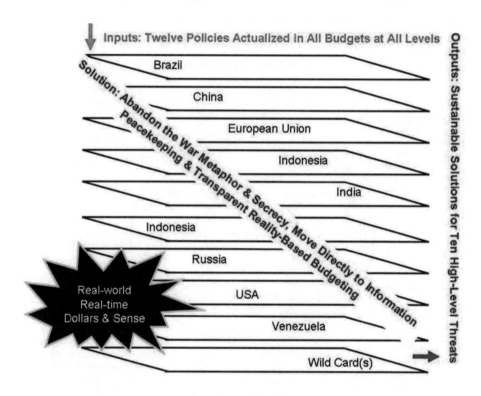

Figure 21. Using Information to Harmonize Major Player Spending

Apart from the major demographic players, the concepts in this chapter are easily implementable within regions, sub-regions, between two countries (e.g. Iran and Turkey), or other alliances (e.g. Brazil and West Africa).

Chapter 9
State of the Regional Unions

Below is a very selective list of major regional organizations, by no means complete, but simply to provide a sense of how many allied networks the UN could energize if it were to champion M4IS2 and an Open Everything approach to the majority of the information-sharing and sense-making opportunities. Some are geographically related, others security related.

African Union (AU)
Association of Southeast Asian Nations (ASEAN)
Central American Integration System (SICA)
Collective Security Treaty Organisation (CSTO)
Commonwealth of Independent States (CIS)
Cooperation Council for the Arab States of the Gulf (CCASG)
European Union (EU)
League of Arab States (Arab League)
North American Free Trade Agreement (NAFTA)
North Atlantic Treaty Organization (NATO)
Organization of American States (OAS)
Pacific Islands Forum (PIF)
Shanghai Cooperation Organisation (SCO)
South Asian Association for Regional Cooperation
South Asian Association for Regional Cooperation (SAARC)
Southeast Asia Treaty Organization (SEATO)
Union of South American Nations (UNASUR)

Some of the organizations above that are not Unions have discussed the possibility, including the Arab League, NAFTA and the Pacific Islands Forum.

African Union

The African Union (abbreviated **AU** in English, and **UA** in its other official languages) is an intergovernmental organisation consisting of 52 African states. Established on July 9, 2002, the AU was formed as a successor to the Organisation of African Unity (OAU). The most important decisions of the AU are made by the Assembly of the African Union, a semi-annual meeting of the heads of state and government of its member states.

Figure 22. African Union (AU)

There are eight Regional Economic Commissions (REC) recognized by the AU, each established under a separate regional treaty, all of which could benefit substantially from sharing transparent trusted information:

- Arab Maghreb Union (UMA)
- Common Market for Eastern and Southern Africa (COMESA)
- Community of Sahel-Saharan States (CEN-SAD)
- East African Community (EAC)
- Economic Community of Central African States (ECCAS)
- Economic Community of West African States (ECOWAS)
- Intergovernmental Authority on Development (IGAD)
- Southern Africa Development Community (SADC)

The African Union has a number of official bodies that could benefit substantially from intelligence (decision-support):

- African Court of Justice
- African Union Authority
- Assembly of the African Union
- Economic, Social and Cultural Council
- Executive Council
- Pan-African Parliament (PAP)
- Peace and Security Council (PSC)
- Permanent Representatives' Committee
- Technical Committees

Both the Abuja Treaty and the Constitutive Act provide for Specialized Technical Committees to be established made up of African ministers to advise the Assembly. In practice, they have never been set up. The ten proposed themes are: Rural Economy and Agricultural Matters; Monetary and Financial Affairs; Trade, Customs, and Immigration; Industry, Science and Technology; Energy, Natural Resources, and Environment; Transport, Communications, and Tourism; Health; Labour, and Social Affairs; Education, Culture, and Human Resources. Taking the latter established need and equally established inaction, imagine the value of having a global common list of committees.

Shanghai Cooperation Organisation (SCO)

The **Shanghai Cooperation Organisation (SCO)** is an intergovernmental mutual-security organisation which was founded in 2001 in Shanghai by the leaders of China, Kazakhstan, Kyrgyzstan, Russia, Tajikistan, and Uzbekistan. Except for Uzbekistan, the other countries had been members of the **Shanghai Five**, founded in 1996; after the inclusion of Uzbekistan in 2001, the members renamed the organisation.

Figure 23. Shanghai Cooperation Organisation (SCO)

The four major areas of cooperation cover security, economics, and cultural exchanges, as well as annual summits.

Subordinate organizations that could benefit from global information-sharing and sense-making include special working groups and non-governmental institutions including a business council, an interbank forum, and a forum.

Of great interest from a global and regional information-sharing and sense-making perspective are the Observers, Dialog Partners, and Guests.

Observers:

- India
- Iran
- Mongolia
- Pakistan

Dialog Partners:

- Belarus
- Sri Lanka

Guests:

- Afghanistan
- ASEAN
- CIS

This chapter is not focused on threats or policies, but is should be obvious that from both a threat and a policy perspective, the participants in the SCO have both a great deal of information to share and a great deal to gain from exchanging information on all of these topics and especially the threat of poverty and the policies of energy and water, with other regional alliances.

Union of South American Countries (UNASUR)

The **Union of South American Nations** (Dutch: *Unie van Zuid-Amerikaanse Naties* - **UZAN**, Portuguese: *União de Nações Sul-Americanas* - **UNASUL**, Spanish: *Unión de Naciones Suramericanas* - **UNASUR**) is an intergovernmental union integrating two existing customs unions: Mercosur and the Andean Community of Nations, as part of a continuing process of South American integration. It is modeled on the European Union.

There is little of substance to UNASUR at this time, but in my personal view, the one thing the USA could do to nurture this region and achieve truth & reconciliation for centuries of predatory policies, is to offer M4IS2 to USASUR.

Figure 24. Union of South American Countries (UNASUR)

Chapter 10

Cultures of Catastrophe, Cheating, Conflict, & Conspiracy

The word **corrupt** (Middle English, from Latin *corruptus*, past participle of *corrumpere*, to destroy : *com-*, intensive pref. and *rumpere*, to break) when used as an adverb literally means "utterly broken".

According to Wikipedia, which can be very useful in generic terms, but itself very corrupt in editorial practice depending on the issue, suggests that the term could refer to Political corruption, , Corporate corruption, Putrefaction, Data corruption, Corruption (linguistics), or Bribery in politics, business, or sport (including match fixing).

Chapter 11 will discuss Information Asymmetries and Data Pathologies, always present alongside corruption; and Chapter 15 our understanding of revolution across the political-legal, socio-economic, ideo-cultural, techno-demographic, and natural-geographic domains.

Accepting Corruption as a high-level term for being outside a State of Grace, this chapter will focus on four predominant representations of corruption in all that we do: our cultures of catastrophe, cheating, conflict, and conspiracy. We create our own catastrophes; we cheat one another with impunity; we choose to invest in war at three times the cost of peace; and we stand idly by as conspiracies murder our presidents, our civil rights leaders, the crew of the USS Liberty, and the most recently, 9-11 and the looting of the US Treasury.

This particular chapter is an essay crafted from the titles of books by others, each linked in the online version of this book to my summary of each book.

Cultures of Catastrophe

The most important insight I have gained in the past three decades of studying humanity as it stumbles about doing damage to all the Earth systems it touches, is that catastrophe is what happens when humans do not plan for, do not respond to, and then either over-react or under-react to the long-term implications of what would ordinarily be nothing more than an isolated disaster. This is IMPORTANT. It means that we are not thinking, and worse, we are not thinking holistically. *Catastrophe & Culture—The Anthropology of Disaster* (Susanna M. Hoffman) is especially helpful in pointing out that no amount of money is going to prevent catastrophe—absent a commitment to creating a culture of attention and interoperability and information-sharing, we will create our own catastrophes each time we are challenged by what could have been nothing more than a localized disaster.

We are the source and the cause of most of our catastrophes. The other three sections focus on cheating, conflict, and conspiracy. Here I emphasize the corruption inherent in how we allow our own industrial practices, our own governmental practices, to destroy, destabilize, and dismiss. *The Next Catastrophe—Reducing Our Vulnerabilities to Natural, Industrial, and Terrorist Disasters* (Charles Perrow) points out that natural disasters impact on six times more people than all the conflict on the planet. Industrial irresponsibility, especially in the nuclear, chemical, and biological industries, is legion, and much more potentially catastrophic than any terrorist attack. Of special concern is the storage of large amounts of toxic, flammable, volatile, or reactive materials outside the security perimeters—this includes spent nuclear fuel rods and tons of chlorine stored without special protection that if combined with fire would put millions at risk.

Perrow's latest book (he also wrote the seminal book, *Normal Accidents—Living with High-Risk Technologies*) is complemented by *Acts of God—The Unnatural History of Natural Disaster in America* (Ted Steinberg) This latter book is a magnificent epistle on the folly of mankind and the duplicity of government, business and the media. The author of totally brilliant as he gently sets forth the myth that we are not responsible for acts of God when in fact we are the perpetrators of complex human, social, economic, and political fabrications and decisions that invariably: 1. Screw over the poor and those of color; 2. Amortize high risks taken by the rich across the entire taxpayer base; and 3. Conceal, lie, deceive as to the actual premeditated decisions that occasioned the disaster turning into a catastrophe.

Another book that closely supports the above conclusions and concerns is _Collapse–How Societies Choose to Fail or Succeed_ (Jared Diamond). The author has conducted arduous research and lined up a number of case studies to support his five part framework of examining the topic of how societies choose to succeed or fail. They are: a. Environmental degradation, whether man-made or natural; b. Climate change (as distinct from desertification, deforestation, etc.); c. Hostile neighbors; d. Less friendly neighbors (loss of support); and e. Societies' responses.

The latter is especially important because it impacts on all the others. What we are all beginning to realize is that our over-all culture is the framework by which we Orient, Observe, Decide, and Act (OODA), a concept best represented in modern times by Col John Boyd, USAF (Ret), eulogized in _Boyd–The Fighter Pilot Who Changed the Art of War_ (Robert Coram).

Critical Path (Buckminster Fuller) speaks to how the economic theory of scarcity and secrecy is evil, benefitting the few at the expense of the many. Fuller believed that Earth is NOT a zero sum Darwinian game for humans and that in fact it is the human role–the human mind's role–to "synergize" Earth into a win-win for all. In time-energy "true cost" accounting, every gallon of oil that we use costs $1 million (in 1981 dollars). He tells us that there are two critical paths that are not understood by the public or those who profess to represent the public: path one is those natural trends that proceed with or without human errors, omissions, and interventions; path two is the human path both local and as a global aggregate. Fuller's wisdom has been reinforced by _Non-Zero_ (Robert Wright) as well as _Holistic Darwinism: Synergy, Cybernetics, and the Bioeconomics of Evolution_ (Peter A. Corning).

79

The emerging solutions that remediate, ameliorate, and obviate these negative cultures are brought forward in Parts III and IV of this book. Here we will just emphasize the break-down of the scientific method of inquiry, and the corruption that has over-taken what should be a pure investigative method that produces intelligence (decision-support). This is not about the fragmentation of knowledge, a strategic problem addressed in Chapter 5, nor is it about Information Asymmetries and Data Pathologies as discussed in Chapter 11, the next chapter. This is about inherent corruption that on the one hand divorces science from the humanities—from the moral and the social—and on the other hand seeks to actively manipulate and misrepresent scientific findings in isolation from the whole.

Voltaire's Bastards–The Dictatorship of Reason in the West (John Ralston Saul) calls into question much about how we organize ourselves politically, economically, and socially. The bottom line, and very consistently with other great books such as *The Manufacture of Evil* (Lionel Tiger) on the low end and *Consilience: The Unity of Knowledge* (E. O. Wilson) on the high end, is that Western thinking has been corrupted to the point that the West has become, as the inside flap of *Voltaire's Bastards* says, "a vast, incomprehensible directionless machine, run by process-minded experts....whose cult of scientific management is bereft of both sense and morality." He concludes that secrecy is pathological, undermining both public confidence and the public dialog. Intelligence should be disseminated actionable knowledge, not secrets.

Now fast forward to ClimateGate, which we will not belabor. Two books capture the fraud inherent in ClimateGate. *The Real Global Warming Disaster* (Christopher Booker) is in brief about bad science, bad media, bad politics, and bad finance. The obsession with climate change denigrates everything else—climate change is a tiny part of the larger and more legitimate threat, Environmental Degradation; and within climate change, carbon emissions are a tiny aspect in relation to emissions of sulfur and mercury as well as human destruction of wetlands and the Amazon. The other book is *Global Warming False Alarm–The Bad Science Behind the United Nations' Assertion that Man-made CO2 Causes Global Warming* (Ralph B. Alexander).

80

Cultures of Cheating

An entire book has been written about _The Cheating Culture–Why More Americans Are Doing Wrong to Get Ahead_ (David Callahan), and another on _The Global Class War –How America's Bipartisan Elite Lost Our Future – and What It Will Take to Win it Back_ (Jeff Faux).

In brief, the men who manage money—money they invent out of thin air and then lend at outrageous rates of interest—have corrupted all aspects of our society, both within the USA and around the world. I have written about this in both a book and a chapter, see _ELECTION 2008: Lipstick on the Pig_ and the chapter Paradigms of Failure as well as the supporting Annotated Bibliography on Reality.

Cheating is so pervasive that I cannot really do it justice in the context of this book that strives to be an overview making the case for a World Brain with embedded Global Game, so below are three sections with recommended readings (all linked in the free online version of this book).

Cheating can occur because of information asymmetries and data pathologies, the subject of our next chapter. This is important—the more we can achieve transparency of all transactions, the more that we can reduce corruption, fraud, waste, and abuse—in other words, cheating.

Cheating at the Top

Cheating at the top is largely driven by money corrupting politics, but in fairness to the banks and corporations, it appears that the "shakedown" for money originates with the politicians who seek to exploit their privileged positions for financial advantage. Categories at Phi Beta Iota that cover this segment include: Banks, Fed, Money, & Concentrated Wealth (37); Budget Process & Politics (18); Capitalism (Good & Bad) (125); Corruption (78); Culture, Research (112); Impeachment & Treason (46); Politics (144); and Power (Pathologies & Utilization) (94). A few representative books are listed in the balance of this chapter.

Breach of Trust—How Washington Turns Outsiders Into Insiders (Tom A. Coburn M.D); *Grand Illusion—The Myth of Voter Choice in a Two-Party Tyranny* (Theresa Amato); *How The World Really Works* (Alex Jones); *National Suicide: How Washington Is Destroying the American Dream from A to Z* (Martin L. Gross); *Running on Empty—How the Democratic and Republican Parties Are Bankrupting Our Future and What Americans Can Do About It* (Peter G. Peterson); *The Broken Branch—How Congress Is Failing America and How to Get It Back on Track* (Thomas E. Mann); *The Crisis of Western Culture* (Thom Hartmann); *The Power of Israel in the United States* (James Petras); *They Dare to Speak Out—People and Institutions Confront Israel's Lobby* (Paul Findley); VICE—Dick Cheney and the Hijacking of the American Presidency (Lou Dubose); *When Corporations Rule the World* (David C Korten). See also *DVD: The AMERICAN Ruling Class.*

Cheating in the Middle

Cheating at the top impacts on the middle and the bottom in an appalling manner. Historically the Middle Class is the buffer between concentrated wealth at the top and terrible scarcity at the bottom—a form of safety valve for those seeking to rise and a means of offering compassion and a safety net through localized direct charity to those at the bottom. When the Middle Class is sharply reduced, the gaps between rich and poor become too evident, and revolutions generally result. In my view, this is where the disenfranchisement of the public goes too far, the center collapses, extremists dominate on both sides of the political divide, and there is a general sense of helplessness in which the Middle Class also collapses from within. See for example *Betrayal: How Black Intellectuals Have Abandoned the Ideals of the Civil Rights Era* (Houston A. Baker); *Big-Box Swindle—The True Cost of Mega-Retailers and the Fight for America's Independent Businesses* (Stacy Mitchell); *Democracy Matters—Winning the Fight Against Imperialism* (Cornel West); *Empire of Illusion: The End of Literacy and the Triumph of Spectacle* (Chris Hedges); *Rage of the Random Actor* (Dan Korem); *Screwed—The Undeclared War Against the Middle Class — And What We Can Do About It* (Thom Hartmann); *Soft Despotism, Democracy's*

Drift: Montesquieu, Rousseau, Tocqueville, and the Modern Prospect (Paul A. Rahe); *The Disposable American–Layoffs and Their Consequences* (Louis Uchitelle); *The End of America–Letter of Warning to a Young Patriot* (Naomi Wolf); *The Life and Death of NSSM 200 –How the Destruction of Political Will Doomed a US Population Policy* (Stephen D. Mumford); *The True Cost of Low Prices–The Violence of Globalization* (Vincent A. Gallagher); *War on the Middle Class–How the Government, Big Business, and Special Interest Groups Are Waging War on the American Dream and How to Fight Back* (Lou Dobbs). See also *DVD: Bonhoeffer (2003)*.

Cheating at the Bottom

Cheating at the bottom, in my view, is simply a matter of survival, not about low moral character. I include one work on the motivation that drives terrorists because terrorism is one logical result of deeply concentrated wealth, sustained injustice, and a feeling of helplessness when combined with the human intelligence to know that it need not be so ugly for all.

Among the books in this area: *Blue Collar Ministry–Facing Economic and Social Realities of Working People* (Tex Sample); *Dying to Win–The Strategic Logic of Suicide Terrorism* (Robert Pape); *Harvest Of Rage–Why Oklahoma City Is Only The Beginning* (Joel Dyer); *Life at the Bottom–The Worldview That Makes the Underclass* (Theodore Dalrymple); *Nickel and Dimed–On (Not) Getting By in America* (Barbara Ehrenreich); *Nobodies–Modern American Slave Labor and the Dark Side of the New Global Economy* (John Bowe); *Off the Books–The Underground Economy of the Urban Poor* (Sudhir Alladi Venkatesh); *Pathologies of Power–Health, Human Rights, and the New War on the Poor* (Paul Farmer); *The Bottom Billion–Why the Poorest Countries are Failing and What Can Be Done About It* (Paul Collier); *The Globalization of Poverty and the New World Order* (Michel Chossudovsky); *The Shock Doctrine–The Rise of Disaster Capitalism* (Naomi Klein); *The Working Poor–Invisible in America* (David K. Shipler); *Unspeakable Truths–Facing the Challenges of Truth Commissions* (Priscilla B. Hayner).

Cultures of Conflict

Cultures of Conflict are a logical companion to cultures of catastrophe, cheating, and conspiracy. All four of these cultures depend on information asymmetries (in which secret plays a substantive role) and data pathologies that allow the few to deceive the many. All four of these cultures represent an abuse of power by the few over the many.

Among the core categories of reviews that are available at Phi Beta Iota are these: Empire, Sorrows, Hubris, Blowback (146); Intelligence (Government/ Secret) (275); Military & Pentagon Power (72); Power (Pathologies & Utilization) (94); and War & Face of Battle (108).

Here are just a few books covering the general topics of covert war, open war, and the consequences of war for large regions such as Africa and Latin America: *A Peace to End All Peace–The Fall of the Ottoman Empire and the Creation of the Modern Middle East* (David Fromkin); *A War Against Truth–An Intimate Account of the Invasion of Iraq* (Paul William Roberts); *Blind Into Baghdad–America's War in Iraq* (James Fallows); *Blood in the Sand–Imperial Fantasies, Right-Wing Ambitions, and the Erosion of American Democracy* (Stephen Eric Bronner); *Blood Money–Wasted Billions, Lost Lives, and Corporate Greed in Iraq* (T. Christian Miller); *Cultures and Globalization–Conflicts and Tensions* (Helmut K. Anheier); *Dark Alliance–The CIA, the Contras, and the Crack Cocaine Explosion* (Gary Webb); *Daydream Believers–How a Few Grand Ideas Wrecked American Power* (Fred Kaplan); *Dogs of God–Columbus, the Inquisition, and the Defeat of the Moors* (James Reston Jr.); *Dunces of Doomsday–10 Blunders That Gave Rise to Radical Islam, Terrorist Regimes, And the Threat of an American Hiroshima* (Paul L. Williams); *Failed States–The Abuse of Power and the Assault on Democracy* (Noam Chomsky); *Fiasco–The American Military Adventure in Iraq (Hardcover)* (Thomas E. Ricks); *First Do No Harm–Humanitarian Intervention and the Destruction of Yugoslavia* (David N. Gibbs); *Foreign Follies–America's New Global Empire* (Doug Bandow); *Imperial Grunts–The American Military on the Ground* (Robert D. Kaplan); *In the Name of Democracy–American War Crimes in Iraq and Beyond* (Jeremy Brecher); *Killing Hope–US Military and*

CULTURES OF CATASTROPHE, CHEATING, CONFLICT, & CONSPIRACY

C.I.A. Interventions Since World War II Through 2003 (William Blum); *Legacy of Ashes–The History of the CIA* (Tim Weiner); *Licensed to Kill–Hired Guns in the War on Terror* (Robert Young Pelton); *Nemesis–The Last Days of the American Republic* (Chalmers Johnson); *Open Veins of Latin America–Five Centuries of the Pillage of a Continent* (Eduardo Galeano); *Overthrow–America's Century of Regime Change from Hawaii to Iraq* (Stephen Kinzer); *Palestine–Peace Not Apartheid* (Jimmy Carter); *Review: Interventions* (Noam Chomsky); *Rumsfeld–His Rise, Fall, and Catastrophic Legacy* (Andrew Cockburn); *Running The World–the Inside Story of the National Security Council and the Architects of American Power* (David Rothkopf); *Silent Steel–The Mysterious Death of the Nuclear Attack Sub USS Scorpion* (Stephen Johnson); *Target Iran–The Truth About the White House's Plans for Regime Change* (Scott Ritter); *The Culture of National Security* (Peter J. Katzenstein); *The End of Iraq–How American Incompetence Created a War Without End* (Peter W. Galbraith); *The Fifty Year Wound–The True Price of America's Cold War Victory* (Derek Leebaert); *The Health of Nations–Society and Law beyond the State* (Philip Allott); *The Looming Tower–Al-Qaeda and the Road to 9/11* (Lawrence Wright); *The Road to 9/11–Wealth, Empire, and the Future of America* (Peter Dale Scott); *The Three Trillion Dollar War–The True Cost of the Iraq Conflict* (Linda Bilmes); *The Trial of Henry Kissinger* (Christopher Hitchens); *War and Decision–Inside the Pentagon at the Dawn of the War on Terrorism* (Douglas J. Feith*); War and Peace and War: The Rise and Fall of Empires* (Peter Turchin); *War is a Racket–The Antiwar Classic by America's Most Decorated Soldier* (Smedley Butler); *Web of Deceit: The History of Western Complicity in Iraq, from Churchill to Kennedy to George W. Bush* (Barry M. Lando); *What We Say Goes* (Noam Chomsky); *Why the Rest Hates the West–Understanding the Roots of Global Rage* (Meic Pearse).

I apologize most earnestly to those readers who do not like the above manner of marshalling information—each live link (from the free online version of the book) leads to a review of the specific book, generally 1,000 words and ten links. My intent with this chapter is to address a very complex and very fundamental aspect of our global reality by acknowledging the enormous body of work created by others.

Cultures of Conspiracy

Conspiracy theories are too often denigrated when they are in fact in the forefront of truth detection. In this short single-page we touch on major conspiracy theories that have subsequently been proven to be well-founded.

Assassination of John F. Kennedy

A Farewell to Justice–Jim Garrison, JFK's Assassination, and the Case That Should Have Changed History (Hardcover) (Joan Mellen); *JFK and the Unspeakable–Why He Died & Why It Matters* (James W. Douglas); *Someone Would Have Talked–The Assassination of President John F. Kennedy and the Conspiracy to Mislead History* (Larry Hancock); *Tears of Autumn–A Paul Christopher Novel* (Charles McCarry).

Assassination of Martin Luther King

An Act of State–The Execution of Martin Luther King (William F. Pepper).

Russian Sinking of USS Scorpion, Attack on USS Liberty by Israel

Scorpion Down–Sunk by the Soviets, Buried by the Pentagon: The Untold Story of the USS Scorpion (Ed Offley); *The Attack on the Liberty–The Untold Story of Israel's Deadly 1967 Assault on a US Spy Ship* (James Scott).

9-11—Allowed to Happen or Made to Happen?

9/11 Synthetic Terror–Made in USA, Fourth Edition (Webster Griffin Tarpley); *Painful Questions–An Analysis of the September 11th Attack* (Eric Hufschmid); *The Hidden History of 9-11* (Paul Zarembka).

See all of the 9-11 materials I have reviewed at 9-11 Truth Books & DVDs (27). Beyond these we now know that both Viet-Nam and Iraq were elective wars with fraudulent public declarations about causes and consequences. We also know that electoral fraud has been widespread. What don't we know? Lots.

Chapter 11
Information Asymmetries
& Data Pathologies

Information is the ultimate arbiter of wealth and various forms of power—as Alvin Toffler so ably discussed in *Powershift–Knowledge, Wealth, and Violence at the Edge of the 21st Century* (Bantam, 1991)—*information is a substitute for wealth and violence, for labor, capital, for space and time.*

The remainder of this book is about information and how to convert information into intelligence (decision-support) and intelligence into a prosperous world at peace. I call this Information Arbitrage.

This short chapter will discuss Information Asymmetries, Data Pathologies, and Missing Information.

- INFORMATION ASYMMETRY. An imbalance in access to relevant information between two parties, such that one party enjoys a considerable advantage over the other.

- DATA PATHOLOGY. A deliberate manipulation of data by one party for the purpose of deceiving, misleading, or defrauding other parties by distorting or withholding relevant data.

- MISSING INFORMATION. A state of poor access to information, generally not from malicious root causes, but rather from poor design and over-all shortcomings in the information industry and the bureaucracies that it serves.

INFORMATION ASYMMETRY is the primary reason why the "hidden hand" of Adam Smith does not actually work—because buyers and sellers do *not* have the same access to information. Mark Lewis did a book on Wall Street and its deceptive and manipulative practices that is still valid today: *Liar's Poker–Rising through the Wreckage on Wall Street* (Penguin, 1990).

From Wikipedia: In economics and contract theory, **information asymmetry** deals with the study of decisions in transactions where one party has more or better information than the other. This creates an imbalance of power in transactions which can sometimes cause the transactions to go awry. Examples of this problem are adverse selection and moral hazard. Most commonly, information asymmetries are studied in the context of principal-agent problems. In 2001, the Nobel Prize in Economics was awarded to George Akerlof, Michael Spence, and Joseph E. Stiglitz "for their analyses of markets with asymmetric information.

Setting aside the ethical aspects of lying to your customers, conflicts of interest, and straight fraud, information asymmetry is achieved through a restriction on the availability of information.

SECRECY is the primary means by which information is restricted. There are two kinds of secrecy:

- DEEP SECRECY. This has only recently earned a term of its own, and is studied by David Pozen in a *Stanford Law Review* article by that title. *When a small group of similarly situated officials conceals from outsiders the fact that it is concealing something, the result is a deep secret.* **The participant has privileged access such as might be provided by interlocking boards of directors.**

- INSTITUTIONAL SECRECY. Practiced by all forms of organization, including governments, corporations, and religions, this is a form of organized information control that is known to exist. In the US Government, one authority suggests that 90% of secrecy is intended to protect turf and budget while avoiding oversight and accountability.

Secrecy can also have detrimental effects, both on those who thrive on the exploitation of secrecy to their own ends, and on those whom they represent, i.e. the public.

- Secrecy as a Negative Internally: *The danger is, you'll become like a moron. You'll become incapable of learning from most people in the world, no matter how much experience they have in their particular areas that may be much greater than yours' [because of your blind faith in the value of your narrow and often incorrect secret information].* Daniel Ellsberg speaking to Henry Kissinger as recounted in *SECRETS: A Memoir of Vietnam and the Pentagon Papers* (Viking, 2002).

- Secrecy as a Negative Externally: *80% of what I needed to know as CINCCENT I got from open sources rather than classified reporting. And within the remaining 20%, if I knew what to look for, I found another 16%. At the end of it all, classified intelligence provided me, at best, with 4% of my command knowledge.* Tony Zinni speaking to a senior national security manager, as recounted in "Open Source Intelligence," *Strategic Intelligence* Volume II, Chapter 6, pp. 95-122.

Obviously criminal gangs, terrorist groups, dictators and secret police forces and others make a substantial commitment to secrecy. The fundamental proposition in this book is that public intelligence (decision-support) is in the public interest; and that clarity, diversity, integrity, and sustainability all require transparency of information to permit truth and reconciliation to be foremost among the participants so as to achieve peace and prosperity for all.

On the next page I provide a few references, each one linked to a full book review (in the free online version of this book) at Phi Beta Iota Reviews.

Agenda for a New Economy: From Phantom Wealth to Real Wealth (Korten)

Global Warming False Alarm–The Bad Science Behind the United Nations' Assertion that Man-made CO2 Causes Global Warming (Alexander)

Hidden Truth–Forbidden Knowledge (Greer)

Imperial Secrets–Remapping the Mind of Empire (Kelley)

Nation of Secrets–The Threat to Democracy and the American Way of Life (Gup)

Report of the Commission on Protecting and Reducing Government Secrecy (Moynihan et al)

Rule by Secrecy–The Hidden History That Connects the Trilateral Commission, the Freemasons, and the Great Pyramids (Marrs)

Secrecy & Privilege–Rise of the Bush Dynasty from Watergate to Iraq (Parry)

Secrecy as Fraud (2002) (Pierre Tristam)

Secrecy Report Card 2009 (Aftergood et al)

Secret Intelligence Costs Taxpayer $75 Billion a Year (Steele)

Spying Blind–The CIA, the FBI, and the Origins of 9/11 (Zegart)

The Foundation–A Great American Secret; How Private Wealth is Changing the World (Fleishman)

The Hidden History of 9-11 (Zarembka)

The Rise of the Fourth Reich–The Secret Societies That Threaten to Take Over America (Marrs)

The Secret Founding of America–The Real Story of Freemasons, Puritans, & the Battle for The New World (Hagger)

The Sorrows of Empire–Militarism, Secrecy, and the End of the Republic (American Empire (Johnson)

The Three Trillion Dollar War–The True Cost of the Iraq Conflict (Bilmes)

These are but a handful of the relevant works. The concealment of "true cost" is an information asymmetry that will be covered later in this book.

DATA PATHOLOGIES are illustrated below, each defined by a book—the full titles for each book, and links are provided on the next page.

- Mass Instruction

- Forbidden Knowledge

- Lost History

- Manufacturing Consent

- Missing Information

- Fog Facts

- Propaganda

- Rule by Secrecy

- Weapons of Mass Deception

CURE

Integrity

Figure 25. Data Pathologies

There are two central ideas in relation to Data Pathologies.

- Elite Wisdom versus Crowd Wisdom. All data pathologies exist because an elite believes that it knows best, and that the "crowd" is ignorant, incapable of "knowing," and therefore best deceived or misinformed.

91

- Hubris. When the public is not educated, or is inattentive, this results in *carte blanche* for those who would exploit the public— and the public's money—to their own end.

Here are a few relevant books, each linked to a full review that summarizes the book as a whole and itemizes key points and in this case, also coupled to a book that represents the antidote to the data pathology.

Weapons *of Mass Instruction* (Gatto); Antidote: *Teaching to Transgress– Education as the Practice of Freedom* (Hooks)

Forbidden Knowledge–From Prometheus to Pornography (Shattuck); Antidote: *Consilience–The Unity of Knowledge* (Wilson)

Lost History–Contras, Cocaine, the Press & 'Project Truth' (Parry); Antidote: *Responsible History* (Baets)

Manufacturing Consent–The Political Economy of the Mass Media (Chomsky & Herman); Antidote: *The Future of Ideas–The Fate of the Commons in a Connected World* (Lessig)

The Age of Missing Information (McKibben); Antidote: *THE NEW CRAFT OF INTELLIGENCE: Personal, Public, & Political* (Steele)

Fog Facts –Searching for Truth in the Land of Spin (Beinhart); Antidote: *Scholarship in the Digital Age–Information, Infrastructure, and the Internet* (Borgman)

Propaganda–The Formation of Men's Attitudes (Ellul); Antidote: *Pedagogy of the Oppressed* (Freire)

Rule by Secrecy–The Hidden History That Connects the Trilateral Commission, the Freemasons, and the Great Pyramids (Marrs); Antidote: *The Transparent Society–Will Technology Force Us to Choose Between Privacy and Freedom?* (Brin)

Weapons of Mass Deception–The Uses of Propaganda in Bush's War on Iraq (Rampton, Stauber); Antidote: *Unspeakable Truths–Facing the Challenges of Truth Commissions* (Hayner)

Chapte

Rebalancing & Re
Instruments of N

There is no finer center for strategic thir
Strategic Studies Institute (SSI) of the US A
conceptualized and managed the annual
topic of Rebalancing the Instruments of N

Below is a severely abridged summary of
version with endnotes, and also available

America has hit bottom. The Comptroller
in the summer of 2007, and—when Congr
later to go public with his concerns reg
future unfunded obligations. The reality is
health, infrastructure, water policies, am
unfunded. It is in this context that the n
elective engagement in a three-trillion d
bankrupted the Nation of blood, treasure
once-proud place as the ultimate champ
stability, and peace.

The gifted speakers in 2008 resembled
conference, with the title then of "Challe
and Asymmetrically," a conference that
Joint Vision 2010. The conclusions of the
My Joint Force Quarterly article summar

MISSING INFORMATION is used in this book to refer to information that is known to exist, but that cannot be accessed easily. Below is one depiction of this situation from an online point of view.

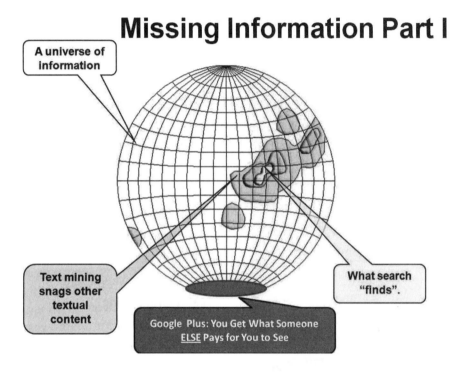

Figure 26. Missing General Information

This slide is borrowed with permission from Steve Arnold, whose chapter, Search panacea or ploy: Can collective intelligence improve findability?, in COLLECTIVE INTELLIGENCE: Creating a Prosperous World at Peace, is a standard in the field. I added the Google Plus at the bottom—with their programmable search engines, you now can get what someone else wants you to see rather than the best available answer. The "universe" includes analog or hard-copy information as well a C drives and email.

Below is a second illustration of h
information, in this case the "true cc
discussed in Chapter 25 along with Ec
here the only point that needs to be
good or service is simply not known to
how much fuel, how much sweatshor

Missing Informati

TRUE COST OF A COTTON SHIR

- Water
- Earth Erosion
- Fuel (in situ & in transit)
- Child & Abused Labor
- Toxic Chemical Waste
- Tax Avoidance
- Waste
- Opportunity Costs (Local)
- Post Purchase Costs (Yours

TRUE COST OF
PRINT CARTRIGES
THAT LIE TO YOU

Figure 27. Missing

Ecological Intelligence—How Know
Can Change Everything matters!
information in all languages all the
its job of conscious evolution, evo
zero "win-win" for all. More on thi

The 1998 Strategy Conference brought out a number of points that are still ver
important and still neglected.   Everything below was brought forward twelve
years ago, and nothing of substance has changed up to today.

- Active-reserve mix needs change
- America is its own worst enemy
- Anonymous attacks coming
- Army-Marine Corps competing with Navy-Air Force for budget
- Civil-military relationships are weak, undefined, unresourced
- Decision-making has forgotten to plan, cannot adapt to change, and is unable to stimulate a serious dialogue
- Dependency on contractors in the battle area is a major Achilles' heel
- Enemies know how to wage war between the seams of our legal systems
- Existing force structure is acutely vulnerable to asymmetric attack
- Intelligence remains an afterthought
- Issue is one of balance across the instruments of national power
- Mobility is more important than mass
- Nation is vulnerable to campaigns that leverage the international and local media
- Need <u>four</u> forces after next: Big; Small; Peace; Home
- Our planning process cannot deal with radical rapid shifts
- Private sector role needs examination
- Soldiers cannot be policemen
- States unlikely to attack directly
- Technology will not replace boots on the ground
- Technology without intelligence is blind
- Time and space favor the asymmetric non-traditional enemy
- Vulnerabilities in the civil sector
- We constantly underestimate willingness of others to do great harm to bystanders
- We don't do offensive asymmetry
- We spread ourselves too thin, this favors asymmetric enemy
- We suffer from fallacy of misplaced concreteness (or more recently, from ideological fantasies unchecked by reality)
- Weapons' cost must be appropriate to the target profile and priority

The good news is that America remains the most powerful and wealthiest Nation on the planet, with infinite potential to create new wealth and thus to promote stabilization and reconstruction around the world. As one individual commented during the April event, you solve illegal immigration by assuring a good life for all, everywhere, not by building walls between what's left of the good life here and the pathos everywhere else that stems from political corruption and the criminal looting of commonwealths that we help facilitate.

Here are the highlights from each segment of the 2008 Army conference.

- We are not well-organized for new era; Challenges and dangers more complex; Threats are more dispersed; Need to organize five D's (Diplomacy, Defense, Development, Domestic Capacity (Private Sector), Decision-Support (Intelligence)); AfricaCom intended to be an inter-agency command able to orchestrate Operations Other Than War (OOTW); Difficult for an outside state to impose peace—we influence other contributors, while supporting indigenous initiatives; Secretary of Defense Robert Gates on record: military alone cannot win the peace; Preventive action prior to crisis is necessary; Active, Stand-By, and Reserve Forces envisioned for Stabilization & Reconstruction missions—nine months out of the year in the field in non-permissive environments.

- Must understand the past; Pearl Harbor "never again" was catalyst; Military gained place at high table and ultimately displaced Diplomacy as top voice; Inter-agency coordination understood to be desirable, but never really achieved; White House militarized via the National Security Council, lost ability to manage economic or other forms of power; Outside secret intelligence, there is virtually no understanding of the proven process of decision-support; Technical intelligence has come to dominate the budget and the process; Need to achieve warning; US suffers from a strategic deficit. We need grand strategists and standing plans for long-term inter-agency and multinational endeavors in our national interest; We are not exercising US influence in an intelligent cost-effective manner.

- Information domain is the key terrain of the 21st Century; Our enemy is lies and half-truths, misinformation, disinformation, any threat to operational security and privacy, and our own complacency and ignorance; Enemy follows no conventional rules; Virtual Caliphate of 6,500 active extremist web sites we are not really understanding; Every soldier is a communicator, all must be able to do timely public truth-telling; Our biggest battle is for the hearts and minds of our own public and their perception of how and why we do battle; We have a *huge* Cultural Knowledge Gap; We have a *huge* Historical Knowledge Gap; Tribes, groups, non-territorial publics are the center of gravity.

- Military personnel want to know:

  - o Who's who (social structure)
  - o What makes them tick (cultural beliefs, values, customs, behavior)
  - o What's with all the tea drinking (cultural forms including myths, narratives, and symbols)
  - o Assessments of risk generally high

- Less than 1% of Department of Defense (DoD) budget spent on social sciences [this is similar to the secret intelligence world's refusal to spend more than a fraction of 1% on open sources of information in all languages]; New money pays for tools, not data—this is the sucking chest wound in Public Diplomacy and Strategic Communication; There is no coordination of research across agencies, Need a proponent within National Security Council (NSC), e.g. a Cultural Advisor to the President; Reach-back capability, 24/7 is valued but non-existent.

- Bureaucratic turf wars continue to set us back—even in the field, inter-agency elements are more about co-location than actual integration into a single team; The innovators are too low in the chain; Need budget and incentives for rotationals, need flexible responsive contingency funding, and need to manage instability rather than seek to resolve outright.

- DoD is going to have to give up major systems to fund peace operations.

- We are being destroyed on the Information Operations (IO) front—it is easier to get approval to drop a bomb than to do a press release; Need the multinational corps for small wars –we must anticipate need for proxies in areas where US presence will incite anger; Air power *claims* persistence and precision but is still not delivering (even with drones).

- Need a professional and brutally honest roles and missions debate; We must plan for advisor wars, hybrid wars; Irregular warfare has *many* categories; We should plan to help others "do" counterinsurgency *not* do it ourselves.

- Greatest success is those wars we can prevent from starting at all. Must do more to intervene in time—great deal of incoherence in this dialogue; Role of Ambassador and country team not well-defined or understood; Resident military advisors and short-term training teams are hugely different offerings; Need to get back in business of sending out many more advisors, while also attracting many more multinational students to our schools— there is no better investment than to field a future president or military leader who's been trained in one of our schools.

- Army purged counter-insurgency capabilities after Viet-Nam; Stability operations are supposed to receive comparable priority with combat operations; Command & Staff College does not offer specialized blocks in counter-insurgency (as of 2008); Need an Advisor Corps with transition teams in permanent being, equivalent to 18th Airborne [Civil Affairs Brigade?]; Consensus is key to organizational learning and willingness to change—politics and existing cultures are pushing back hard; Services must discipline their appetites, move big war stuff into reserve, do wholesale examination of naval aviation.

- Today inter-agency operations are characterized by collocation, not by integration of inputs or outcomes; At the tactical level there is no time for Constitutional, legal, policy, political review virtually impossible, initiatives such as building a road quickly to help nurture the local economy too hard.

- Ultimate flexibility is in real money that can be spent locally [ideally not on imported Private Military Contractors (PMC)] but rather within the local economy]; Somebody has to be in charge in the field; UN is actually a good model with the Secretary General's Special Representative (SGSR) and the Force Commander; Need to seek feedback at all times.

- DoD recognizes it cannot do it all, and in 2006 called for revitalization of civilian agencies and of integrated statecraft; Key problem is staffing of expertise across all fronts from justice and policing, public administration, business recovery, essential services, diplomacy, diplomatic security; "Whole of government" means upfront involvement in planning, not just in final stages before implementation; Same process [and program dollars] used for Continuity of Government (COG) and contingency responses overseas could be used to refine our inter-agency endeavors; We could learn a great deal from other countries, every bit of it unclassified; Agencies and Departments continue to play games with one another, the President, and Congress; Trust is the coin of the realm, we're bankrupt.

- Recreating state institutions is not enough—must rebuild locally owned and operated capabilities and create an enabling environment at the local level; We live in a 24/7 media coverage environment; Attacks on UN and NGO people and buildings have changed their attitudes about collaboration for the better, but within strict rules of engagement; After 9/11 all environments are non-permissive—NGOs recognize this, have security officers and security training; Our goal is to leverage *all* actors; United Nations (UN) has amazing capabilities that we need to understand and integrate into our plans; 38,000 NGOs should be of immediate interest to us; some of them such as Children Care and Mercy Corps have substantial budgets and capabilities; NGOs are very concerned about the militarization of foreign assistance.

- Excessive dependence on military instrument has negative consequences; Must transform entire structure of national security including domestic security; Our institutions are out-moded—systemic failures will be often.

- We have *horizontal* challenges and a *vertical* form of government [in the Collective Intelligence citizen wisdom environment, they speak of the need to end pyramidal organizations that rely on top down command and control, and the need to adopt circle organizations that allow for very rapid adaptation and resilience at all levels]; Complexity has sky-rocketed. Newt Gingrich says we have met the enemy and it is our bureaucracy; We can learn a great deal from the business community about just enough, just in time horizontal collaboration and partnerships; We cannot preserve our national security without having 21st Century capabilities.

- Our national system for planning, programming, budgeting (PPBS), and allocating simply does not work. In the absence of a strategy all can understand, stabilization & reconstruction is not going to get the authority, budget, staff, or attention; Most endeavors will not include the military, but those that should be executing civil missions do not have the resources, training, and so on to get to the field; We cannot answer the question: what is being spent by each element of the US Government in any given country?; It takes too long to obtain budgets and field capabilities—we need to be able to act much more quickly; Each country is different—one size team does not suit all countries or conditions.

- Today we are right where the US was on 6 December 1941, the day before Pearl Harbor. Even with 9/11, which should have been a wake-up call, we've hit the snooze button and are waiting for the next big hit; We have to understand the linkages between all the sectors. We have no integrators in government or in the private sector, no one whose job it is to connect the dots, craft a message and a strategy, and implement with a carrot-stick campaign plan; Where in the USG do we go for indications and warning? We have to focus on prevention, we have to achieve a whole of government harmonization, and we have to create equally solid relationships with a vast range of NGOs, private sector elements, even key individuals around the world.

Complete notes (19 pages) and a full article expand on all of the above points.

101

Below I reproduce the core distinction that General Gray made in his 1989 article, Global Intelligence Challenges in the 1990's, on the basis of the strategic generalizations that were achieved very quickly by the Marine Corps Intelligence Center (MCIC) in its pioneering Open Source Intelligence (OSINT) study, _Overview of Planning and Programming Factors for Expeditionary Operations in the Third World_, eventually published in 1990.

Conventional Threat	Emerging Threat
+ Governmental	+ Non-Governmental
+ Conventional/Nuclear	+ Non-Conventional
+ Static Orders of Battle	+ Dynamic or Random
+ Linear Development	+ Non-linear
+ Rules of Engagement	+ No Constraints
+ Known Doctrine	+ Unknown Doctrine
+ Strategic Warning	+ No Existing I&W Net
+ Known Intelligence Assets	+ Unlimited 5th Column

Figure 28: What the Marines Knew in 1988

On 19 December 1995 I was one of a handful of Americans invited to address the French national conference on "War and Peace in the 21st Century." Dr. Robert Gates, Dr. Samuel Huntington, and Dr. Charles Cogan (a former covert operations personality) were the others, with Sir Michael Howard from England being memorable as well.

Below is the original 1995 outline of my remarks.

DIAGNOSIS of the Failure of Intelligence (INT)
1. Four Warrior Classes
2. Dependency on Information
3. Information Explosion-Drowning
4. Technological Complexity and Vulnerability
5. Ascendancy of the Disposed

STRUCTURAL IMBALANCE in Defense and INT
1. States Assume Borders, Citizens, Tax Base
2. Defense Assumes Conventional Enemy
3. Intelligence Assumes Conventional Enemy, Optimizes for Secrets
4. Information Infrastructure Assumes No Threat, No Attack
5. Law Assumes General Obedience, Domestic Criminals

NEW FORMS OF VIOLENCE and INT Challenges
1. Information Warfare (Global, Corporate, and Individual)
2. Transnational Gangs—Money, Computers, Fifth Column, Ruthlessness
3. Proliferation—Sowing Dragon's Teeth
4. Disease—Socio-Economic, Ideo-Cultural, Techno-Demographic
5. Economic Competition and National Attractiveness

EARLY WARNING through Virtual Communities
1. Chaos and "Just in Time" Order via Virtual INT
2. Voluntary Sharing & Integration of Information
3. Public Makes Policy, Public Must Understand Threat
4. Political Accountability Essential—Leadership
5. Warning for Integration of Defense and Police

PREVENTION & ACTION with Information Strategies
1. Domestic Intelligence—Statecraft as Soulcraft
2. Environmental Intelligence—Eliminate External Diseconomies
3. Technical Intelligence—Bad Engineering ("Gov Spec Cost Plus")
4. National Information Strategies—Four Pillars
5. Bottom Line: Know When to Kill, Kill Wisely

I take no pleasure in seeing such anticipatory insight ignored by those gathered in Paris for the event but I also hold the USG blameless—I failed to impress—Dr. Gates, who followed me, said "I'm not even going to touch that."

Next are two of the original 1990's graphics with a few comments, followed by a new graphic on changing our national security paradigm.

As Senator Sam Nunn (D-GA) said when serving as Chairman of the Senate Armed Services Committee (SASC), *understanding the threat comes first*—it comes before strategy, before force structure and policy development, and before action of any kind. It took the UN High-Level Panel to finally arrive at a holistic understanding of the ten high-level threats to humanity (Chapter 1). Below is a "type" threat graphic intended to set the stage for organizing Whole of Government operations along four complementary tracks.

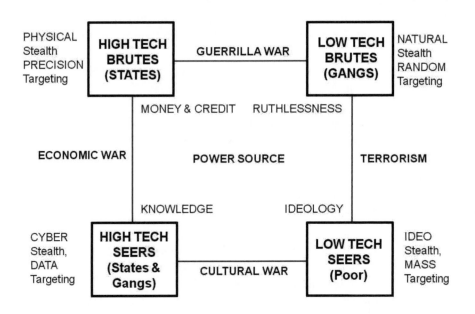

Figure 29. Different Threat Classes Require Different Approaches

This was developed in 1992 while creating a class for the Marine Corps University (MCU), Command & Staff College (C&SC). It should be obvious, but still is not understood within most governments, that there are four major threat "types" and that each requires a different mix of Whole of Government planning, programming, budgeting, and operational campaign management (as well as multinational and unilateral information-sharing and sense-making).

Following logically from the above conceptualization, below is what I briefed to the annual Army Strategy Conference in 1998—the need for four forces after next instead of the "one size fits all" then in vogue. This is discussed in much greater detail in my related article for SSI, Threats, Strategy, and Force Structure: An Alternative Paradigm for National Security, finally published in 2001 but written in 1997-1998.

1	i	i	i
CINCWAR	**CINCSOLIC**	**CINCPEACE**	**CINCHOME**
Strategic NBC	**Small Wars**	**State/USIA**	**Public Health**
Big Wars	**Constabulary**	**Peace Corps**	**Education**
Reserve	**Ground Truth**	**Peace Navy**	**E-Security**
TOP SECRET US	**Reserve**	**Peace Airlift**	**Port Security**
SECRET MULTINATIONAL		**Civil Affairs++**	**Border Patrol**
UNCLASSIFIED MULTINATIONAL Education, Intelligence & Research			
⬇ 50%	⬆ 15%	⬆ 20%	⬆ 15%
US$300B/Yr	US$100B/Yr	US$150B/Yr	US$100B/Yr

- Cost of National Guard redirections split among all four CINCs
- CINHOME intelligence includes citizen continuing education, life-long service

Figure 30. Rebalancing the Security Budget—Four Forces

In light of the huge expansion of the "big war" budget for Iraq and Afghanistan (and soon Yemen, Sudan, and Somalia), and the coincident devaluation of the dollar in the aftermath of a decade of inflationary money mis-management, we're better off discussing percentages than actual dollar amounts.

When one takes the trouble to catalog all of the missions being executed by the US military (many of them because we have only one foreign affairs action default option: the military (or worse, covert paramilitary operations)), one discovers that our military is optimized for just 10% of the actual threat—what the UN High-Level Panel calls Inter-State Conflict.

Despite the massive amounts of money moved toward both secret intelligence and homeland security since 9/11, the reality is that both the $75 billion a year we now spend on secret intelligence, and the $44 billion a year for homeland security are being very badly spent for lack a Strategic Analytic Model that properly represents both the ten high-level threats (Chapter 1) and the twelve core policies (Chapter 8).

We are still planning , programming, and budgeting on an old war paradigm in which virtually all of the discretionary funding authority goes to the Pentagon, and virtually no discretionary (or surge) spending authority is assigned to all of the other elements of national power. Below is a comparison of the old war paradigm with the new peace paradigm (which is just as violent initially, but sharply reduces violence through intelligent global multinational operations).

OLD WAR PARADIGM	NEW PEACE PARADIGM
• Obsession with Current "Intelligence" (Actually Classified News), Driven by Fear, Partisan Ideology, & Greed	• Respect for History & Cultural Heritage, Striving for Truth & Reconciliation
• Emphasis on Secrecy & Inner Circle Dialog Ignoring Congress & Public	• Open Dialog that Implements Article 1 of the Constitution, is Reflective
• Unilateral Aggression without Serious Diplomacy or Negotiation	• Multinational Diversity as Primary Approach to All Challenges
• Spend More Making War than Peace, Focusing on Optimizing Wealth for One Billion Rich	• Create Stabilizing Infinite New Wealth by Sharing Free Knowledge "One Cell Call at a Time" for Five Billion Poor

Figure 31. Old War Paradigm versus New Peace Paradigm

106

Others, such as Medard Gabel, have demonstrated that we are spending over $1.3 trillion a year on the instruments of war, at the same time that we could create a prosperous world at peace for under $250 billion a year. *Peace and prosperity, in other words, cost less than a quarter of what we spend on war, with one big difference: war enriches a few, while peace enriches everyone.* We can learn from the Chinese, below are highlights from a Memorandum on Chinese Irregular Warfare.

- Chinese Irregular Warfare strategy appears to be more advanced than our own, and consists of the juxtaposition of 7th Generation Electronic Warfare EW7), and a juggernaut of Presidential-level agreements and penetrations Waging Peace across the entire southern hemisphere, using trade, immigration, and cultural outreach, to gain ascendancy without fighting.

- Chinese success stories include forcing Dick Cheney's aircraft to land in Singapore for an unscheduled demarche (2007-02-25); killing the ability of the Japanese Reconnaissance Satellite (2007-03-25); possibly forcing down a B-52 "accidentally" armed with nuclear missiles (2007-08-30); hacking the Secretary of Defense's personal security system (2007-09-07); and impeding the High-Frequency Active Auroral Research Program (HAARP) a top Chinese target (2007-09-23). There are other successes and scares, including access to computers at the Northern Air Defense Command (NORAD) not connected to the Internet—the Chinese appear to have mastered use of electronic circuits to penetrate computers running on public power, one reason I speculate that the National Security Agency desperately wants to create its own power generation plants at each of its major locations.

- Chinese successes in both Latin America and Africa as well as increasingly in Central Asia have been noted but not really appreciated by US policy-makers, although some seem to harbor the delusion that they can push the Chinese back. *Charm Offensive–How China's Soft Power Is Transforming the World* is one book I recommend. What we do in Public Diplomacy does not compare favorably with the vastly more coherent and better-funded Chinese program.

In comparison with the Chinese effort that is coherent, peaceful, sustained, and scalable, our own Public Diplomacy, Strategic Communication, and Foreign Assistance programs are pathetic. We are losing the total war for total peace. These are the major elements of China's strategy:

- Old: **Chinese business** diasporas across Asia and especially strong in Singapore, Indonesia, and the Philippines, very strong in Argentina, growing stronger in former Portuguese colonies including Brazil, via operations from Macao.

- Old: Massive global **student populations** in the sciences, with a presence in virtually every major laboratory relevant to national security and the national infrastructure.

- New: **Presidential-level push** across the entire Southern Hemisphere, to establish trade agreements, subsidize processing and transport of needed raw natural resources, and facilitate the unrestricted immigration of Chinese nationals. Macao is base for accessing former Portuguese colonies.

- New: Substantive surge in **cultural outreach** that can fairly be described as three to five times better than ours, with free Chinese lessons, cultural centers 3-5 times better than ours, free construction of headquarters buildings (no extra charge for the electronic monitoring grid that comes with each).

- Worst-case scenarios see us losing access and respect to exploding Chinese populations that move into **majority status in Argentina and elsewhere around 2025.**

We have more military musicians than we have diplomats. That sums up our distorted and ignorant priorities.

On the next page, with pointers to fuller treatments online, are two graphics on intelligence reform, without which I expect the USG specifically, and other governments generally, to remain deaf, dumb, and blind, making decisions out of touch with reality and driven by partisan ideology instead of the truth.

Below are depicted how I believe the US $75 billion a year community must be restructured so as to create a Smart Nation that could be the catalyst for achieving a World Brain.

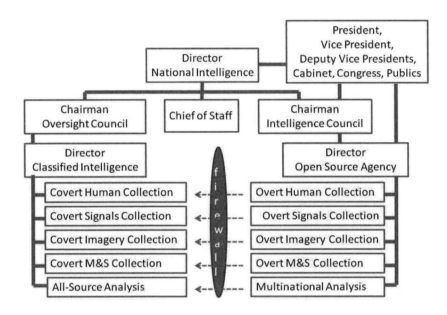

Figure 32: Essential Restructuring of US "Intelligence" Community

Apart from my various books, my latest thinking on all this is provided by my Human Intelligence (HUMINT) Trilogy at Phi Beta Iota, consisting of:

- **Intelligence for the President–AND Everyone Else**, as published in *CounterPunch*, Weekend Edition, February 27 – 1 March 2009

- **Fixing the White House and National Intelligence**, *International Journal of Intelligence and Counterintelligence*, Spring 2010

- **Human Intelligence (HUMINT): All Humans, All Minds, All the Time** (SSI Monograph Draft, NEW)

Chapter 13
Regional Centers & Networks

This chapter will gore three sacred (but stupid) oxen among the varied government intelligence communities, but ultimately to the benefit of all concerned.

SACRED OX #1: National Security is about threats and the only really important subject for national intelligence to focus upon.

SACRED OX #2: Secret sources and methods are more valuable and more important and more relevant than open sources and methods.

SACRED OX #3: Bi-lateral secret discussions are better than multilateral open discussions—the inefficiencies are worth the implied bi-lateral trust.

No, no, and no. The 21st Century is seeing global recognition of at least three major epiphanies (the fancy word for "aha"):

HOME RULE IS POSSIBLE. Unilateral militarism, virtual colonialism, and predatory immoral capitalism can be resisted and refused.

INFORMATION IS POWER. The quickest route to local and regional self-governance, peace, and prosperity is through multinational information-sharing and sense-making, particularly with respect to external influences and "true cost" (Chapter 25) of proposed goods and services, both local and global.

GROUP SHARING OPTIMIZES WEALTH. The sharing of information among the members of the regional group and its Eight Tribes increases wealth for all.

With both personal humility and total respect for the reader, it is not possible to lay out a complete foundation within this book for certifying that the World Brain and Global Game will produce a prosperous world at peace. All I can do is "tell the story" and hope that at least one region will test these ideas. I am myself immediately available for adoption by any region wishing to use me in the pursuit of the vision this book describes.

What we do know, from the London School of Business, is that for every ten out of one hundred individuals who acquire and begin using cell phones, the national Gross Domestic Product (GDP) jumps one half of one percent. I believe that the documented result is under-stated for two reasons:

1. The intangible benefits of being "connected" are vastly more than just what can be measured by formal monetary metrics; and

2. GDP is not a good measure of a society's health—Genuine Progress Indicator (GPI) is better. It is my view that at the bottom of the pyramid among the very poor, a cell phone yields 100% positive results and therefore its value is at least twice what can be measured using only monetary metrics.

A core references now available on this point is "When a cell phone is like a cow," *The Financial Express*, Apr 07, 2007, from which the following gems are taken for sharing here:

> *While econometric research by the London School of Business has shown that 10 phones per 100 people add 0.6% to the GDP of a country, the United Nations estimates that 0.6% growth cuts poverty by 1.2%.*
>
> *Today GrameenPhone has 10 million subscribers, connects 100 million people through 2,50,000 phone ladies, who buy phones on microloans from the Grameen Bank and lease air time to villagers to make a living after paying off their loans. Today a phone lady earns on an average $750 a year, which is double the average annual income of a Bangladeshi. GrameenPhone has revenues of $1 billion and annual profits of $200 million.*

112

A second reference, "Can the Cellphone Help End Global Poverty?," is featured within the ICT for Development web site, adding commentary that supplements a *New York Times* story by Sara Corbett of April 13, 2008.

According to statistics, 80 percent of the world population lives in cellular network range, which is double the level in 2000; and 68 percent of the world's mobile subscriptions by the end of 2006 were in developing countries, according to figures from the International Telecommunications Union. This reflects the demand, served by various network proliferation strategies.

The pressure to increase networks comes from the more than 3.3 billion mobile-phone subscriptions worldwide. "According to statistics from the market database Wireless Intelligence, it took about 20 years for the first billion mobile phones to sell worldwide. The second billion sold in four years, and the third billion sold in two." However, as stated here, there are at least three billion people who don't own cellphones, the bulk of them to be found in Africa and Asia. [Emphasis added.]

When given an opportunity by cellphone researchers like Chipchase, the residents of economically poor sections of cities express their ideas of dream phones - a bottom-up approach to design. Their ideas reflect their needs, from add-on air quality monitors to land mine detectors to weather predictors to a global positioning device (GPS) that will point to Mecca.

And, in a top-down approach, futuristic cellphone prototypes are being tested in this same socio-economic category - from phones that can recharge by being swung around for 15 minutes to those that have photos rather than numbers in their address book. Though the design focus may not appear to be directed towards ending global poverty, the connectivity of cellphones, according to designer Chipchase, may increase people's productivity and well-being because they can be reached.

113

Connecting the last three billion people will save humanity for the simple reason that it will unleash the entrepreneurial power of all those minds.

REGIONAL INTELLIGENCE. A regional intelligence centre should be organized to assure both the exploitation of all knowledge available locally and globally among the Eight Tribes of intelligence using the military as the hub in each national jurisdiction; and to qualify for membership in an emergent global network of regional intelligence centers that will ultimately comprise the foundation for the World Brain. An illustration of a USA-centered Multinational Decision-Support Centre (MDSC) is provided in Figure 18 on pager 52 (Chapter 6). Below is a depiction of a proposed organization for an Asian Regional Multinational Decision-Support Centre fully-capable of sharing and exploiting both secret and open information.

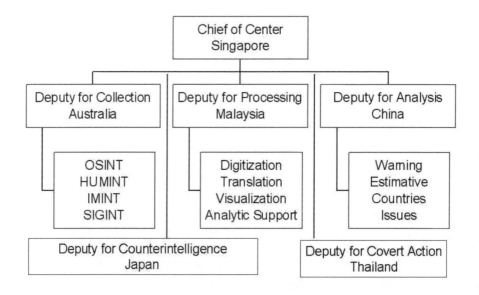

Figure 33. Regional Multinational Decision-Support Centre (RMDSC)

Below is depicted a simple form of organization where a military "watch center" provides a service of common concern for the nation (or province or district), using cell phones and the Internet to harness what I have called "the distributed intelligence" of the collective.

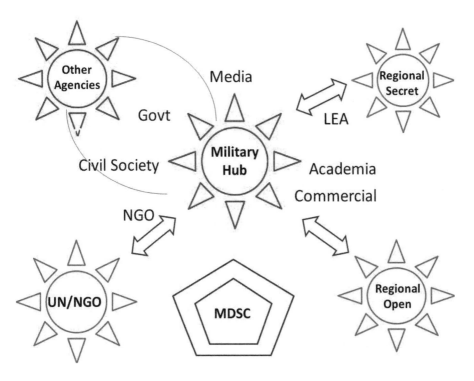

Figure 34. Home Country Military Hub for M4IS2

M4IS2 is the Swedish concept of Multinational, Multiagency, Multidisciplinary, Multidomain Information-Sharing and Sense-Making. This depiction places the home country military as the central actor for internal, regional, and global information-sharing and sense-making, both secret and open, because the military has the communications and computing resources to fulfill this role, and the military is the one "culture" that is virtually uniform around the world.

115

REGIONAL "ON DEMAND" EDUCATION. The poor may be illiterate, but they are not stupid. Once empowered with a cell phone, even if only a borrowed cell phone, the way is open to educate the poor "one cell call at a time." This requires a combination of a call center or a series of call centers, and a Global Volunteer Virtual Translation Network (GV2TN) that can fully satisfy national and regional needs for educated mentors who have Internet access, language competency, and a willingness to volunteer some time—as little as 30 minutes a day—to be helpful.

There are a handful of concepts that are associated with this approach.

CULTURAL HERITAGE. Diversity is our salvation, for within diversity we find innovation in the face of adversity. The loss of a language is the loss of a culture. Creating call centers and providing a means of connecting all those who speak a particular language or dialect regardless of where they are on the planet is a superb means of both maintaining a cultural heritage, and providing the members of that culture with "global reach."

EARLY WARNING. Over fifteen years ago, while attending a Hackers Conference (the Silicon Valley conference started by Stewart Brand), we discussed the future value of information and concluded that in the future the QUESTION is more valuable than the ANSWER. Imagine the value of ten farmers calling in with cell phone photos of the same plant disease, or the same kind of dead bird—this is a form of early warning that no country can afford, but if a call center is in place, this kind of warning comes free and in real time.

TIME-ENERGY SAVINGS. Minister Mentor Lee Kuan Yew has written (in 2005) "demography, not democracy, will be the most critical factor for security and growth in the 21st Century." Nations need policies to reduce poverty and these include discouragement of excess procreation, and the use of ICT to conserve demographic time and energy. If a call center can save man-hours that would otherwise have to be used (e.g. going to the market to learn prices), this is a net productivity gain for the country as a whole.

Chapter 14
Conclusions & Recommendations

Conclusions

The INTEGRITY of the information available to decision-makers is the root factor in determining all else.

At the Operational level there must be agreement on twelve core policies about which truthful information must be shared and evaluated.

There are eight demographic challengers who will determine the future of humanity, both within their own borders, and across the Southern Hemisphere.

The regional unions are both closer to their own challenges than the UN or other international bodies, and more effective in the aggregate than any single national entity.

The USA in particular, Western countries in general, and the dictators of the planet (44 of them) now represent, with the exception of Cuba, cultures of catastrophe, cheating, and conflict.

Recommendations

Regardless of their ideological or cultural viewpoints, all parties should accept TRUTH as a factor.

The twelve core policies are Agriculture, Diplomacy, Economy, Education, Energy, Family, Health, Immigration, Justice, Security, Society, and Water.

We must acknowledge, embrace, and respect Brazil, China, India, Indonesia, Iran, Russia, Venezuela, and Wild Cards such as the Congo, Malaysia, South Africa, and Turkey.

Simultaneously with an effort to create UNODIN, emphasis must be placed on helping and encouraging each regional union to become master of its own information net.

The only viable antidote to cultures of catastrophe, cheating, and conflict is a competing culture of "the truth at any cost" that demonstrates that truth reduces all other costs for the larger good.

117

The primary source of inequality, poverty, and other ills challenging humanity as a whole and the impoverished regions especially is Information Asymmetry.

The secondary source of inequality, poverty, and other ills challenging humanity is missing information.

Governments and organizations are dysfunctionally organized and more responsive to special interests than to the public interest—decisions "in our name" are bankrupting the many in favor of the few.

An alternative and complementary view of the global challenge matrix is that of four threats—high tech brutes, low tech brutes, high tech seers, low tech seers.

The global distribution of legacy ICT systems compartmented by organization, issue, location, and multiple forms of secret control cannot address our challenges.

Within most governments, the military is the only organization that combines discipline, adequate funding, and C4I expertise.

The fastest way to remediate poverty and injustice is to connect the five billion poor with cell phones, and to educate them one cell call at a time.

In tandem with empowering all humans with connectivity, the determination of true costs is vital.

Budget accountability and transparency must be achieved through public demands for electoral reform including referendums and posting of all proposed legislation prior to a vote.

Governments must restructure and rebalance themselves in order to create four forces after next, one focused on waging peace, another on domestic prosperity.

Regional centers and networks that leverage open software, sources, and spectrum are the essential foundation for creating a global information-sharing environment.

The military should serve as the hub for creating national and regional and then international information-sharing and sense-making networks.

Part III

Tactical Intelligence—Diversity
All Humans, All Minds, All the Time— The World Brain

Part III consists of seven chapters addressing the practical tactical aspects of creating a World Brain that can create accurate timely intelligence (decision-support) in every clime and place. It includes chapters on analytic tradecraft, the power of indigenous demographics that no government can suppress, the new craft of intelligence, a broader understanding of human intelligence (HUMINT) than is now accepted among governments, and a culminating point—the center of gravity—a global to local range of needs table.

This part of the book emphasizes DIVERSITY in the sense intended by all of the modern sages who have studied the inherent order and inter-dependence of all natural systems—what Stewart Brand called Co-Evolution and what others today call Bio-Mimicry. Diversity is what gives us options.

Whereas the final part of the book focuses on technical matters, this part is about human interaction—the human craft of intelligence that demands multinational information-sharing and sense-making, predominantly without secrets, and able to harness what I have for decades called "the distributed intelligence of the Whole Earth."

A short anecdote first. Howard Bloom, in *Global Brain—The Evolution of Mass Mind from the Big Bang to the 21st Century* (Wiley, 2001) speaks of Eskimos having 50 words for snow—and how our brain cells corresponding to the 49 words we do not learn at an early age vanish before we are teen-agers. Linguistic and cultural diversity is the essence of the World Brain, and we must all recognize that not only do the indigenous peoples have vast stores of knowledge that are essential to the future of humanity; but that every loss of any language, any culture, sharply reduces the diversity of innovative ideas that could be helpful to our evolutionary activism, to our conscious evolution, to our integral consciousness as a species.

Chapter 15. Tactical Intelligence Sources and Methods. The gravest problem we have within the "organized" intelligence communities (generally just governments and selected corporations) apart from technical inadequacies discussed in Part IV, is the lack of a Strategic Analytic Model that is all-encompassing. Governments focus excessively on military and criminal threats, and do not apply the due diligence necessary to the non-military threats.

Chapter 16. Indigenous Peoples—Demographic Poverty & Power. The West, and "modern" capitalism, focus on the one billion rich with an annual income of one trillion dollars. The future is at the bottom of the pyramid, where five billion poor have a total annual income of four trillion. Within that population, there are over 5,000 distinct indigenous ethnic groups with their own cultures, language, and centuries of deep knowledge.

Chapter 17. The New Craft of Intelligence (Collection & Processing). I will not repeat the contributions made in two earlier books, _THE NEW CRAFT OF INTELLIGENCE: Personal, Public, & Political_; and _INFORMATION OPERATIONS: All Information, All Languages, All the Time_. Here we will focus only on the globally-relevant concepts needed to enable multinational multifunctional information-sharing and sense-making. Suffice to say that it is impossible for any one country, even one as nominally wealth (but grotesquely mis-managed) as the USA, to get a grip on all relevant information inclusive of historical and cultural information as well as information in 183 languages we simply do not comprehend. To achieve Intelligence for Earth demands a coherent, holistic, universal acceptance of multinational information-sharing.

Chapter 18. The New Craft of Intelligence (Analysis & Decision-Support). The sad reality is that even with $75 billion a year being spent on secret intelligence, the USA still does not do decision-support for the President (who gets "at best" 4% of what he needs) or anyone else. A complete restructuring—indeed a reinvention—of intelligence analysis and decision-support is needed. Such reform is not expensive, but it does require a comprehensive re-education of the public, policymakers, acquisition managers, operational commanders, and intelligence practitioners.

Chapter 19. Human Intelligence (HUMINT): All Humans, All Minds, All the Time. The information in the monograph from the Strategic Studies Institute (SSI) will not be replicated here (and is free online). Here we focus on the broad strokes needed to reconnect human intelligence to decision-making.

Chapter 20. 21ˢᵗ Century Counterintelligence: Evaluating Health of the Nation. This chapter focuses on what counterintelligence should be addressing in the 21ˢᵗ Century, not on the minutia of counterintelligence. Mindful of Sun Tzu's dictum that one must know oneself, this chapter applies the framework for the analysis of revolutionary potential from Figure 37 at page 136 to the USA specifically, the world generally, providing citations (and links in the free online version of the book) to hundreds of books by others who are authoritative on the various means by which we are subverting ourselves.

Chapter 21. Conclusions and Recommendations. The findings of this part, and related recommendations, are presented side by side.

Chapter 15
Tactical Intelligence Sources & Methods

This is not a book about tradecraft, but rather about mind-set. The material that follows, both in this chapter and in the other chapters in this third part of the book, seeks to illuminate how broadly—holistically—we must think if we are to be effective at understanding and then adapting to reality.

Three core points will be made in this chapter:

1. Everything is connected. It is not possible to get an accurate understanding of any single threat, or any single domain, without understanding the whole system.

2. There are four levels of analysis that are now blending depending on the circumstances: strategic, operational, tactical, and technical; these in turn have three "slices" that interact: civilian, military, and environmental.

3. The threat changes depending on the level of analysis. This is hugely important in part because policymakers who have no idea about strategy and who receive truly mediocre intelligence (decision-support) tend to over-react or assume ideologically or politically-motivated extremist positions that end up costing all concerned, including international businessmen.

We will begin with a comparison from a book by Charles Hampden-Turner, _Radical Man: The Process of Psycho-Social Development_ (Gerald Duckworth, 1971). It is the single best book we have found in the past fifty years of reading focused on humanity and the nature of man, who can be either an animal or a radical innovative _human_ being, a _conscious_ human being.

On this page and the next are two graphics from the book that were used to create one axis of my 1975-1976 graduate thesis on understanding revolution.

Man's anemic failure to exist renders
a) His PERCEPTION *narrow* and *impoverished*
b) His IDENTITY *"locked in"* and *stagnant*

i) He accepts little or no *responsibility* for FEEDBACK, which leads to *dis*INTEGRATION and lack of COMPLEXITY in himself and his victim.

h) But seeks domination of, or submission to, others' perspectives in a non-dialectical, negantropic failure of SYNERGY

g) And is often unable to make a SELF-CONFIRMING, SELF-TRANSCENDING IMPACT (even over shorter distances)

c) Leading to an overall sense of *in*COMPETENCE and anticipated *loss*

d) He fails to INVEST authentically or intensely

e) And by devising non-SUSPENDING, RISK-reducing strategies

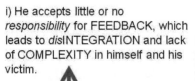

f) Avoids trying to BRIDGE THE (wider) DISTANCES to others

Figure 35. Man as Anemic Failure

This is not the place to replicate the magnificent work done by Charles Hampden-Turner (who not so incidentally, produced this work against great opposition from a "multitude of academic Know-Nothings" who trashed his "naïve idealism" and focused mostly on maintaining their own status).

If there were one book that could be said to have radicalized me, this is it. A strong complement, but a totally different book, is Robert Carkhuff's *The exemplar—The exemplary performer in the age of productivity* (Human Resource Development Press, 1984).

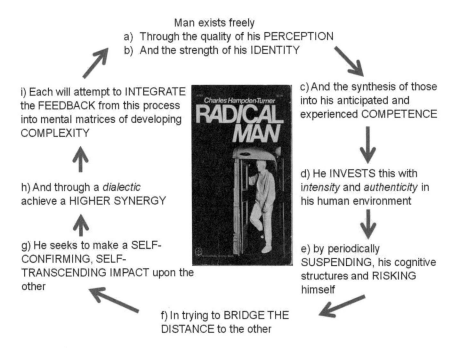

Figure 35. Radical Man Fulfilled

The descriptive terms used by Charles Hampden-Turner comprise the vertical axis of the original theory for thinking about revolution in very human terms.

The horizontal axis was fleshed out after examining common explanations of revolution (generally political-legal or socio-economic) and realizing that ideo-cultural, techno-demographic, and natural-geographic needed to be added.

A short version of my thesis, _Thinking About Revolution_ , was created in 1992 and is the recommended first step beyond this chapter.

	Political-Legal	Socio-Economic	Ideo-Cultural	Techno-Demographic	Natural-Geographic
Perception	Isolation of elites; inadequate intelligence	Concentration of wealth; lack of public disclosure	Conflicting myths; inadequate socialization	Acceptance of media distortions; inadequate education	Reliance on single sector or product; concentrated land holdings
Identity	Lack of elite consensus; failure to define priorities	Loss of economic initiative; failure to do balanced growth	Loss of authority; failure to provide and honor national myth system	Failure to accept and exploit new technologies and new groups	Failure to integrate outlying territories into national system
Competence	Weak or inefficient government; too much or too little bureaucracy	Break-down of fiscal, monetary, development, or welfare policies	Humiliation of leaders; loss of confidence by population	Failure to enforce priorities, with resulting loss of momentum	Failure to prepare for or cope with major national disasters
Investment	Ego-centric or parochial government	Excessive or insufficient mobility; lack of public sector	Cynicism; opportunism; corruption	Failure to nurture entrepreneurship or franchise all groups	Failure to preserve or properly exploit natural resources
Risk	Elite intransigence; repression; failure to adapt	Failure to deal with crime, especially white collar crime	Failure to deal with prejudice; desertion of intellectuals	Failure to develop national research & development program	Failure to honor human rights; failure to protect animal species
Extroversion	Ineffective tension management; failure to examine false premises	Structural differentiation; lack of national transportation network	Elite absorption of foreign mores; failure to deal with alienation	Failure to develop communications infrastructure, shared images	Failure to explore advantages of regional integration
Transcendence	Foreign control of government; arbitrary or excessive government	Loss of key sectors to foreign providers; loss of quality control	Media censorship; suppression of intellectual discourse	Failure to control police, army, or terrorists; failure to employ *alphas*	Failure to respect natural constraints or support organic growth
Synergy	Failure to assimilate all individual or respond to all groups	Status discrepancies; lack of economic motivators	Absence of sublimating myths; failure of religion	Failure to provide program and technology assessment	Failure to distribute benefits between urban and rural
Complexity	Garrison, industrial, or welfare states	Unstable growth; excessive defense spending	Cultural pre-disposition toward violence	Excessive urbanization, pollution, or development	Lack of land for expansion; inefficient use of land

Figure 37. Framework for the Analysis of Revolution

In the preceding matrix, one can appreciate the enormous contribution made by Charles Hampden-Turner only if one first understands that when this matrix was first created, only a third of the squares could be filled from the existing literature. His startlingly original work was both essential to the discovery of other pre-conditions of revolution in domains not previously considered by scholar-practitioners, and helpful in understanding that concentrations of anything are bad for society—humanity requires moderation and balance.

Below is a single illustration of the analytic model underlying the Expeditionary Environment Analytic Model used by the Marine Corps Intelligence Center (MCIA) of which the author was both the senior civilian, and Study Director for the flagship study, *Overview of Planning and Programming Factors for Expeditionary Operations in the Third World*.

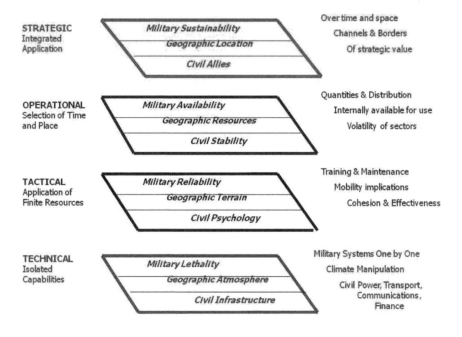

Figure 38. Levels of Analysis and Vertical Analytic Domains

Finally, we come to a very important point that neither the US Intelligence Community nor the policy makers, acquisition managers, and operational commanders, appear to have grasped despite its being presented from 1988 onwards in a variety of public forums. *The threat changes depending on the level of analysis.*

Level of Analysis	Threat Grade	Comment
Strategic Sustainability	LOW (2.0)	Not sustainable for more than two weeks.
Operational Availability	MEDIUM (3.0)	Many of them scattered around.
Tactical Reliability	LOW (2.0)	Cannibalized parts, stored in open, poorly trained crews.
Technical Lethality	HIGH (4.0)	Best tanks money could buy at the time from Russia. US IC Official Threat on Worst Case Basis
General Threat Factor	<MEDIUM (2.75)	Proper analysis differentiated threat at each level which means each level commander is *individually* informed.
Military Difference	1.25 (31%)	Being wrong by 31% is significant— nuances matter. On balance, at two of four levels, threat is a LOW threat.

Figure 39. Threat (or Factor) Changes at Each Level of Analysis

The test case for arriving at this understanding was the Libyan T-72 tank from Russia, at the time the best tank money could buy. Then, as now, the evaluation was focused only on its technical merits, without regard to strategic sustainability, operational availability, or tactical reliability.

That will have to suffice for this overview. A great deal more information can be found via the links in the online version of this book, or by searching at Phi Beta Iota, the Public Intelligence Blog.

Chapter 16

Indigenous Peoples
Demographic Poverty & Power

The "poverty zone" shown <u>below</u> depicts those countries of the world where a substantial percentage of the population lives on less than one dollar a day.

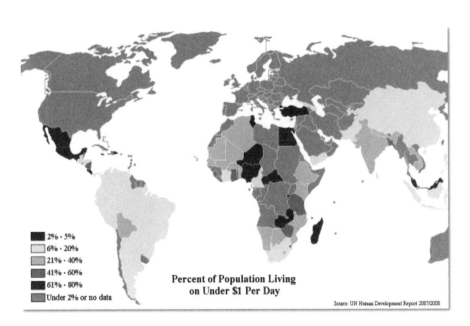

Figure 40. The Poverty Zone

About 1 billion people globally live in extreme poverty - less than $1 per day. Nearly 3 billion (half the world) lives on less than $2 per day.

Poverty, rightfully and righteously declared the single greatest high-level threat to humanity by the UN High-Level Threat Panel, tends to be consistent with gender inequality, child mortality, illiteracy (not the same as idiocy), untreated infectious diseases, and water scarcity.

There are a number of excellent and ably illustrated Atlases of the world where this constellation of burdens can be explored. However, there is a point about poverty that is not well-made in many publications, and that is that in the so-called affluent nations, the concentration of wealth in the top 1% of the population has become so outrageously inequitable as to place much larger percentages of the broader public into poverty status. Below is a depiction of poverty in the USA as of 2000. I believe it has tripled as of 2010.

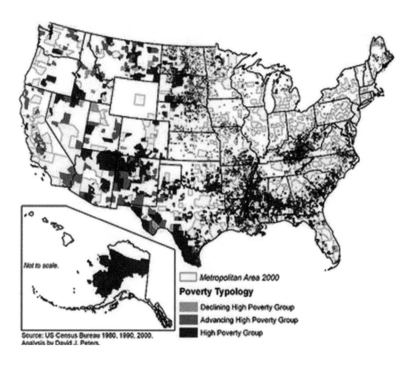

Figure 41: Poverty in the USA 2000

Before turning to the more positive aspect of indigenous peoples, I merely want to observe that one reason poverty is properly ranked by the High-Level Panel above all other threats is because poverty is in and of itself the foundation for all of the other threats.

Poverty is where infectious diseases thrive without treatment. Poverty causes billions to do vastly more damage to the environment than all the corporations in the world combined. While this entire book and the website created to support this book, Phi Beta Iota, come at the above assertion from all sides, there are a few books I wish to mention here:

Deer Hunting with Jesus–Dispatches from America's Class War (Joe Bageant)

Eco-Imperialism–Green Power, Black Death (Paul Driessen)

Environment, Scarcity, and Violence (Thomas Homer-Dixon)

Environmental Security and Global Stability–Problems and Responses (Paul G. Gaffney II and Max Manwaring, Editors)

The Health of Nations–Infectious Disease, Environmental Change, and Their Effects on National Security and Development (Andrew Price-Smith)

The Real Environmental Crisis–Why Poverty, Not Affluence, Is the Environment's Number One Enemy (Jack M. Hollander)

In all of these books, the real eye-opener for me was Joe Bageant's *Deer Hunting with Jesus,* which illuminated the reality that across every small town in America, there is a small "cabal" that cheats the citizens of corporate tax revenues and income by exchanging tax waivers, free public land, and pollution exemptions to corporations in return for commissions and consulting fees. Corruption is not limited to dictators or the two-party tyranny in America (in the service of its Wall Street barons), corruption is everywhere, and the only antidote to corruption is complete transparency. As I observe at the beginning of this book, there is plenty of money with which to create a prosperous world at peace, we simply have to stop the few from stealing it all.

With the reality of global poverty firmly in mind as our highest-priority high-level threat to humanity, in the three remaining pages of this chapter I want to itemize some books along two lines of inquiry: first, the power of the people, whatever their condition; and second, the infinite possibility of poverty eradication and wealth creation if we can connect the people to one another and to information.

A Power Governments Cannot Suppress (Howard Zinn)

Counterculture Through the Ages—From Abraham to Acid House (Ken Goffman a.k.a. R.U. Sirius)

Dignity for All—How to Create a World Without Rankism (Robert Fuller)

Escaping the Matrix—How We the People can change the world (Richard Moore)

Improper behavior—when misconduct is good for society (Elizabeth Janeway)

Orbiting the Giant Hairball—A Corporate Fool's Guide to Surviving with Grace (Gordon MacKenzie)

Pedagogy of Freedom—Ethics, Democracy, and Civic Courage (Paulo Freire)

Pedagogy of the Oppressed (Paulo Freire)

Philosophy and the Social Problem—The Annotated Edition (Will Durant)

Society's Breakthrough!—Releasing Essential Wisdom and Virtue in All the People (Jim Rough)

Teaching to Transgress—Education as the Practice of Freedom

The Power of the Powerless—Citizens Against the State in Central-Eastern Europe (Vaclav Havel)

The Unconquerable World—Power, Nonviolence, and the Will of the People (Jonathan Schell)

The Unrepresented Nations and Peoples Organization: Diplomacy's Cutting Edge (Jeff Greenwald)

These books barely scratch the surface. *Free will is our power, our destiny.*

Demographic Purchasing Power

C. K. Prahalad's _The Fortune at the Bottom of the Pyramid–Eradicating Poverty Through Profits_ (Wharton, 2004) is cited in my Preface as one of four life-changing books in my reading history.

His core point cannot be over-emphasized or repeated too often: the one billion rich around whom modern capitalism and its toxic companion consumerism are organized has an aggregate income of roughly one trillion a year; the five billion poor, despite the fact that billions are living on $1 to 3 dollars a day, has an aggregate annual income of four trillion—_four times as much._

Most capitalists are still in the throes of the Industrial Era, where money buys politicians; environmental costs can be externalized to the public and future generations; and the public can be influenced to want—even enjoy—dirty water, contaminated air, unhealthy food, and toxic material goods.

It will take another quarter century to turn back the "Red Tide" of capitalism run amok, but that era is over, and as public intelligence in the public interest gains ground, accelerated by its attributes of being free, useful, and infinitely shareable, I anticipate huge changes in the marketplace such that the blind who think they are "too big to fail" coming crashing down, and the small, fleet of foot willing to _listen_ to the public thrive across an infinite variety of niches, most of them local in nature.

We have, I believe, three kinds of waste in our "modern" system of systems:

1. Waste inherent in complexity and an attendant absence of accountability. The PriceWaterHouseCooper documentation of how 50% of every US health dollar is spent on waste is a perfect example.

2. Waste inherent in ignorance of the consequences of our mis-behavior. Paving over wetlands, converting agriculture to a factory-based system and allowing animals bred for meat to spread disease, exposing our children to toxins and

electronic emissions whose ill-effects the power companies and others are quick to obscure, all of this imposes unnecessary costs.

3. Finally, we have waste inherent in the destruction of the commons and the adoption of exclusive ownership of portions of Mother Earth, especially inland waters, below-ground aquifers, and ocean shorelines, such that the many are deprived solely to benefit a few.

The time has come to eliminate all three forms of waste by empowering the poor to create infinite wealth—stabilizing wealth that enables peace for all— at the same time that we re-invent governance, capitalism, education, and everything else that could, that should, that does not today, characterize *homo sapiens* ascendant.

C. K. Prahalad is—by his own acknowledgement—the tip of the iceberg of knowledge that could unleash the entrepreneurial energy and time (time-energy was always Buckminster Fuller's core measure) of the five billion poor.

Muhammad Yanus, in *Creating a World Without Poverty–Social Business and the Future of Capitalism* offers us a very real implementation plan.

Featured in his book, in the middle, is the French company Danone, and the joint venture to create a yogurt for the poor children, ultimately being delivered in a bio-degradable cup that converts into fertilizer.

This product at whatever price was created within a poor economy where the cost to produce was less; it was designed to cost less and use inexpensive bio-degradable packaging, and it delivered just as much nutrition as a more expensive product in heavy plastic and needing refrigeration.

The conflict—one that I hope will be rapidly resolved on the basis of common sense standing firm on a foundation of public intelligence (discussed in the next two chapters)—is between corporations that have plundered the Third World backed up by the US Marine Corps and other Armed Forces—and the "home cultures" that are now ready to blossom in their own right, overcoming the colonialization, predatory capitalism, and unilateral militarism of the past.

As C. K. Prahalad observes, there is a fortune at the bottom of this pyramid, and they are *not* going to spend that fortune on "Western" consumer goods or on predatory pricing.

The Innovator's Solution–Creating and Sustaining Successful Growth by Clayton M. Christensen and Michael E. Raynor, offers three "litmus tests" helpful to those seeking to monetize disruptive new ideas:

1) Is there a population of clients that has historically been under-funded, under-staffed, and have as a result *gone without*?

2) Is this group likely to appreciate lower cost "good enough" solutions?

3) Is it possible to be profitable while providing these clients lower cost good enough solutions?

The Power of Women

I still remember being startled by Michael O'Hanlon's discussion, in *A Half Penny on the Federal Dollar–The Future of Development Aid* (Brookings, 1997), of how even a few years of education for women resulted in substantive progress across a number of fronts including family health and the recognition of the value of keeping families small in number.

As I recollect concluding, the single best return on investment for foreign aid or assistance of any kind, dollar for dollar, lies in the education of women. This is one reason why I believe that the "telephone lades" of India are at the very beginning of their rise to wealth and a much greater role in the political and economic and cultural affairs of their communities from local to national to global. Putting a cell phone in the hands of a poor woman is in my view the perfect antidote to putting a gun in the hands of a man.

Infinite Wealth to the Wealth of Networks

Other books address poverty eradication, most of them very poorly because they try to address poverty in isolation from all else. A central premise of this book is that we must eradicate all ten high-level threats simultaneously, by using shared information to harmonize how we behave and how we spend on all twelve policies. Our objective is nothing less than the empowerment of the eight demographic challengers such that they avoid our mistakes while leveraging the entrepreneurial imagination and energy of their huge publics.

Here I will simply honor several books that have informed me, in order of their publication, with respect to the power of an informed public as a means of creating infinite stabilizing wealth. I have mentioned them before, this is where I wish to cite them fully and together.

1991. Alvin Toffler, _Powershift—Knowledge, Wealth, and Violence at the Edge of the 21st Century_ (Bantam, 1991)

1999. Barry Carter, _Infinite Wealth—A New World of Collaboration and Abundance in the Knowledge Era_ (Butterworth-Heinemann, 1999)

2002. Thomas Stewart, _The Wealth of Knowledge—Intellectual Capital and the Twenty-first Century Organisation_ (Nicholas Brealey, 2002)

2006. Yochai Benkler, _The Wealth of Networks—How Social Production Transforms Markets and Freedom_ (Yale, 2006)

2006. Alvin Toffler, _Revolutionary Wealth_ (Knoph, 2006)

There is a difference between the literature on collective intelligence, including smart mobs, wisdom of the crowds, and so on, and the literature on wealth creation.

Chapter 17
The New Craft of Intelligence
(Collection & Processing)

I have written an entire book on the topic of this and the next chapter, _THE NEW CRAFT OF INTELLIGENCE: Personal, Public, & Political_ (OSS, 2002), and also a book on _INFORMATION OPERATIONS: All Information, All Languages, All the Time_ (OSS, 2003). As with all books that I write or publish, they are free online at Phi Beta Iota, the Public Intelligence Blog.

The intent of this book is to focus on the highest-level issues that must be addressed by national, regional, and international networks in the practical domains of information collection and information processing.

My two illustrated lectures with notes, COLLECTION: Know Who Knows (2004) and PROCESSING: Make the Most of What You Know (2004) are recommended for study—this chapter is an executive summary, nothing more.

There are four principal areas that require strong leadership if they are to be properly embraced as part of a coherent intelligence endeavor:

- Lessons of History (Inclusive of Culture and _Multi-Lingual_)
- Global to Local Burden Sharing
- Private Sector Exploitation
- Secret Endeavors (Unilateral, Bi-Lateral, Multi-Lateral)

As a general rule, no less than 80% and usually closer to 95% of all information needed to make the most important decisions is openly available, with the added advantage that it can be shared with legislators, media, and the public.

There are five core domains in collection as relevant to most of the world:

- Open Source Information
- Human Information
- Signals Information
- Imagery Information
- Leadership Integrity

The first and the last are generally very poor within most "secret" intelligence communities. I ignore Measurements & Signatures Information as being much too expensive and not at all satisfying in terms of return on investment.

Although ninety countries are reported to have Open Source Intelligence (OSINT) units, including all of the <u>North Atlantic Treaty Organization</u> (NATO) and Partnership for Peace (PfP) countries as well as many of the countries in the Southern Hemisphere, this specific discipline is not well developed because the Western nations—with the exception of The Netherlands and the Nordics—<u>refuse to acknowledge inexpensive open sources</u> that can be shared with anyone are in fact 80% or more of the proper solution.

Use the two books cited above, and all of the <u>handbooks</u> and <u>other guides</u> at <u>Phi Beta Iota, the Public Intelligence Blog</u>, to advance in this area.

Leadership Integrity is about more than simply being honest. Every leader, whether a recipient of intelligence (decision-support) or a provider of intelligence (decision-support), is the sole responsible person for emphasizing the importance of the truth.

The truth at any cost reduces all other costs.

The purpose of this book is to better explain the value of intelligence (decision-support) to every leader of every developing country and all organizations within those countries, so that we can put a stop to fraud, waste, and abuse both within countries, and as imposed from outside by colonialist powers, predatory immoral corporations, and unilateral military incursions. Chapter 20 discusses counterintelligence in the sense of knowing ourselves—we cannot overcome external challenges if we remain oblivious to our internal failures.

Each country enjoys eight distinct "tribes of intelligence," each with its own access to specific types of information unique to its direct interests, and each offering distinct internal capabilities as well as distinct forms of global to local outreach that can be harnessed by the national and regional authorities. They are, in alphabetical order:

ACADEMIA. This includes all schools, not just universities but elementary and high schools, vocational schools, corporate training centers, and so on.

CIVIL SOCIETY. This includes citizen advocacy and neighborhood organizations and it specifically includes labor unions and religions.

COMMERCIAL. This includes all decision-support needs for private sector decision-making, and is much larger than business or competitive intelligence.

GOVERNMENT. This includes municipal, county or district, provincial and state, as well as tribal, territorial, regional, and global governance networks.

LAW ENFORCEMENT. This is intended to include those authorized to use force against citizens as well as all investigative elements including forensics.

MEDIA. This includes both the dying traditional media (print and broadcast) as well as niche publishers, Internet zines, and all other forms of one to many broadcasting. **Investigative journalism is included, but is not decision-support.**

MILITARY. This includes the state and local militia, national gendarmes and border control forces, and all civilians in direct support of the military.

NON-GOVERNMENTAL. The proliferation of non-governmental organizations has not helped reduce poverty or address the many other global issues that governments have also failed to deal with responsibly. Like the other tribes, this one is very ignorant, does not share information well, and needs to learn how to do information-based action.

None of these communities share information properly with one another.

Today the single most expensive challenge—both in costs incurred and in opportunities lost, is the challenge of enabling information-sharing and sense-making among the existing eight tribes within any given nation or region.

It is the task of the leader to ensure that all eight tribes are being exploited to achieve his or her intelligence (decision-support) objectives; that the process being followed respects historical and cultural diversity and engages all possible regional and global collaborators; and finally, that legal ethical sources and methods are used to the fullest extent possible.

The emphasis on legal ethical sources and methods is important because they are generally the least expensive in terms of time and money, and also the least risky in terms of political or cultural "blow-back."

It is also the task of the leader to ensure that the very best people are attracted to the intelligence (decision-support) profession, and that they are treated with the utmost respect and care. There are six considerations.

Getting and Keeping the Right People

- Seek out the innovators with open-minds
- Train them before and throughout their service
- Sustain them with proper pay and good working conditions

Getting and Keeping the Right Managers

- Intelligence professionals are "gold collar" workers—they are race horses, not plow horses
- Intelligence is tough—the highest alcoholism, adultery, divorce, and suicide rates—managers must nurture, coach, mentor, and protect
- Judge your managers by their worst employee

Collection is the foundation for analysis—if the best people are not managing collection, all the smart analysts in the world will be helpless, for they are only as good as the sources, the processing, and (only then) their own gifts.

Requirements Definition is where most intelligence processes fail. To be specific, one can spend $75 billion a year as the USA does for secret intelligence, and still know little of value. Virtually all of that money is being spent on collection without ever actually talking to a customer about what their *requirements* are; and without processing 80% or more of the collection.

The most recent National Intelligence Strategy (2009) of the USA is an example of a document that was created without ever talking to customers, allies, or any of the other seven tribes of intelligence.

Everyone needs decision-support—from Cabinet Ministers to individual action officers. The most fundamental mistake made by most governments is to treat intelligence as a classified news service rather than as a decision-support service essential not just to Cabinet ministers, but to all action officers.

Every person receiving intelligence (decision-support) services should be asked three questions each day:

1. What would you have liked to know yesterday that we failed to provide?

2. What do you need to know today that we did not discuss yesterday?

3. What do you need to know tomorrow, next week, next month, next year?

All of these answers should then be collated to establish the specific collection management objectives with priorities and spending and level of effort or detail being established as part of the plan.

Collection Management is about "knowing who knows," a phrase introduced to the larger intelligence community of the world by Dr. Stefan Dedijer speaking to the first international conference on Global Security & Global Competitiveness: Open Source Solutions in December 1992.

Collection Management consists of four parts, each of which has a Processing component.

- FIND. Do we already know this?
- GET. Can we get this from the other seven tribes or another nation?
- BUY. Can we buy this at low cost quickly from the private sector?
- TASK. Which specific person or capability shall we order to do this?

Processing is central to every part of the intelligence (decision-support) cycle from defining requirements (who else has the same need, have we met this need before) through collection, analysis, and dissemination.

National Security C3I3H3—Command, Communications, & Computing, Inter-Agency, Inter-Disciplinary, Inter-Operability, Heuristics of the Community Intelligence Cycle, a 1987 graduate-level study of three US Embassies, came to the conclusion that the total Country Team collected less than 20% of the relevant available information spanning all US information requirements, for three reasons:

- US diplomats were in the minority in their own Embassy, outnumbered by a broad range of individuals from many US agencies
- US diplomats have no money with which to entertain (below the Ambassadorial level) and are limited to the physics of a 24-hour day and who will be seen with them in public
- US spies have lots of money but will only listen to traitors

Worse, because most of the information received in bulk is in hard-copy (e.g. university yearbooks, commercial reports, local directories, local journals), the information is either discarded locally or returned to Washington in hard-copy via the diplomatic pouch or the postal service. Once in Washington the information is discarded or filed away and is not shared.

The bottom line: Spilling 80% of the 20%, it can be said that the average Embassy provides its national government with less than 2% of the available relevant information in usable form—and that is without considering language translation challenges, where the US is notoriously ill-equipped, particularly for complex languages characteristic of the most unstable areas of the world.

Modern technology allows for inexpensive scanners to be distributed at all reasonable collection points—in a typical embassy there should be one in the political, economic, visa, and security offices. Essential hard-copy information that needs to be shared should be scanned in at the collection point so that it can be shared digitally and immediately with the "wide area network."

As Multinational Engagement, also known as M4IS2 (Multinational, Multiagency, Multidisciplinary, Multidomain Information-Sharing and Sense-Making) gains acceptance, three very good things will happen:

1. Embassies will have shared networks so that information is only scanned in once and then shared across all Embassies (e.g. economic reports)

2. Each Embassy can mobilize its respective "tribes" into a local national network so that its counterpart academics, commercial representatives, media, and non-profits have an incentive to participate in the local wide area network

3. Countries and local businesses will recognize that digital information goes further and faster and reaches more minds, and will be incentivized to provide as much information as possible in digital form—helping them achieve this should be a major focus on all assistance programs.

There are two aspects of data entry that merit emphasis:

1. Open Source data standards are very helpful. Many countries are moving to Free/Open Source Software (F/OSS) because they do not feel that their citizens should have to buy proprietary Microsoft or other products in order to access information created or purchased with taxpayer funds. While the Internet makes it easy to share, the form in which the original data is provided makes a difference, especially in the Southern Hemisphere.

2. Most organizations understand <u>Date Time Group</u> (DTG) attributes for information; few understand the equal importance of geospatial attributes provided via a <u>Spatial Reference System</u> (SRS) sometimes called a Coordinate Reference System (CRS). It is not possible to do machine-speed processing to isolate all information about a specific location without some form of SRS being associated with all information. SRS is the referential aspect, not to be confused with <u>Geographic Information System</u> (GIS), which is the combination of hardware, software, and data.

Processing has two major objectives:

1. To assure the preservation and ease of retrievability of all information that is collected regardless of discipline (open, signals, images, or human), medium (hard-copy, analog, digital) or source (time, location, authenticity).

2. To permit geospatially & time-date machine-speed detection of alerts, anomalies, patterns, and networks ("connecting the dots").

Processing can provide, if properly managed, for increased information-sharing among governments, corporations, international organizations, and citizens, along three lines of advance:

1. Summaries of known information that do not disclose sources & methods can be used to <u>inspire agreements to exchange more detailed information.</u>

2. Leveraging open source data standards can dramatically reduce costs by incentivizing burden-sharing so that common data is collected once and shared with all interested parties.

3. Summaries of information that is NOT known can inspire national (eight tribe), regional, and global burden-sharing agreements, for example with respect to the threat posed by rapidly vanishing fresh water supplies. The <u>Planetary Skin</u> initiative is an example of a possible approach to interaction.

In the modern era Collection and Processing are merging in Cloud Computing but it is most helpful to retain a clear distinction between human beings, data objects, and the means as well as the social networks that make collection and processing possible. Below is an illustration of the four quadrants of knowledge that lead to the creation of Organizational Intelligence.

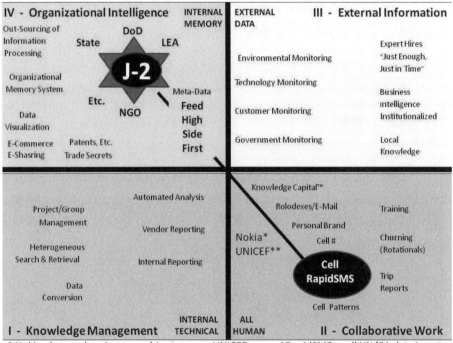

Figure 42: Four Quadrants Leading to Organizational Intelligence

Neither collection nor processing is about technology in isolation from its human employers. The "Cloud" integrates all human minds all the time, and finally makes possible—in theory—the availability to all humans of all information in all languages all the time. This is the "Omega Point" for human consciousness, a global mind, and the World Brain.

Quadrant I: Knowledge Management

The organization or network must not forget what it knows; it must not lose data, links, or the history (provenance) of aggregated data. In this quadrant, where most organizations still reside, the focus is on internal information and helping internal employees make use of internal data.

Quadrant II: Collaborative Work

Known today as Web 2.0, or as "social networking," this is the human cloud connected by cell phones and electronic mail and services such as Twitter, Facebook, and LinkedIn. Below is an illustration of Twitter as an intelligence collection and networking tool.

Figure 43: Twitter as a Collection Tool

146

The first photographs out of Haiti on 12 January 2010 after the worst earthquake in 200 years, came from Twitter. While Twitter Trends and other Twitter-related tools are emergent, this is not yet to a point where a "360 degree view" (for example, of a disaster site or a landing zone's perimeter) can be easily plotted, nor can all individuals at a specific time and place be "harnessed" from a remote location. Never-the-less, in combination, cell phones are the "brain cells" of the World Brain, and Twitter is one of its nervous systems.

Quadrant II is about Human Capital. The one inexhaustible resource we have on Earth is humanity and the ability of humanity to think and imagine. Over time two separate developments will occur in this quadrant:

1. *All Rise—Somebodies, Nobodies, and the Politics of Dignity*. Every single human mind is unique and in its diversity, a source of innovation. Example: top executives for a sporting shoe company were meeting trying to imagine profitable ideas for the future. Hours after they started, a security guard who kept passing them sat in and then interrupted: "What about us?" Security guards need sports-type shoes that look business-like. The company did $28 million in sales in its first year of sales to this new niche.

2. Micro-Tasking "By Name." Over time, individuals will have a visible identity and known interests and competencies. Within limits prescribed by the individual and the group, it will be possible to know who knows who, how they know, what they know, what they do, who they are talking to, where they are sitting, and how they feel. A fisherman at a specific lake could volunteer his availability as a source on the conditions there at that time. In the Haiti disaster, individuals could be using the UNICEF RapidSMS system to dial in specific urgent needs including insulin and other person-unique needs, to a Range of Needs Table that is then acted upon by all governments and relief organizations in a voluntary visible manner.

The ability to *first* empower and *then* harness the distributed intelligence of the Earth will be the defining characteristic of the 21st Century.

Quadrant III: External Information Acquisition

Peter Drucker, writing in *Forbes ASAP* on 28 August 1998, said that we have spent fifty years focusing on the "T' in IT (Information Technology), and that we must now spend the next fifty years focusing on the "I" or Information. The *old* IT model spends money on information technology, the *new* IT model spends money on information access within the Cloud and on empowering individuals so they can acquire and exploit "just enough, just right, just in time" sources of external information. Most governments, corporations, and organizations are very marginally-attentive to this quadrant.

Quadrant III demands Collection Management ("Know Who Knows") as well as sophisticated processing so as to not lose the value of any of the external information. It includes the monitoring of customers, government regulations, technology, and the environment. Within Quadrant III any organization should be able to access any needed information—including unpublished information created "just in time" for a specific new need—for any time, place, or issue.

Quadrant IV: Organizational Intelligence

This was inspired by Harold Wilenski's book, *Organizational Intelligence (Knowledge and Policy in Government and Industry)* (Basic, 1967) and is largely about the memory of the organization or network regardless of how many of human and technical "generations" might pass. It includes turnover files, meta-data, archives of intellectual property, and the complete integration of all that each employee knows relevant to the affairs of the organization, now stored in "shoeboxes" under the employees desk in most organizations (metaphorically speaking).

It is useful to compare Figure 42 with Nova Spivak's Meta-Web illustration to see a convergence of the technical-centered (Spivak) and the human-centered (Steele).

Technical matters related to collection and processing are discussed in Part IV of this book.

Chapter 18

The New Craft of Intelligence
(Analysis & Decision-Support)

As with the previous chapter, all of the detailed information for this and the last chapter can be found in *THE NEW CRAFT OF INTELLIGENCE: Personal, Public, & Political* (OSS, 2002), and also a book on *INFORMATION OPERATIONS: All Information, All Languages, All the Time* (OSS, 2003). As with all books that I write or publish, they are free at Phi Beta Iota, the Public Intelligence Blog.

My two illustrated lectures with notes, ANALYSIS: All-Source Analysis, Making Magic (2004) and NEW RULES for the New Craft of Intelligence (2004) are recommended for study—this chapter is an executive summary, nothing more.

The first portion of this chapter (and the matching briefing) draws on the historic and still valuable *A Compendium of Analytic Tradecraft Notes* (1997) by Jack Davis. A number of other handbooks and historic contributions are easily accessible at Phi Beta Iota, the Public Intelligence Blog.

"The New Rules for the New Craft of Intelligence" are also discussed in detail in Chapter 15 of *THE NEW CRAFT OF INTELLIGENCE: Personal, Public, & Political* (OSS, 2002).

Put most simply, Analysis is how one converts information into intelligence (decision-support) that will support decisions that produce outcomes. The purpose of this book is to inspire *Intelligence for Earth* such that all of us together can *do* Analysis to create a prosperous world at peace. We must create Smart Nations, Clever Continents, and the World Brain.

In Chapter 5 we discussed the fragmentation of knowledge. It is the work of the analyst to bridge the gap between what the decision-maker *needs to know*, and what can be known in the time and with the resources available.

As discussed in Chapter 17, Requirements Definition is a critical first step. In my view, Analysts should be in direct inter-action with the decision-maker or group of decision-makers they are supporting, and the Analyst should be determining—and defining—what the decision-makers need to know on the basis of their explicit demands, pending schedule, and future concerns.

It is not acceptable for a decision-maker to tell the Analysts "give me everything you have, I will pick out what I need." That is unprofessional, irresponsible, and also a certain prescription for decision failure.

Similarly, it is not acceptable for a decision-maker to decide to be their own intelligence officer, doing their own collection and their own analysis. Intelligence (decision-support) is both an art and a science—decision-makers are generally skilled at the direct leadership of people, and they are generally not skilled at deep broad reading, at culling anomalous and predictive patterns from vast amounts of disparate data, and at simplifying complex studies into easily understood basic points that can be used politically.

Finally, it is not acceptable for a decision-maker to withhold from the Analysts supporting them any information they acquire while engaged in diplomatic or other substantive conversations or negotiations. The decision-maker drives the car, but the analyst prepares the car for the anticipated road conditions, repairs the car after a hard ride, and generally helps the decision-maker—the driver— by providing an *information carriage* that protects and supports the decision-maker in their daily work.

Globalization and the Internet have made it significantly more difficult for a decision-maker to keep track of many core lines of inquiry, and at the same time have made it easier for properly trained and organized Analysts to do excellent work that is comprehensive, multi-cultural, and timely.

The single most important foundation for proper analytic support to a decision-maker is the devising of the Strategic Analytic Model in which the organization as a whole agrees on what threats it wishes to focus on; what policies it is able to organize; and what other stakeholders are important to the prosecution of the organizational mission. See one example at Figure 19 on page 60. Similar detail is needed for the other three levels of analysis.

Such a model—and the underlying agreement—rarely exist in governments, corporations, or international organizations. For this reason, and here we quote Ben Gilad, one of the top people in the commercial intelligence arena, writing in *Business Blindspots–Replacing Your Company's Entrenched and Outdated Myths, Beliefs and Assumptions With the Realities of Today's Markets*

> ***Top manager's information is invariably either biased, subjective, filtered, or late.***

As the Brahimi Report (2003) made clear for the United Nations, and the Aspin-Brown Commission and 9-11 and many other commissions have made clear for the USA, there is nothing "modern" about decision-support in today's archipelago of Industrial-Era organizations. They are all top-down "command & control" hierarchies that make decisions based on assumptions, history, ideology, or undue influence by others, rather than on a sound appreciation of all relevant information.

Analysis is where all of the sins—all of the shortcomings—of an organization or nation or region's approach to intelligence (decision-support) come to rest.

If the parent organization has not provided resources for the collection of external information and the exploitation of already known information, the Analyst is handicapped.

If the parent organization has not provided resources for the processing of information, including analytic desktop analytics that will be discussed in Part III of this book, the Analyst will be limited to "cut and paste" methods.

Figure 16 on page 44 illustrated the new leadership and decision-making environment in which bottom-up multinational consensus must replace top-down unilateral decision-making. I repeat that figure here in cleaner form because it is central to practicing the new craft of intelligence in the new era.

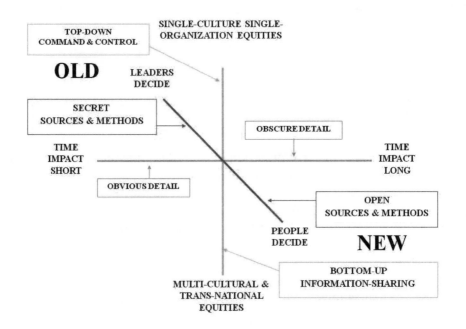

Figure 44: Keep 20% of the Old, Get a Grip on the 80% We've Ignored

The "new" approach is actually the "old old" approach of the Native American Indians who held councils and thought about the impact of any decision "seven generations out," and of the indigenous Mayan and other Indian cultures in South America. With the shift toward open sources, the acme of skill for today's analyst lies less with "tasking" a classified asset to collect something specific, and more with knowing exactly which expert to connect the decision-maker with "in the moment," with the expert, not the analyst, creating new knowledge precisely tailored to the need in current context.

Some of the nuances of analysis, such as how the threat changes depending on the level of analysis (strategic, operational, tactical, technical) were mentioned in Chapter 15.

Both managers and the analysts supporting them need to know the historian of the organization, and the librarian of the organization.

If the organization does not have a historian, it is making a common mistake, for the historian is the catalyst for organizational memory and ensures that the lessons learned by one generation are not forgotten—this is part of Organizational Intelligence.

Most organizations have librarians, but many have not yet realized that the role of the librarian has changed in the 21st Century. In the past librarians were primarily archivists, cataloguing and ensuring ready access to hard-copy materials acquired to support the mission of the organization.

Today librarians are more like digital scouts, helping the analysts—or in the absence of analysts the individual employees—discover, discriminate, distill, and develop external sources of information.

So—do you have a librarian? Do you have a historian? Sit down with them and ask them about what they have been doing and what they need to do better. This is the first step in creating a "Smart" organization.

I will not review analytic competencies here, for that use any of the handbooks available at Phi Beta Iota, the Public Intelligence Blog. The North Atlantic Treaty Organization (NATO) Handbooks are still the best available for the military, and the United Nations has produced some excellent handbooks for law enforcement managers, analysts, and front-line officers.

Other sources of handbooks abound. The best over-all source of regularly updated guidance on open source intelligence methods is the *2009 Handbook Online for Internet Tools and Resources for Creating Open Source Intelligence*

(OSINT) by Dr. Ran Hock, Chief Training Officer, Online Strategies, Inc.. See also *2009 OSINT Links Directory by Ben Benavides.*

Analysts, apart from subject domain knowledge and a knowledge of the collection disciplines available for them to task, must have the following competencies:

- **Internet Competency.** Understand multiple search engines and their limitations, as well as multiple means of doing both Deep Web and multi-lingual search and translation; understand multiple means of accessing images, maps, videos, and audio files; understand how to use the Internet to identify, screen, contact, and then validate any expert on any topic in less than one hour. Generally Internet tasks that require more than one hour should go to a specialist in the library or the Open Source Intelligence (OSINT) Cell, discussed in the next section.

- **Commercial Online Competency.** Understand the capabilities and limitations of the major global online fee-for-service offerings, and how to ask the librarian for a specific search— commercial online databases have very old search systems where mistakes can be very costly. Generally complex searches should be out-sourced to an information broker with over a decade of experience with the specific commercial database most likely to satisfy the requirement.

- **Gray Literature Competency.** Understand how to identify, access, and exploit "gray literature," limited edition publications, generally in hard-copy or in removable digital media such as flash drives or CD-ROM discs; this usually requires a knowledge of what is available (it is not generally listed on the Internet); and a human path to the materials.

- **Primary Research Competency.** Direct human-to-human contact is still the best means of exploiting knowledge that has not been published; of rapidly exploiting deep knowledge that is not susceptible to machine processing; and of creating new knowledge tailored to the need on a "just right, just in time" basis. Between Citation Analysis, Media Analysis, and skill in using personal communications, a great deal can be achieved by going direct to an expert or a person on the scene.

- **Analytic Toolkit Competency.** The existing "best in class" practitioner of OSINT, the US Special Operations Command (USSOCOM) J-23, uses over 23 different softwares, many proprietary, to accomplish as many different analytic tasks. This will be discussed in more detail in Part III on Technical Intelligence. Analysts must be competent in using desktop as well as back-office tools; must understand geospatial and time analysis tools; must understand structured analysis and other detection tools; and must be skilled with multi-media exploitation and presentation tools.

- **Geospacial Competency.** Despite the advent of Google Earth, few analysts are skilled at connecting structured databases to Google Earth, and most do not know how to acquire and then integrate detailed maps such as are offered by East View Cartographic for the developing world, drawing on the Russian military maps created for the wars of national liberation—the Americans ignored the requirement and do not have maps at the 1:50,000 level for most of the developing world.

- **Analytic Tradecraft.** This is covered in the previously mentioned *Compendium* by Jack Davis but nine factors are listed below.
  01 Trade-Off Analysis in Client Context
  02 Nine Evaluation Criteria for Credibility

155

03 Assumptions Must Be Specified
04 Alternative Outcomes Must Be Specified
05 Distinguish Between Facts, Opinions, and Sources
06 Harness Both Internal and External Expertise
07 Know the Art of Distillation and Summarization
08 Understand Deception, Counterintelligence, Timeliness
09 Analysts are Managers Of:
----Customer Relations and Requirements Definition
----Money for Open Source Information Procurement
----External Experts Under Contract or Influence
----Secret Collection Management If Available

Below is a single illustration from that briefing, of a standard OSINT Cell, created as part of the first report for the Defense Intelligence Agency in 1994.

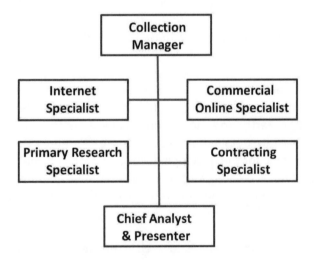

Figure 45. Standard Open Source Intelligence Cell

There are two additional concepts that must be presented to the executive readership of this book, prior to outlining the New Rules.

Below is the "Herring Pyramid" as devised by Jan Herring, the first National Intelligence Officer for Science & Technology (NIO S&T) within the US Intelligence Community, and then the father of commercial intelligence in the USA, along with a few others such as Leonard Fuld.

Figure 46. Herring Pyramid of Analytic Focus and Cost

Jan Herring, co-founder of Academy of Competitive Intelligence, along with George Marling, pioneered open source exploitation in the 1970's.

The next illustration is my own, created in support of the Earth Intelligence Network, a 501c3 Public Charity that is the proponent for a World Brain Institute and an embedded Global Game. It emphasizes the vital importance of adopting a Whole Systems approach in doing analysis. By adopting such an approach, the leader can use analysis to move away from the "stovepipe" nature of government, and toward Whole of Government analytics and Whole of Government planning, programming, budgeting, and operations.

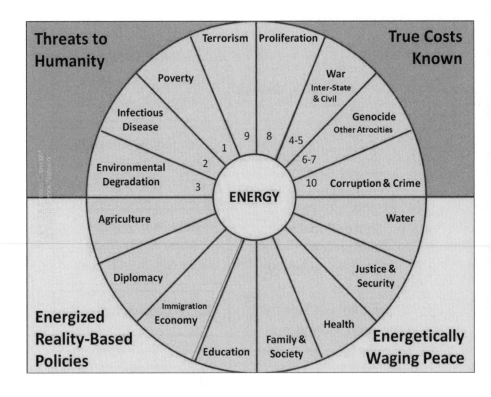

Figure 47. Holistic Analysis—All Threats, All Policies, All the Time

Properly done, any of the threats or any of the policies can be placed in the central position, the point being to evaluate the trade-offs across all threats and all policies all the time. This is the only way to be effective at governing.

Now, finally, to the new rules. The briefing NEW RULES for the New Craft of Intelligence (2004) and the original chapter, "The New Rules for the New Craft of Intelligence," Chapter 15 of *THE NEW CRAFT OF INTELLIGENCE: Personal,*

Public, & Political (OSS, 2002), provide more detail. This is the quick tour of the horizon for busy executives and citizen leaders.

Rule 01. Decision-Support is the Raison d'être. Intelligence is defined by the value it delivers to the leader, not by the inputs or costs.

Rule 02. Value-Added Comes from Analysis, Not Secret Sources. The problem with spies is they only know secrets, and at least 80% if not 95% of the global relevant information is not secret—it is openly available.

Rule 03. Global Coverage Matters More. Surprise is to be avoided by casting a very wide net and being able to focus more attention on a moment's notice.

Rule 04. Non-Traditional Threats Are of Paramount Importance. We knew this in 1988, but were delighted to have the UN High-Level Panel confirm it in 2004. Poverty, Disease, Environmental Degradation—these are the real threats to humanity, along with the other seven threats they identify.

Rule 05. Intelligence without Translation is Ignorant. Today, eight years after 9/11, neither the US secret intelligence community nor the diplomats nor the military has an adequate inventory of trusted foreign language interpreters.

Rule 06. Source Balance Matters More. Less technical, more human; less secret, more open; less collection, more processing; less production for the sake of production, more reflection for the sake of insight.

Rule 07. "Two Levels Down." Dr. Stephen Cambone understood this perfectly when he spoke in 2004 about the need for universal coverage at neighborhood levels of granularity. The new standard is local; this is *a double order of magnitude increase in difficulty* of collection, processing, analysis, and integration as well as purposeful dissemination.

Rule 08. Processing Matters More, Becomes Core Competency. Multilingual networks have dramatically increased the complexity and amount of multimedia data—today, to take one small example, analysts are overwhelmed with imagery from drones—as is usual in the US Intelligence Community, collection systems are created without planning for the processing of what they collect. This could be a "center of gravity" for a multinational network.

Rule 09. Cultural Intelligence is Fundamental. This is now more important than political or economic or military intelligence, and it requires deep knowledge of history, language, and of course culture. This cannot be taught—we must leverage multinational access to trusted sources in whom the knowledge is inherent.

Rule 10. Geospatial and Time Tagging is Vital. Machine-speed processing of multidisciplinary data is not possible without both date time groups (DTG) and Spatial Reference Data (SRD); it is also important to be able to interpret different standards and ultimately arrive at a common standard.

Rule 11. Global Open Source Benchmarking. In order to detect change around the world, a multi-national effort to benchmark global open sources is mandatory. This will set a foundation against which spikes and chatter and other anomalies can trigger additional attention and collection.

Rule 12. Counterintelligence Matters More. As we have learned in recent years, non-state terrorists who are already citizens of Western countries are a major threat. All threats are now transnational, generally sub-state in their componency, and therefore very difficult to detect without substantive investments in counterintelligence—religious counterintelligence included.

Rule 13. Cross-Fertilization Matters More. The old approach was the linear paradigm, from consumer to collector to source to analyst to consumer. The new intelligence paradigm places emphasis on connecting the consumer in direct contact with the source or sources—generally not secret at all—who can create new knowledge in the moment, precisely tailored to the need.

Rule 14. Decentralized Intelligence Matters More. In the age of distributed information, "central intelligence" is an oxymoron. Knowing who knows, knowing how to find who knows, and being able to collect, process, and analyze on a "just enough, just in time" basis is the acme of skill for the new craft of intelligence.

Rule 15. Collaborative Work and Information Communications Rise. As we discussed in reviewing the four quadrants of knowledge (Figure 42 on page 145), it is vital to nurture the uniqueness of each individual—each will create a personal "brand" over time; and it is vital to advance electronic sharing across time and space—physical collocation is neither achievable nor desirable for the most complex problems. Formal communications systems are inadequate; the entire range of Web 2.0 to Web 4.0 tools and practices must be used.

Rule 16. New Value is in Content + Context + Speed. In a globalized world that moves faster and faster each day (changes to the Earth that used to take 10,000 years now take three), context matters, as does speed of delivery of the tailored answer. "Good enough" *now* is better than perfect too late.

Rule 17. Collection Based on Gaps versus Priorities. Everything matters in a connected world. Priorities should be respected on a first pass, but gaps are dangerous. Something on everything is a more useful starting point for new challenges than everything on the one wrong thing.

Rule 18. Collection Doctrine Grows in Sophistication. It is foolish and expensive to use sensitive assets to collect open information. First find the answer if it is already in the data base; then get the answer from an ally if possible; if not, buy the answer from a commercial provider. Tasking a sensitive asset should be the last resort.

Rule 19. Citizen "Intelligence Minutemen" are Vital. "Hive mind" is the essence of 21st Century Intelligence. Witness the value of Twitter as a tool for rapidly assessing the Haitian earthquake of 12 January 2010. A Smart Nation nurtures, mobilizes, and harnesses the distributed intelligence of all citizens.

Rule 20. Production Based on Needs versus Capabilities. Forget about routine or recurring production—nothing should be produced that does not support a specific decision. Analysts must spend more time thinking, traveling, and talking to consumers, less time writing for the sake of production.

Rule 21. Strategic Intelligence Matters More. Estimative intelligence must be restored as a primary object of analysis, with a special emphasis on identifying peaceful preventive measures that can stop a threat from maturing.

Rule 22. Budget Intelligence is Mandatory. Analysis of one's own national budget is a form of counterintelligence with respect to the degree that Whole of Government policy is strategically sound or ideologically mis-directed. Similarly, other countries can be evaluated based on their actual budgets.

Rule 23. Public Intelligence Drives Public Policy. 80% to 90% of secrecy is about avoiding accountability and concealing fraud, waste, and abuse. Public intelligence estimates are an essential element in assuring sound public policy.

Rule 24. Analysts are Managers. Analysts are managers of people, money, priorities, and information. Collectors must be analysts in order to improve the precision and timeliness of their collection endeavors.

Rule 25. New Measures of Merit. Gross results are no longer acceptable (the numbers game). Evaluation must be based on the usefulness and timeliness of intelligence (decision-support) in relation to actual decisions and outcomes.

Rule 26. Multi-Lateral Burden Sharing is Vital. While national spies and secrets will still be needed, especially against violent sub-state groups such as transnational criminal gangs, predatory multinational corporations, and terrorists, the great majority of intelligence (decision-support) will only be achievable if we work together in multi-lateral teams that assure a diversity of sources, a diversity of methods, a diversity of viewpoints, and ultimately, a comprehensive aggregation of all relevant information in all languages all the time. In this context, the United Nations becomes an important facilitator.

Chapter 19

Human Intelligence (HUMINT): All Humans, All Minds, All the Time

This chapter summarizes the Strategic Studies Institute (SSI) monograph by the same title, scheduled for publication in April 2010. That monograph is in turn the third part of a trilogy on Human Intelligence (HUMINT) that includes Intelligence for the President–AND Everyone Else, as published in *Counterpunch*, Weekend Edition, February 27 – 1 March 2009 and Fixing the White House and National Intelligence, *(International Journal of Intelligence and Counterintelligence*, Spring 2010).

The human factor has been central to my thinking about the future of humanity, of governance, and of life on Earth. From being the son of an international oil engineer to being a Marine Corps infantry officer and then a clandestine case officer (C/O) or spy, the human factor has been vital. In the past two decades of pioneering Open Source Intelligence (OSINT) and now Multinational, Multiagency, Multidisciplinary, Multidomain Information-Sharing and Sense-Making (M4IS2), the human factor has become even more central, because the acme of skill in the 21st century is *not* to steal one secret from one person for the benefit of the few, but instead to harness the distributed intelligence of the Whole Earth for the benefit of all of humanity.

The Resilient Earth does *not* need us, but we do need the Earth. The human factor is all we have to work with if we are to achieve a sustainable prosperous world at peace and survive as a species. I approach this topic respectful of what technology can offer, but highly skeptical of technology as a panacea in the face of fast-moving complexity—there is nothing to equal the capacity of the human brain or—even better—the collective intelligence of all humans.

I believe that no one nation—and certainly no one organization—can understand, much less address, the complex challenges of today. This is why I am devoting the balance of my life to M4IS2.

However, I also believe that we are at the very beginning of realizing our human potential, and that we have been wrong in allowing humans to segment themselves and fragment their knowledge as discussed in Chapter 5.

Three books have been especially helpful to me on this topic.

- Charles Hampden-Turner, _Radical Man—The Process of Psycho-Social Development_ (Gerald Duckworth, 1971)

- Robert Carkhuff, _The exemplar—The exemplary performer in the age of productivity_ (Human Resource Development Press, 1984)

- Harlan Cleveland, _The Knowledge Executive—Leadership in an Information Society_ (Dutton Adult, 1985)

As I have gone on in life to observe the dysfunctionality of industrial-era organizations that "commoditize" humans and threat them as "cogs" in a "machine", I have come to appreciate the reliability of military organization. While it has its own pathologies, on balance the military can be relied upon to be where it is supposed to be and do what it is asked to do—including the functions of global communications, logistics, and mobility in often austere environments.

This is why I believe the US Department of Defense (DoD) must become a "core force" for the USA, a broader deeper foundation for national security than merely war-fighting, with two major support functions:

1. Be the strategic "glue" for Whole of Government operations.

2. Be the global general service for multinational multifunctional operations.

It is in that context that I conceptualized "full spectrum" HUMINT. Below is a depiction of the "Core Force" that I developed for a lecture to Eastern European and Russian parliamentarians visiting the George C. Marshall Center in Germany in the 1990's.

Figure 48. Core Force with Eight Human Functions

Of the missions depicted in Figure 48, none is more important than the Ground Truth mission. The reality is that our Embassies have become little fortresses from which few dare to venture far afield. The diplomats are in the minority within their own embassy, and have virtually no funds for entertaining diverse constituencies, and even less so for commissioning local commercial sources

165

of legal ethical information for specific products. Indeed, the only people with money to spend in the US overseas community are the spies. How we relate to foreign cultures and entities is pathologically inept.

Peace and prosperity are more difficult to orchestrate than war and poverty. The first two require complex harmonization of effort within shared intentions that are inherently multi-cultural and multi-generational, while the latter two simply call for a willingness to do wanton violence. Below is an illustration of the increasing complexity of what we need to know in relation to war, and implicitly, in relation to peace.

Warfare Era	What Do We Need to Know?
1st Generation	Easy: Where is the army?
2nd Generation	Easy: Where are the trenches?
3rd Generation	Moderate: How many with what?
4th Generation	Hard: Watch every non-state actor.
5th Generation	Hard: Watch everything on the fly.
6th Generation	Hard: Make sense of billions of bits.
7th Generation	Very Hard: 24/7, 183 languages *and put our own strategy, policy, structure & budget in order.*

Figure 49. War & Peace: The Seventh Generation

I take the trouble to isolate the seventh generation of complexity, building on the work of Dr. Col Max Manwaring, one of a very small handful of American strategic pioneers, because I want to strongly emphasize that the World Brain comprised of human brains in the aggregate can do what no complex network of machines can do now or in the foreseeable future. The following quotation from Jim Bamford's *Body of Secrets* is helpful:

Eventually NSA may secretly achieve the ultimate in quickness, compatibility, and efficiency—a computer with petaflop and higher speeds shrunk into a container about a liter in side, and powered by only about ten watts of power: the human brain.

166

Digital Natives

A major challenge facing all of us as leaders is the changing nature of our population. Marc Pensky's _Don't Bother Me Mom–I'm Learning!_ makes the distinction between those who are born into the digital era, and those like myself who struggle to cope with digital complexity. There is now also a book by the title _Digital Natives & Digital Immigrants_.

Below are summarized the competing—the starkly distinct—natures of the population that we want to lead (Digital Natives) and the population now in "command and control" positions (Digital Immigrants).

Digital Natives (Rising)	Digital Immigrants (Retiring)
Prefer receiving information quickly from multiple multimedia sources	Prefer slow and controlled release of information from limited sources
Prefer parallel processing and multitasking	Prefer singular processing and single or limited tasking
Prefer processing pictures, sources, and video before text	Prefer to provide text before pictures, sounds and video
Prefer random access to hyperlinked multimedia information	Prefer to provide information linearly, logically and sequentially
Prefer to interact/network simultaneously with many others	Prefer students to work independently rather than network and interact
Prefer to learn "just in time"	Prefer to teach "just in case" (it's on the exam)
Prefer instant gratification and instant rewards	Prefer deferred gratification and deferred rewards
Prefer learning that is relevant, instantly useful and fun	Prefer to teach to the curriculum guide and standardized tests

Figure 50. Human Generational Differences

At its most fundamental, 7th Generation Warfare is total, pervasive, sustained, nuanced, and can only be won by fighting ideas, not weapons. Not only do we need to empower every human being with connectivity (cell phones) and access to information (education one call at a time), but we also need to completely re-invent education, intelligence (decision-support), and research.

I continue to believe that education, intelligence (decision-support), and research must be managed together if we are to create Smart Nations, Clever Continents, and the World Brain.

Brainpower, not Firepower, is what we need to bring to bear, and we need to do this 24/7 in all languages and all mediums. Thomas Jefferson said *"A Nation's best defense is an educated citizenry."* Voltaire's version:

When a nation begins to think, it is impossible to hold it back.

Humanity Ascending is the mission, HUMINT is the foundation.

"Humanity Ascending" is a phrase I learned from Barbara Marx Hubbard, and the DVD series by the same title. She cited Benjamin Franklin's reference to the "divinity in our humanity." HUMINT is not about spying. HUMINT is about learning, deciding, and evolving—humanity ascending.

The good news is that **Public (Human) Intelligence** in is here to stay:

- Collective (social networks)
- Peace (harmonization of peaceful preventive measures)
- Commercial (from moral green to golden peace)
- Gift (mobilization and harmonization of giving by all)
- Cultural (raising a new generation without embedded biases)
- Earth (eliminating human consumption of the Earth)

168

In 1994 speaking to a Canadian conference, and later in writing in <u>Private Enterprise Intelligence: Its Potential Contribution to National Security</u>, I conceptualized the end of the linear paradigm of intelligence, and the emergence of the diamond paradigm.

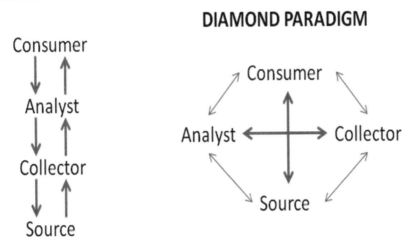

Figure 51. Linear versus Diamond Intelligence Process

In the arena of human intelligence, the linear paradigm is the "command and control" paradigm that seeks to micro-manage and is therefore never adaptive, responsive, or coherent when facing nuanced challenges, while the diamond paradigm is how real people should approach the real world—as a network that easily permits cross fertilization. Another way of describing the new craft of intelligence, as conceptualized by the director of the South African <u>National Intelligence Agency</u> (NIA) in the 1990's, is as a DNA spiral, such that all of the humans in the different collection, processing, and analysis disciplines are constantly cross-fertilizing and exploiting information at all stages from initial contact to final finished presentation. As General Mike Hayden pointed out while serving as director of the National Security Agency (NSA), information must be shared and exploited <u>from the moment of ingestion</u>, and not have to wait until the very end of the process to be "seen."

The linear process is what we still have in place today, and "intelligence" is placed before the President just once a day, in a largely sterile *President's Daily Brief* (PDB). Intelligence is *not* "at his side" throughout the day. Now imagine a completely new process in which the President (or whatever "decider" is being served) is exposed to the complete range of all human knowledge in all languages, most of it not secret and shareable, as needed.

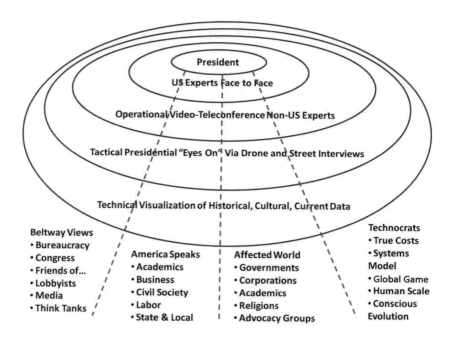

Figure 52: Putting the President in Touch with Humanity and Reality

The above construct is equally applicable for every policy-maker in every Cabinet or Ministry, for every acquisition manager, for every commander, for every staff action officer all the way to every A Team commander or company commander in the field. It is also applicable to the leaders and action officers of corporations, foundations, and international organizations.

We can no longer manage anything without intelligence (decision-support).

170

This chapter does not repeat lengthy critiques of HUMINT published elsewhere, nor does it address the specific organizational recommendations made to the US Government (USG). Here we focus only on constructive highlights.

Human Intelligence (broadly and properly defined) will be the heart, soul, and brain of 21st Century intelligence, not only within governments, but within all eight tribes of intelligence. In addition to CI and Security, I explicitly include both analysts of individual technical collection disciplines and all-source analysts; and consumers at every level from President to Action Officer (AO).

AOs today are one deep and have zero resources for securing OSINT, nor do they receive any support at all from the US IC. This is a principal reason why global multinational issues networks such as envisioned by J. F. Rischard, at the time Vice President for Europe of the World Bank, in his still-precious book, _HIGH NOON—Twenty Global Problems, Twenty Years to Solve Them_ are so urgently needed.

HUMINT at the strategic level will be about Smart Nations, Clever Continents, and the World Brain. At the operational level it will be about multinational information-sharing and sense-making to achieve mutual objectives by harmonizing up to $1 trillion a year in spending via an online Global Range of Needs Table that harmonizes organizational budgets by location and policy objective while also inducing direct charitable giving by the 80% of the one billion rich that do not now give now. The harmonization will occur voluntarily through the use of shared decision-support. The latter is discussed in more detail in Chapter 26.

At the tactical level, HUMINT will become the Queen of the intelligence chessboard, providing direct support to the King—_any_ decision-maker—by harnessing the distributed intelligence of all humans in all languages all the time—both those in the specific area of interest, and those outside who have something to contribute—and by restoring human primacy in relation to all technical intelligence operations—technical will excel _with_ HUMINT, not alone.

The HUMINT Trifecta educates and nurtures the all-source analysts *and* consumers including the public—especially the public—and provides the decision-maker with concise, contextually-grounded all-source insights in a "just enough, just in time" manner that leaves no decision—whether of policy, acquisition, or operations—without a firm foundation that eliminates waste and redundancy.

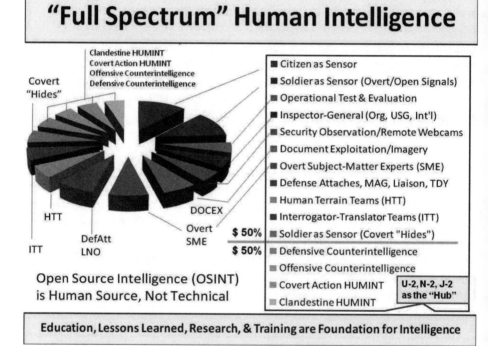

"Full Spectrum" Human Intelligence

Clandestine HUMINT
Covert Action HUMINT
Offensive Counterintelligence
Defensive Counterintelligence

Covert
"Hides"

HTT

DefAtt

ITT   LNO

DOCEX

Overt
SME

$ 50%

$ 50%

Open Source Intelligence (OSINT)
is Human Source, Not Technical

- Citizen as Sensor
- Soldier as Sensor (Overt/Open Signals)
- Operational Test & Evaluation
- Inspector-General (Org, USG, Int'l)
- Security Observation/Remote Webcams
- Document Exploitation/Imagery
- Overt Subject-Matter Experts (SME)
- Defense Attaches, MAG, Liaison, TDY
- Human Terrain Teams (HTT)
- Interrogator-Translator Teams (ITT)
- Soldier as Sensor (Covert "Hides")
- Defensive Counterintelligence
- Offensive Counterintelligence
- Covert Action HUMINT
- Clandestine HUMINT

U-2, N-2, J-2
as the "Hub"

Education, Lessons Learned, Research, & Training are Foundation for Intelligence

Figure 53: Integrated Full-Spectrum HUMINT Management

In the above figure LNO = Liaison Officer and SME = Subject-Matter Expert.

This figure is the culmination of my thirty or so years in the intelligence business. I emphasize the inclusion of OSINT as part of HUMINT, while specifying that OSINT is also the only discipline that is both a supporting discipline to both

HUMINT and the technical disciplines, and a stand-alone discipline where secret sources are not appropriate. Those organizations and nations that treat it as Technical Intelligence (TECHINT) are mistaken and consequently accessing less than 20% of what they should be.

I will not belabor the fact that other Nations are superior to the USA in their management of "full spectrum HUMINT," but I will mention three: the People's Republic of China (PRC), the Islamic Republic of Iran; and Cuba.

My own examination of _The Foreign Affairs System of the People's Republic of China_ (Lehigh University, 1975) remains quite valid and is available online in my Early Papers.

A current and concise definition of the "five circles" of Iranian HUMINT has been provided by Amir Taheri, As the US Retreats, Iran Fills the Void, _Wall Street Journal_, 4 May 2009. The five circles are

1) commercial companies and banks, many of them fronts;

2) charities and scholarships;

3) "cultural" centers offering language and religion;

4) Hezbollah operating openly; and

5) clandestine operations with and without indigenous Sunni radicals in support.

For an overview of Iran's penetration of Latin America, see Samuel Logan, Iran's Inroads and Deepening Ties in Latin America, Mexidata.info, 4 May 2009, including the phrase "as Iran continues to strengthen relationships, more Iranian doctors, diplomats, teachers, businessmen and officials are arriving in Latin America."

On the next two pages I outline fifteen HUMINT slices, each of which receives a full page in my monograph as published by SSI (forthcoming April 2010).

Citizen as Sensor & Sense-Maker. "Put enough eyeballs on it, no bug (or threat) is invisible." Similarly, put enough human brains to work, generate innovation beyond any industrial-era giant's wildest imagination. Web data templates and RapidSMS (Short Message System) are making extraordinary things possible, along with Twitter and other emerging offerings.

Soldier as Sensor (Overt/Open Signals). The concept of the strategic corporal is well established, both by Field Marshall Erwin Rommel, and more recently (1999) by General Charles Krulak, USMC. The soldier is the ultimate HUMINT asset. The contrast between the Eastern way of war emphasizing human intelligence and stealth with a small logistics footprint, and the Western way of war that emphasizes very expensive technical mass with a very big logistics footprint, is ably made by H. John Poole in various books.

Operational Test & Evaluation (OT&E). Speaking "truth to power" cannot apply only to "red" forces, and now as we understand it, to "white," "yellow," and "green" forces, but to our own "blue" forces as well. Lies kill one's comrades. We must stop lying to ourselves!

Inspector-General (Organizational, USG, International). We need an IG inspection of our fundamental assumptions about war and peace in the 21st Century. At the strategic level, the IGs should all be in alliance with the GAO and OMB and GSA, seeking to define completely new 21st Century objectives that are transformative of the means, ways, and ends of government. This should be a multinational network.

Security Observation/Remote Webcams/Floating Periscopes. We have been slow to empower our distributed forces with both modern security surveillance technology, and the *tactical* processing power needed to do "face trace" or find other anomalies that might be missed by the human eye. Also, between solar power, relay stations, and satellite communications, there is no reason why we cannot field persistent ground surveillance, for example, along the Somali coast. Security is a form of static HUMINT combined with "on demand" HUMINT, and only a robust educational program can make it effective. We still do not do multinational security collaboration that would offer enormous dividends when we get around to it. In any given foreign capital for example, the Regional Security Officers (RSO) speak among themselves, but their video surveillance systems, their watch lists, and other technical and human measures are not integrated among Embassies, and even less so with corporate general managers, NGO security networks, etc.

Document Exploitation/Imagery. I am told that it still takes 4-6 weeks for ten pages of captured Dari documents to be translated and returned to the tactical commander. I can do Dari translations from the field within 4-6 hours. Why we have not implemented a global grid using www.telelanguage.com, and field digitization (to include pen-based digitization) that can go directly from the field to a Dari translator on call in that given instant. Why is this still a problem? Old minds and processes, lack of new knowledge or imagination.

All-Source Analysts & Global Experts. Over the next ten years we must migrate away from putting new hires into anything other than OSINT exploitation, and emphasize mid-career hires for the senior all-source analytic positions as well as HUMINT collection and CI positions (the latter retaining their life's pattern as legitimate cover). At the same time, we must empower all-source analysts with the resources and the multinational social skills with which to leverage global experts regardless of nationality, and with the ability to draw on the MDSC for reach-back to all eight tribes of any given country.

Defense Attaches, Technical Liaison. We are long overdue for a review of how Departments and Ministries as a whole, and individual services and agencies, handle the selection, assignment, and on-going oversight and exploitation of all officers as well as non-commissioned and enlisted personnel serving in external billets. We are also long over-due for actually addressing—with responsible planning, programming, budgeting, hiring, training, and exercises—the short- to long-term operations under conditions more often than not hazardous that require Whole of Government as well as Multinational, Multifunctional task forces. I'd especially like to see Military Advisory Groups (MAG) modernized and given Information Operations (IO) responsibilities.

Human Terrain Teams (HTT). Done right, HTT should be inter-disciplinary and multinational, and should not require clearances at all. Anthropologists with language skills should be the heart of HTT, and most of them should not be Americans or even Europeans.

Interrogator-Translator Teams (ITT). I want to broaden the ITT category to include Military Police (MP), Civil Affairs (CA), Combat Engineers (CE), and all the folks that come into contact with both Prisoners of War (POW), which in the Marine Corps is an S-1/Adjutant housekeeping job rather than an S-2 intelligence exploitation job, and with civilians, including our logisticians (who are constantly starved for intelligence support at the same time that they have so much to offer in terms of practical insights about access and trafficability). We must conceive and execute a new form of HUMINT campaign plan that simultaneously educates, trains, informs, empowers, and ultimately protects every member of the inter-agency team that is being supported, and that is both conscious of—and able to exploit—every human several times removed in their respective networks.

Soldier as Sensor (Patrolling, Force Reconnaissance, Covert "Hides"). Patrolling is a fundamental element of infantry operations, and appears to rise and fall in cycles. Its companion, force reconnaissance, also tends to rise and fall. There is no substitute for a human brain attached to human eyes and ears, particularly when real-time contextual understanding and warning is needed. While Unmanned Aerial Vehicles (UAV) and Forward Air Controllers (FAC) and Aerial Observers (AO) can be most helpful, it is the human on the ground that produces "ground truth," a "360 degree" appreciation that cannot be achieved by any combination of technologies, close-in or remote. A great deal more can be done in using force reconnaissance to emplace close-in remote monitors, including webcams and live audio devices, in enemy encampments and criminal enclaves.

Defensive Counterintelligence and Offensive Counterintelligence are best discussed elsewhere. Chapter 20 addresses the need for 21st Century Full-Spectrum Counterintelligence, simply understanding our own deep problems of our own making.

176

Covert Action HUMINT. There is no finer overview on covert action that is legally available to the public than Alfred Cumming, *Covert Action: Legislative Background and Possible Policy Questions* (Congressional Research Service, February 9, 2009). I am persuaded by my own direct experience and a lifetime of reading that policymakers are not sufficiently informed, nor ethically grounded, and therefore should not be authorizing covert actions, with two exceptions: the capture or assassination of key terrorist or gang leaders and the interdiction of key ingredients of Chemical, Biological, Radiological, and Nuclear (CBRN) weapons of mass destruction (WMD).

Clandestine HUMINT. From where I sit, CIA has become useless. It refuses to abandon official cover and it has proven incapable of scaling up non-official cover despite spending tens of millions if not more on up to 21 "pseudo-companies," 20 of which had to be shut down recently. At the same time, CIA's young case officers (C/O) and analysts (the majority of the CIA analytic population now has less than five years employment at CIA) deprive CIA of any claim to special competence in HUMINT or all-source intelligence. CIA's alleged successes are in my opinion those of the foreign liaison services of the many dictators that we now pay huge sums of money to while turning a blind eye to their practice of torture and the raw fact that most of our money ends up in their bank accounts.

Bottom line: with the sole exception of deep penetrations of white collar corporate criminal networks; transnational criminal gangs; and local to global terrorist organizations, neither covert action nor clandestine HUMINT are worth the cost, the risk, or the moral hazard.

The major obstacles to HUMINT success are our consumers, out-dated security guidelines, and ignorant lawyers. To be successful, HUMINT managers must first educate all those "inside the wire." Consumers who say "tell me everything about everything," or "you figure it out," have not been properly educated or trained. Finally, lawyers....they say no when they mean they do not know, and they advise the destruction of useful intelligence (ABLE DANGER) rather than reveal their ignorance about whether it was legal or not.

177

HUMINT costs less, requires less time, and is much more responsive than technical collection, in part because with HUMINT, "processing" is embedded all along the human chain, from source to collector to analyst to consumer.

Below is a very high-level view of everything except the technical disciplines, which are assumed to be subordinate to HUMINT rather than out of control and costing billions of unnecessary dollars.

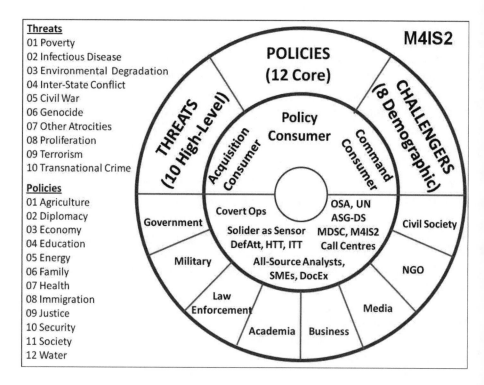

Figure 54: HUMINT Field—Sources, Targets, and Consumers

Chapter 20

21st Century Counterintelligence: Evaluating the Health of the Nation

This chapter focuses on what counterintelligence should be addressing in the 21st century, not on the minutia of the practice of counterintelligence. A fine overview of the later in traditional (secret world) terms is at Wikipedia.

Sun Tzu is well-known for his translated dictum

> *If you know your enemies and know yourself, you will not be imperiled in a hundred battles... if you do not know your enemies nor yourself, you will be imperiled in every single battle.*

What he does not address is the focus on this chapter: what if you know your enemy but do not know yourself? While I firmly believe that no government really knows its "enemy," I am more concerned at this time with the costs of any government—and by extension, the public that government represents—not knowing itself. I address Paradigms of Failure as well as Legitimate Grievances in general terms, in the chapter by that name in *ELECTION 2008: Lipstick on the Pig* (EIN, 2008), and also recommend the Annotated Bibliography for an internationally-oriented overview of reality.

This entire book is about knowing ourselves. This book also accepts the Santayana Institute's Twelve Principles, several of which make the point that every enemy is in fact part of the larger We, and knowing one's enemy is to have empathy for the whole comprised of "them" and "us" forming one We.

The question of "who knows" within a nation is fundamental. For example, from 1974-1979 both the US White House and the US Senate were fully briefed on Peak Oil and knew with precision that a "<u>long emergency</u>" would begin early in the new century. Similarly, in that timeframe, the Central Intelligence Agency (CIA) issued very fine reports on both the future lack of clean potable water, and the threat of HIV/AIDS. Back then, the information was communicated in briefings and hearings. Today the books are flooding the marketplace, but the public is not reading these books nor agitating for reform. See, for instance: *The Party's Over—Oil, War and the Fate of Industrial Societies* and *Twilight in the Desert—The Coming Saudi Oil Shock and the World Economy*.

The politicians chose to ignore these "clear and present" dangers in part because the policymakers—the civil servants—did not alert or alarm the public—and in part because the public had become inert and largely uninformed, a condition that persists today.

Today *The Next Catastrophe—Reducing Our Vulnerabilities to Natural, Industrial, and Terrorist Disasters* is readily anticipatable and preventable, but neither the politicians and their policy advisors, nor the public, are paying attention.

The above situation, drawing a distinction between a few "in the know" that chose not to pursue the public interest, and the public being unwitting, is a vital one. Thomas Jefferson put it this way:

> **A Nation's best defense is an educated citizenry.**

James Madison, like Thomas Jefferson a Virginian, said this:

> **Knowledge will forever govern ignorance; and a people who mean to be their own governors must arm themselves with the power which knowledge gives.**

There are at least three ways to evaluate the "health of the Nation," and no doubt many others depending on your point of view. Below I simply address three ways to think about our "home front" strength or lack thereof.

Health of the Budget

9/11 is a useful starting point for evaluating the current health of the nation in budget terms. Immediately after 9/11 a literature emerged on asymmetric warfare that quickly observed that for every $1 a terrorist group spent to attack us, we were spending $500,000 to fight back, much of this as a result of our own decisions imposing costs that many believe are not justifiable. Today that figure is probably closer to $5 million for every $1, and the cost of the Iraq war alone is now understood to be $3 trillion.

By 2006 the Republic was insolvent, according to the Comptroller General of the United States (the head of the General Accountability Office or GAO).

1. An economic meltdown beginning in February 2008 that has led to unemployment close to 22% when counting both underemployed and those who have given up looking for work; and been exacerbated by a federal government willing to give trillions it did not have to keep immoral incompetent banks "too big to fail" from losing their bonus money;

2. A series of decisions leading to a three-trillion dollar war in Iraq; and finally

3. A health-care "plan" that fails to address three of the four essentials for national health (healthy lifestyle, healthy environment, natural cures) while committing to trillions in costs for the fourth part (medical remediation) without doing the obvious, reducing the costs of medications to 1% of what we pay now (what the rest of the world pays for generic bulk drugs).

It is not the purpose of this chapter to "investigate and document" the bankruptcy of the US Government and indirectly, of the Republic, only to bring this specific aspect of national counterintelligence forward.

181

Health of the Government

The health of the government can be evaluated at multiple levels, and I will just list these:

1. Is the government well-designed and structured to make informed decisions in the public interest, decisions that utilize all of the instruments of national power in a "whole of government" manner, balancing means, ways, and ends?

2. Is the government well-staffed, with a mix of political leaders, policy appointees, and civil servants who are knowledgeable, replete with integrity, and able to discharge their duties?

3. Is the government responsive to the public it is supposed to serve, or overly responsive to special corporate or religious or foreign interests that demand, buy, and obtain decisions and allocation of the public budget to programs inimical to the public interest?

4. Is the government, on a day to day basis, operating with integrity, meaning that it is collecting and processing relevant information, it is making decisions in a timely coordinated manner, and those decisions are being implemented in a cost-effective timely manner that ably serves the public interest?

I deliberately avoid what I consider to be the tactical issue of detecting and neutralizing espionage against the government because 80% or more of what the government is supposed to be doing is intended to be publicly accountable. Chapter 12 on the instruments of power is relevant here.

The reality is that the answer to all of the above questions is a resounding "NO!" The USA—and many other nations—have governments constituted of stove-pipes dedicated to meeting the interests of the special interests that bribe office holders so as to transfer money from the taxpayer to the special interest. In the case of the USA, the government is dysfunctional—broken.

Health of the Public

The health of the public within a Republic should be—but has not been—the principal pre-occupation of the elected, appointed, and employed leaders of the government at each level. A government, I would add, that is intended to be a servant of the public, not its master.

Sadly, focusing only on the USA but with general applicability to other nations, some less than others (there is much that is good about various other countries, and especially the Nordic countries and The Netherlands), the health of the public in the USA is low by all standards.

I will not repeat nor apply the varied points from previous chapters that bear on this analytic situation, but will just highlight:

- Chapter 5—knowledge is fragmented and the eight tribes do not share information nor make sense together

- Chapter 10—we have a culture of catastrophe, cheating, conflict, and conspiracy

- Chapter 11—the few enjoy information asymmetries in their favor, and impose data pathologies on all of us, including the externalization of costs to the public and the concealment of the "true cost" of all goods and services in terms of water, clean air, non-renewable energy, and persistent toxins.

- Chapter 15—the "average American," once a standard-bearer for all that is good in the world, is now an anemic failure, unwitting, inattentive, and ineffective as a member of the Republic

From my review of Noam Chomsky's *Interventions*:

We are losing the global war of belief systems because we refuse to recognize our grotesque migration from a free people to an evil empire in which the people have no say over what is being done "in their name." Sun Tzu knew that only those who know BOTH themselves, AND their enemy, will be victories. We know NEITHER ourselves nor our enemies, most of them of our own making. There are reasons for this, but the most important reason lies with our own failing as a public willing to demand the public interest in lieu of special interests.

On the next twenty pages I list the broad categories from the framework for the analysis of revolution that appears in Chapter 15, Figure 37, page 126, focused on the domestic health of the USA, with links to summary reviews of each book (in the free online version of this book) at Phi Beta Iota. Most of these complaints are not new—what is new is that they are being noticed and acquiring resonance with the public, a power government cannot suppress.

This chapter was going to be just a few pages long, but after I began listing books documenting the "negatives" that we do not seem to be understanding as a public, I ended going through all 1,500 of my reviews, sorting them into two groups. This is the "negatives" group. Part III of this book will end with the "good news" group in the Annotated Bibliography, and I want to stress that— however much the USA might be off its game, I have absolutely no doubt that We the People are going to restore America the Beautiful, and that ultimately we will all come together to create a prosperous world at peace. This book is intended to contribute to that end.

I decided to limit the Annotated Bibliography to lists of my reviews of books that are generally constructive about the future, while placing the more negative books here as a foundation for understanding the precarious status of the Republic when viewed objectively and with integrity.

It troubles me when colleagues suggest that my critical posture on national matters is evidence of a "hatred" for America. Nothing could be further from the truth. America, and the ideals it represents, are in my DNA*. False patriotism is where idiots, ideologues, and white-collar criminals converge; in a time of trials and tribulations, the greatest service a patriot can render is to speak truth to power, for only by achieving the fullest possible access to the truth can we attend to all that ails us. Tough love is, in my view, patriotic.

Political-Legal

Corruption
Congress Candid Camera
Review: *Breach of Trust–How Washington Turns Outsiders into Insiders* (Hardcover)
Review: *Crashing the Party–Taking on the Corporate Government in an Age of Surrender*
Review: *Gold Warriors–America's Secret Recovery of Yamashita's Gold*
Review: *Hostile Takeover–How Big Money and Corruption Conquered Our Government–and How We Take It Back* (Hardcover)
Review: *Off Center–The Republican Revolution and the Erosion of American Democracy* (Hardcover)
Review: *One Market Under God–Extreme Capitalism, Market Populism, and the End of Economic Democracy* (Paperback)
Review: *Secrecy & Privilege–Rise of the Bush Dynasty from Watergate to Iraq*
Review: *Selling Out*
Review: *Sleeping With the Devil: How Washington Sold Our Soul for Saudi Crude*
Review: *The Attack on the Liberty–The Untold Story of Israel's Deadly 1967 Assault on a US Spy Ship*
Review: *The Broken Branch–How Congress Is Failing America and How to Get It Back on Track (Institutions of American Democracy)*
Review: *The Power of Israel in the United States*
Review: *The Trouble with Africa–Why Foreign Aid Isn't Working*
Review: *The Underground Empire–Where Crime and Governments Embrace*
Review: *They Dare to Speak Out–People and Institutions Confront Israel's Lobby*

Dereliction of Duty (Defense)

Budget Malfeasance
Review DVD: *Why We Fight* (2006)
Review: *Averting the Defense Train Wreck in the New Millennium* (CSIS Report)
Review: *Blank Check–The Pentagon's Black Budget*
Review: *Making America's Budget Policy–From the 1980s to the 1990s* (Paperback)

---

* Deoxyribonucleic acid (**DNA**) is a nucleic acid that contains the genetic instructions used in the development and functioning of all known living organisms

Review: *National Defense*
Review: *The Fifty Year Wound–The True Price of America's Cold War Victory*
Review: *The Three Trillion Dollar War–The True Cost of the Iraq Conflict*
Review: *Transformation Under Fire–Revolutionizing How America Fights*
Review: *Wastrels of Defense–How Congress Sabotages US Security*

Consequences
Imperial Hubris: Why the West is Losing the War on Terror
Review: *Imperial Grunts–The American Military on the Ground* (Hardcover)
Review: *Tiger Force–A True Story of Men and War* (Hardcover)
Review: *Unintended Consequences–The United States at War*

Central Asia
Review: *Descent into Chaos–The United States and the Failure of Nation Building in Pakistan, Afghanistan, and Central Asia*
Review: *Seeds of Terror–How Heroin Is Bankrolling the Taliban and al Qaeda*

Contractors & Contractor-Related Corruption
Review: *Licensed to Kill–Hired Guns in the War on Terror* (Hardcover)
Review: *The Devil's Garden*

Culture
Review: *House of War* (Hardcover)

Homeland Insecurity
Review: *America the Vulnerable–How Our Government Is Failing to Protect Us from Terrorism*
Review: *American Jihad–The Terrorists Living Among Us*
Review: *Open Target–Where America Is Vulnerable to Attack* (Hardcover)
Review: *Osama's Revenge–THE NEXT 9/11: What the Media and the Government Haven't Told You*
Review: *Willful Neglect–The Dangerous Illusion of Homeland Security*

Hubris & Incompetence
Review (Guest): *Bathtub Admirals* (Hardcover)
Review: *Against All Enemies–Inside America's War on Terror*
Review: *An End to Evil–How to Win the War on Terror*
Review: *Blind Into Baghdad–America's War in Iraq*
Review: *Endgame–The Blueprint for Victory in the War on Terror*
Review: *Fiasco–The American Military Adventure in Iraq* (Hardcover)

186

Review: *How Did This Happen? Terrorism and the New War*
Review: *Iraq and the Evolution of American Strategy*
Review: *Losing the Golden Hour–An Insider's View of Iraq's Reconstruction*
Review: *Rumsfeld–His Rise, Fall, and Catastrophic Legacy*
Review: *Squandered Victory–The American Occupation and the Bungled Effort to Bring Democracy to Iraq* (Hardcover)
Review: *The End of Iraq–How American Incompetence Created a War Without End* (Hardcover)
Review: *The Mission–Waging War and Keeping Peace with America's Military*
Review: *The One Percent Doctrine–Deep Inside America's Pursuit of Its Enemies Since 9/11* (Hardcover)
Review: *The Rules of the Game–Jutland and British Naval Command*
Review: *Treachery–How America's Friends and Foes Are Secretly Arming Our Enemies* (Hardcover)
Review: *War and Decision–Inside the Pentagon at the Dawn of the War on Terrorism*
Review: *War in a Time of Peace–Bush, Clinton, and the Generals*
Review: *What Went Wrong? Western Impact and Middle Eastern Response*

Middle East
Review: *Marching Toward Hell–America and Islam After Iraq*
Review: *Target Iran–The Truth About the White House's Plans for Regime Change*
Review: *The Power of Israel in the United States*
Review: *They Dare to Speak Out–People and Institutions Confront Israel's Lobby*

Dereliction of Duty (Health)
Review DVD: *Pandemic*
Review: *Betrayal of Trust–The Collapse of Global Public Health*
Review: *Pathologies of Power–Health, Human Rights, and the New War on the Poor* (Hardcover)
Review: *Who Killed Health Care?–America's $2 Trillion Medical Problem – and the Consumer-Driven Cure*

Dereliction of Duty Other Than Defense)
Review (Guest): *Integrity–Good People, Bad Choices, and Life Lessons from the White House*
Review: *A Season of Inquiry–The Senate Intelligence Investigation*
Review: *Afghanistan's Endless War–State Failure, Regional Politics, and the Rise of the Taliban*
Review: *America the Vulnerable–How Our Government Is Failing to Protect Us from Terrorism*

Review: *Betrayal of Trust—The Collapse of Global Public Health*
Review: *Blue Frontier—Dispatches from America's Ocean Wilderness*
Review: *Bureaucratic Politics and Foreign Policy*
Review: *Collapse—How Societies Choose to Fail or Succeed*
Review: *Defense Facts of Life—The Plans/Reality Mismatch*
Review: *Downsizing Democracy—How America Sidelined Its Citizens and Privatized Its Public*
Review: *Genocide in the Congo (Zaire)*
Review: *Gomorrah*
Review: *Inside Sudan—Political Islam, Conflict, and Catastrophe*
Review: *Leave Us Alone—Getting the Government's Hands Off Our Money, Our Guns, Our Lives*
Review: *My Year in Iraq—The Struggle to Build a Future of Hope*
Review: *Politics Lost—How American Democracy Was Trivialized By People Who Think You're Stupid* (Hardcover)
Review: *Risk and Reason—Safety, Law, and the Environment*
Review: *Running The World—the Inside Story of the National Security Council and the Architects of American Power* (Hardcover)
Review: *See No Evil—The True Story of a Ground Soldier in the CIA's War on Terrorism*
Review: *Seven Sins of American Foreign Policy* (Paperback)
Review: *Shake Hands With The Devil—The Failure Of Humanity In Rwanda*
Review: *The Assault on Reason*
Review: *The Collapse of Complex Societies*
Review: *The Edge of Disaster—Rebuilding a Resilient Nation*
Review: *The Life and Death of NSSM 200 —How the Destruction of Political Will Doomed a US Population Policy*
Review: *The New American Story*
Review: *The Next Catastrophe—Reducing Our Vulnerabilities to Natural, Industrial, and Terrorist Disasters*
Review: *The Political Junkie Handbook (The Definitive Reference Book on Politics)*
Review: *Where Have All the Leaders Gone?*
Review: *While America Sleeps—How Islam, Immigration and Indoctrination Are Destroying America From Within*
Review: *White Nile, Black Blood—War, Leadership, and Ethnicity from Khartoum to Kampala*
Review: *Wilson's Ghost—Reducing the Risk of Conflict, Killing, and Catastrophe in the 21st Century*
Review: *Your Government Failed You—Breaking the Cycle of National Security Disasters*

188

Disinformation, Other Information Pathologies, & Repression

9/11
Review: *9-11*
Review: *9-11 Descent into Tyranny–The New World Order's Dark Plans to Turn Earth into a Prison Planet*
Review: *Access Denied–The Practice and Policy of Global Internet Filtering*
Review: *Painful Questions–An Analysis of the September 11th Attack*
Review: *The 9/11 Commission Report–Omissions And Distortions* (Paperback)
Review: *The Big Wedding–9/11, the Whistle Blowers, and the Cover-up* (Paperback)
Review: *The Hidden History of 9-11*
Review: *The New Pearl Harbor–Disturbing Questions About the Bush Administration and 9/11* (Paperback)
Review: *The Terror Timeline–Year by Year, Day by Day, Minute by Minute: A Comprehensive Chronicle of the Road to 9/11–and America's Response* (Paperback)
Review: *The War On Truth–9/11, Disinformation And The Anatomy Of Terrorism* (Paperback)

Censorship
Review DVD: *The US vs. John Lennon*
Review: *Censorship of Historical Thought–A World Guide, 1945-2000*
Review: *Forbidden Knowledge–From Prometheus to Pornography*
Review: *Gag Rule–On the Suppression of Dissent and Stifling of Democracy*
Review: *Into the Buzzsaw–Leading Journalists Expose the Myth of a Free Press*
Review: *Soft Despotism, Democracy's Drift: Montesquieu, Rousseau, Tocqueville, and the Modern Prospect*
Review: *The Age of Missing Information*

Cover-Ups
Review: *Scorpion Down–Sunk by the Soviets, Buried by the Pentagon: The Untold Story of the USS Scorpion*
Review: *Silent Steel–The Mysterious Death of the Nuclear Attack Sub USS Scorpion*

Extra-Terrestrial Withholding
Review: *Hidden Truth–Forbidden Knowledge*

Iraq
Review: *A War Against Truth–An Intimate Account of the Invasion of Iraq* [ILLUSTRATED] (Paperback)

Propaganda
Review (Guest): *Propaganda—The Formation of Men's Attitudes*
Review DVD: *Fahrenheit 9/11* (2004)
Review: *Big Lies—The Right-Wing Propaganda Machine and How It Distorts the Truth*
Review: *Disinformation –22 Media Myths That Undermine the War on Terror* (Hardcover)
Review: *Fog Facts –Searching for Truth in the Land of Spin* (Nation Books) (Hardcover)
Review: *HOW ISRAEL LOST*
Review: *Interventions*
Review: *It's Not News, It's Fark—How Mass Media Tries to Pass Off Crap As News*
Review: *Manufacturing Consent—The Political Economy of the Mass Media*
Review: *State of Fear*
Review: *The Infernal Machine—A History of Terrorism*

Secrecy
Review: *Lost History—Contras, Cocaine, the Press & 'Project Truth'*
Review: *Nation of Secrets—The Threat to Democracy and the American Way of Life*
Review: *Secrecy—The American Experience*
Review: *Secrets—A Memoir of Vietnam and the Pentagon Papers*
Review: *Secrets and Lies—Operation "Iraqi Freedom" and After: A Prelude to the Fall of US Power in the Middle East?*
Review: *The American Truth*

Two-Party Tyranny
Review: *Grand Illusion—The Myth of Voter Choice in a Two-Party Tyranny*
Review: *Running on Empty—How the Democratic and Republican Parties Are Bankrupting Our Future and What Americans Can Do About It*

Empire as a Cancer Including Betrayal & Deceit
Review: *A Peace to End All Peace—The Fall of the Ottoman Empire and the Creation of the Modern Middle East*
Review: *Acts of Aggression*
Review: *After Iraq—The Imperiled American Imperium*
Review: *Blowback—The Costs and Consequences of American Empire*
Review: *Day of Empire—How Hyperpowers Rise to Global Dominance—and Why They Fall*
Review: *Enforcing the Peace—Learning from the Imperial Past*
Review: *Failed States—The Abuse of Power and the Assault on Democracy* (American Empire Project) (Hardcover)

Review: *Foreign Follies–America's New Global Empire*
Review: *Imperial Ambitions–Conversations on the Post-9/11 World* (American Empire Project) (Paperback)
Review: *Killing Hope–US Military and C.I.A. Interventions Since World War II-Updated Through 2003*
Review: *Nemesis–The Last Days of the American Republic*
Review: *Overthrow–America's Century of Regime Change from Hawaii to Iraq* (Hardcover)
Review: *The Folly of Empire–What George W. Bush Could Learn from Theodore Roosevelt and Woodrow Wilson*
Review: *The Folly of War–American Foreign Policy, 1898-2005*
Review: *The Looming Tower–Al-Qaeda and the Road to 9/11*
Review: *The Road to 9/11–Wealth, Empire, and the Future of America*
Review: *The Sorrows of Empire–Militarism, Secrecy, and the End of the Republic* (American Empire Project)
Review: *The Vulnerability of Empire* (Cornell Studies in Security Affairs)
Review: *War and Peace and War: The Rise and Fall of Empires*
Review: *War, Evil, and the End of History*
Review: *Web of Deceit: The History of Western Complicity in Iraq, from Churchill to Kennedy to George W. Bush*
Review: *What We Say Goes*

Impeachable Offenses (Modern)
Review DVD: *9/11 Mysteries – Part I: Demolitions*
Review DVD: *Behind Every Terrorist There Is a Bush*
Review DVD: *Bush's Brain* (2004)
Review *DVD: Death of a President* (Widescreen)
Review: *9/11 Synthetic Terror–Made in USA, Fourth Edition*
Review: *A Pretext for War–9/11, Iraq, and the Abuse of America's Intelligence Agencies*
Review: *Articles of Impeachment Against George W. Bush*
Review: *Bush at War*
Review: *How Bush Rules–Chronicles of a Radical Regime*
Review: *In the Name of Democracy–American War Crimes in Iraq and Beyond*
Review: *Prelude to Terror–the Rogue CIA, The Legacy of America's Private Intelligence Network the Compromising of American Intelligence* (Hardcover)
Review: *Royal Flush–Impeach Bush Now Cards*
Review: *Rumsfeld–His Rise, Fall, and Catastrophic Legacy*
Review: *The American Truth*

Review: *The Case for Impeachment–The Legal Argument for Removing President George W. Bush from Office* (Hardcover)
Review: *The Great Unraveling–Losing Our Way in the New Century*
Review: *VICE–Dick Cheney and the Hijacking of the American Presidency*
Review: *Where the Right Went Wrong–How Neoconservatives Subverted the Reagan Revolution and Hijacked the Bush Presidency*
Review: *You're Not Stupid! Get the Truth–A Brief on the Bush Presidency*

Impeachable Offenses (Historic)
Review: *A Farewell to Justice–Jim Garrison, JFK's Assassination, and the Case That Should Have Changed History* (Hardcover)
Review: *An Act of State–The Execution of Martin Luther King, New and Updated Edition*
Review: *Buried in the Bitter Waters–The Hidden History of Racial Cleansing in America*
Review: *Imagery of Lynching–Black Men, White Women, and the Mob*
Review: *JFK and the Unspeakable–Why He Died & Why It Matters*
Review: *Someone Would Have Talked–The Assassination of President John F. Kennedy and the Conspiracy to Mislead History*
Review: *The Trial of Henry Kissinger*
Review: *Without Sanctuary: Lynching Photography in America*

Institutionalized Ineptitude
Review DVD: *Idiocracy*
Review DVD: *The Fog of War – Eleven Lessons from the Life of Robert S. McNamara*
Review: *At War with Ourselves–Why America Is Squandering Its Chance to Build a Better World*
Review: *Blind Into Baghdad–America's War in Iraq*
Review: *Breaking the Real Axis of Evil–How to Oust the World's Last Dictators by 2025*
Review: *Daydream Believers–How a Few Grand Ideas Wrecked American Power*
Review: *Devil's Game–How the United States Helped Unleash Fundamentalist Islam* (American Empire Project)
Review: *Dunces of Doomsday–10 Blunders That Gave Rise to Radical Islam, Terrorist Regimes, And the Threat of an American Hiroshima*
Review: *Fiasco–The American Military Adventure in Iraq* (Hardcover)
Review: *Glenn Beck's Common Sense–The Case Against an Out-of-Control Government, Inspired by Thomas Paine*
Review: *National Suicide: How Washington Is Destroying the American Dream from A to Z*
Review: *Our Undemocratic Constitution–Where the Constitution Goes Wrong (And How We the People Can Correct It)*

Review: *Strategery–How George W. Bush Is Defeating Terrorists, Outwitting Democrats, and Confounding the Mainstream Media* (Hardcover)
Review: *The Powers of War and Peace–The Constitution and Foreign Affairs after 9/11* (Hardcover)

Intelligence (Lack Of)

All
2000 ON INTELLIGENCE: Spies and Secrecy in an Open World
Review DVD: *Traitor*
Review: *Bombs, Bugs, Drugs, and Thugs–Intelligence and America's Quest for Security*
Review: *Breakdown–How America's Intelligence Failures Led to September 11*
Review: *Comrade J*
Review: *Fixing Intelligence–For a More Secure America*
Review: *Flawed by Design–The Evolution of the CIA, JCS, and NSC*
Review: *How We Missed the Story–Osama Bin Laden, the Taliban and the Hijacking of Afghanistan*
Review: *Imperial Secrets–Remapping the Mind of Empire*
Review: *Intelligence Failure–How Clinton's National Security Policy Set the Stage for 9/11* (Hardcover)
Review: *National Insecurity–US Intelligence After the Cold War*
Review: *Piercing the Veil of Secrecy–Litigation Against US Intelligence*
Review: *Preventing Surprise Attacks–Intelligence Reform in the Wake of 9/11 (Hoover Studies in Politics, Economics, and Society)* (Hardcover)
Review: *Secrecy and Democracy–The CIA in Transition*
Review: *Spies for Hire–The Secret World of Intelligence Outsourcing*
Review: *Spy Wars–Moles, Mysteries, and Deadly Games*
Review: *Spying Blind–The CIA, the FBI, and the Origins of 9/11*
Review: *Spying on the Bomb–American Nuclear Intelligence from Nazi Germany to Iran and North Korea* (Hardcover)
Review: *State of War–The Secret History of the CIA and the Bush Administration* (Hardcover)
Review: *The Human Factor–Inside the CIA's Dysfunctional Intelligence Culture*
Review: *Turmoil and Triumph My Years As Secretary of State* (Hardcover)
Review: *US Intelligence at the Crossroads–Agendas for Reform*
Review: *Uncertain Shield–The US Intelligence System in the Throes of Reform* (Hoover Studies in Politics, Economics, and Society) (Hardcover)
Review: *Why Secret Intelligence Fails*
Review: *Winning Modern Wars–Iraq, Terrorism, and the American Empire*

CIA

Reference: *Global Outlook Special on False Flag Operations*
Review: *A SPY FOR ALL SEASONS–My Life In The CIA*
Review: *At the Center of the Storm–My Years at the CIA*
Review: *Beyond Repair: The Decline and Fall of the CIA*
Review: *Blond Ghost*
Review: *Blowback–The First Full Account of America's Recruitment of Nazis and Its Disastrous Effect on The cold war, Our Domestic and Foreign Policy*
Review: *Charlie Wilson's War–The Extraordinary Story of the Largest Covert Operation in History*
Review: *Dark Alliance–The CIA, the Contras, and the Crack Cocaine Explosion*
Review: *Denial and Deception–An Insider's View of the CIA from Iran-Contra to 9/11*
Review: *Edward Lansdale's Cold War (Culture, Politics, and the Cold War)* (Paperback)
Review: *In Search of Enemies–A CIA Story*
Review: *Informing Statecraft–Intelligence for a New Century*
Review: *INSIDE THE COMPANY–CIA DIARY*
Review: *Legacy of Ashes–The History of the CIA*
Review: *Lost Promise*
Review: *Spymaster–My Life in the CIA*
Review: *The CIA and the Cult of Intelligence*
Review: *The Phoenix Program*
Review: *The Very Best Men–Four Who Dared–The Early Years of the CIA*

DIA

Review: *Firepower In Limited War*
Review: *None So Blind–A Personal Account of the Intelligence Failure in Vietnam*
Review: *Slow Burn–The Rise and Bitter Fall of American Intelligence in Vietnam*
Review: *Still Broken–A Recruit's Inside Account of Intelligence Failures, from Baghdad to the Pentagon*
Review: *The Tet Offensive–Intelligence Failure in War*
Review: *The Tunnels of Cu Chi*
Review: *War Without Windows*
Review: *Who the Hell Are We Fighting?–The Story of Sam Adams and the Vietnam Intelligence Wars* (Hardcover)

FBI

Review DVD: *Breach* (Widescreen Edition)
Review: *Inside–A Top G-Man Exposes Spies, Lies, and Bureaucratic Bungling in the FBI*
Review: *Merchants of Treason–America's Secrets for Sale*

Review: *My FBI–Bringing Down the Mafia, Investigating Bill Clinton, and Fighting the War on Terror* (Hardcover)
Review: *Robert Maxwell, Israel's Superspy–The Life and Murder of a Media Mogul*
Review: *Wedge–From Pearl Harbor to 9/11–How the Secret War between the FBI and CIA Has Endangered National Security*

NRO
Review: *Deep Black–Space Espionage and National Security*

NSA
Review: *Body of Secrets–Anatomy of the Ultra-Secret National Security Agency*
Review: *The Puzzle Palace–Inside the National Security Agency, America's Most Secret Intelligence Organization*
Review: *The Shadow Factory–The Ultra-Secret NSA from 9/11 to the Eavesdropping on America*
Review: *The Sigint Secrets–The Signals Intelligence War, 1900 to Today–Including the Persecution of Gordon Welchman*

Theocracy
Review: *America's "War on Terrorism"* (Paperback)
Review: *American Theocracy–The Peril and Politics of Radical Religion, Oil, and Borrowed Money in the 21st Century* (Hardcover)
Review: *Blood in the Sand–Imperial Fantasies, Right-Wing Ambitions, and the Erosion of American Democracy* (Hardcover)
Review: *Dreaming War–Blood for Oil and the Cheney-Bush Junta*
Review: *Foreign Follies–America's New Global Empire*
Review: *Hegemony or Survival–America's Quest for Global Dominance* (The American Empire Project)
Review: *Losing America–Confronting a Reckless and Arrogant Presidency*
Review: *Obama–The Postmodern Coup – Making of a Manchurian Candidate*
Review: *Power Trip* (Open Media Series)
Review: *The Ambition and the Power–The Fall of Jim Wright : A True Story of Washington*
Review: *The Bush Tragedy*
Review: *The Price of Loyalty–George W. Bush, the White House, and the Education of Paul O'Neill*

Socio-Economic

Bankruptcy of US Economy, Federal Reserve Malfeasance
Review (Guest) DVD: *I.O.U.S.A. DVD on US Bankruptcy*
Review: *In an Uncertain World–Tough Choices from Wall Street to Washington*
Review: *Maestro–Greenspan's Fed And The American Boom*
Review: *Petrodollar Warfare–Oil, Iraq and the Future of the Dollar*
Review: *The Age of Turbulence–Adventures in a New World*

Blue Collar
Review: *Blue Collar Ministry–Facing Economic and Social Realities of Working People*
Review: *Deer Hunting with Jesus–Dispatches from America's Class War*
Review: *Exporting America–Why Corporate Greed Is Shipping American Jobs Overseas*
Review: *Talking Politics with God and the Devil in Washington, D.C.*

Class War (Global)
Review: *Bad Samaritans–The Myth of Free Trade and the Secret History of Capitalism*
Review: *Eco-Imperialism–Green Power, Black Death*
Review: *Global Inc.–An Atlas of the Multinational Corporation*
Review: *Global Reach–The Power of the Multinational Corporations*
Review: *Open Veins of Latin America–Five Centuries of the Pillage of a Continent*
Review: *Opening America's Market–US Foreign Trade Policy Since 1776* (Luther Hartwell Hodges Series on Business, Society and the State)
Review: *Operating Manual for Spaceship Earth*
Review: *SAVAGE CAPITALISM AND THE MYTH OF DEMOCRACY–Latin America in the Third Millennium*
Review: *The Global Class War –How America's Bipartisan Elite Lost Our Future – and What It Will Take to Win it Back* (Hardcover)
Review: *The WTO* (Open Media Pamphlet Series)

Corporate & Transnational Crime
Review DVD: *American Drug War: The Last White Hope*
Review: *Bulletproof*
Review: *Confessions of an Economic Hit Man*
Review: *Conspiracy of Fools–A True Story* (Hardcover)

196

Corporate Lack of Integrity or Intelligence or Both

Elite Rule

Review DVD: *The AMERICAN Ruling Class*
Review: *All the Money in the World–How the Forbes 400 Make–and Spend–Their Fortunes*
Review: *How The World Really Works*
Review: *Rule by Secrecy–The Hidden History That Connects the Trilateral Commission, the Freemasons, and the Great Pyramids*
Review: *Superclass–The Global Power Elite and the World They Are Making*
Review: *The New Rulers of the World*
Review: *The Rise of the Fourth Reich–The Secret Societies That Threaten to Take Over America*
Review: *The Secret Founding of America–The Real Story of Freemasons, Puritans, & the Battle for The New World*

Middle Class

Review: *Screwed–The Undeclared War Against the Middle Class — And What We Can Do About It*
Review: *War on the Middle Class–How the Government, Big Business, and Special Interest Groups Are Waging War on the American Dream and How to Fight Back*

Poisons, Toxicity, Trash, & True Cost

Review: *A Consumer's Dictionary of Household, Yard and Office Chemicals: Complete Information About Harmful and Desirable Chemicals Found in Everyday Home Products, Yard Poisons, and Office Polluters*
Review: *High Tech Trash–Digital Devices, Hidden Toxics, and Human Health*
Review: *Made to Break–Technology and Obsolescence in America*
Review: *Pandora's Poison–Chlorine, Health, and a New Environmental Strategy* (Paperback)
Review: *The Blue Death–Disease, Disaster, and the Water We Drink*
Review: *The Omnivore's Dilemma–A Natural History of Four Meals*
Review: *The True Cost of Low Prices–The Violence of Globalization*
Review: *Toxin* (Fiction)
Review: *Wal-Mart–The High Cost of Low Price* (2005)

Poverty

Review: *An Atlas of Poverty in America–One Nation, Pulling Apart, 1960-2003*
Review: *Life at the Bottom–The Worldview That Makes the Underclass*
Review: *Nickel and Dimed–On (Not) Getting By in America*
Review: *Nobodies–Modern American Slave Labor and the Dark Side of the New Global Economy*
Review: *Off the Books–The Underground Economy of the Urban Poor*
Review: *The Globalization of Poverty and the New World Order* (Paperback)
Review: *The Working Poor–Invisible in America*

War Complex—War as a Racket

Review DVD: *Lord of War* (Widescreen) (2005)
Review: *Betraying Our Troops–The Destructive Results of Privatizing War*
Review: *Blood Money–Wasted Billions, Lost Lives, and Corporate Greed in Iraq*
Review: *Hope of the Wicked*
Review: *The Price of Liberty–Paying for America's Wars*
Review: *The Shock Doctrine–The Rise of Disaster Capitalism*
Review: *The Swiss, The Gold And The Dead–How Swiss Bankers Helped Finance the Nazi War Machine*
Review: *The True Cost of Conflict/Seven Recent Wars and Their Effects on Society*
Review: *War is a Racket–The Antiwar Classic by America's Most Decorated Soldier*

Ideo-Cultural

Anger

Review DVD: *The Believer* (2001)
Review: *Harvest Of Rage–Why Oklahoma City Is Only The Beginning*
Review: *Kids Who Kill–Confronting Our Culture of Violence*
Review: *Rage of the Random Actor*

Anthropology

Review: *Anthropological Intelligence–The Deployment and Neglect of American Anthropology in the Second World War*
Review: *Catastrophe & Culture–The Anthropology of Disaster*

Corruption

Review: *Dude, Where's My Country?*
Review: *Just How Stupid Are We?—Facing the Truth About the American Voter*
Review: *The Cheating Culture—Why More Americans Are Doing Wrong to Get Ahead*
Review: *The Culture of National Security*
Review: *The Deepening Darkness—Patriarchy, Resistance, and Democracy's Future*
Review: *The End of America—Letter of Warning to a Young Patriot*
Review: *The Final Move Beyond Iraq—The Final Solution While the World Sleeps*
Review: *The Pathology of Power*
Review: *Thieves in High Places—They've Stolen Our Country—And It's Time to Take It Back*

Culture

Review: *The Crisis of Western Culture*

Dissent

Review: *Access Denied—The Practice and Policy of Global Internet Filtering*
Review: *Gag Rule—On the Suppression of Dissent and Stifling of Democracy*
Review: *NOW Who Do We Blame?—Political Cartoons by Tom Toles* (Paperback)
Review: *Speaking Freely—Trials of the First Amendment* (Paperback)
Review: *Why Societies Need Dissent* (Oliver Wendell Holmes Lectures)

Evil

Review: *The Lucifer Principle—A Scientific Expedition into the Forces of History* (Paperback)
Review: *The Marketing of Evil—How Radicals, Elitists, and Pseudo-Experts Sell Us Corruption Disguised As Freedom* (Hardcover)

Family & Values

Review: *How Would a Patriot Act? Defending American Values from a President Run Amok* (Paperback)
Review: *Liberty and Tyranny—A* Conservative Manifesto
Review: *Love You, Daddy Boy—Daughters Honor the Fathers They Love*
Review: *Our Endangered Values—America's Moral Crisis* (Hardcover)
Review: *The Conservative Soul—How We Lost It, How to Get It Back*

Intellectuals
Review: *Betrayal: How Black Intellectuals Have Abandoned the Ideals of the Civil Rights Era*
Review: *Waiting for Lightning to Strike–The Fundamentals of Black Politics*

Religion
Review: *American Fascists–The Christian Right and the War On America*
Review: *American Gospel–God, the Founding Fathers, and the Making of a Nation* (Hardcover)
Review: *Dogs of God–Columbus, the Inquisition, and the Defeat of the Moors* (Hardcover)
Review: *Fighting Identity–Sacred War and World Change (The Changing Face of War)*
Review: *God's Politics–Why the Right Gets It Wrong and the Left Doesn't Get It* (Hardcover)
Review: *Pagan Christianity?: Exploring the Roots of Our Church Practices*
Review: *Palestine Inside Out–An Everyday Occupation*
Review: *Piety & Politics–The Right-Wing Assault on Religious Freedom*
Review: *Religion Gone Bad–The Hidden Dangers of the Christian Right*
Review: *Tempting Faith–An Inside Story of Political Seduction*
Review: *The End of Faith–Religion, Terror, and the Future of Reason* (Paperback)
Review: *The Left Hand of God–Taking Back Our Country from the Religious Right* (Hardcover)
Review: *The War After Armageddon*
Review: *While Europe Slept–How Radical Islam is Destroying the West from Within* (Hardcover)

Techno-Demographic

Abuse & Atrocities
Review: *Human Security and the New Diplomacy–Protecting People, Promoting Peace*
Review: *In the Absence of the Sacred–The Failure of Technology and the Survival of the Indian Nations*

Communications & Computing
Review: *Computer-Related Risks*
Review: *Cuckoo's Egg*
Review: *CYBERPUNK–Outlaws and Hackers on the Computer Frontier, Revised*
Review: *Cybershock–Surviving Hackers, Phreakers, Identity Thieves, Internet Terrorists and Weapons of Mass Disruption*

201

Review: *Database Nation –The Death of Privacy in the 21st Century* (Paperback)
Review: *Masters of Deception–The Gang That Ruled Cyberspace*
Review: *Networks and Netwars–The Future of Terror, Crime, and Militancy*
Review: *Pearl Harbor Dot Com*
Review: *Stealing the Network–How to Own a Continent*
Review: *Terminal Compromise*
Review: *The Hacker Crackdown–Law And Disorder On The Electronic Frontier*

Education
Review: *Anthropologists in the Public Sphere–Speaking Out on War, Peace, and American Power*
Review: *Voltaire's Bastards–The Dictatorship of Reason in the West*
Review: *Weapons of Mass Instruction*

Falsehoods
Review: *Empire of Illusion: The End of Literacy and the Triumph of Spectacle*
Review: *Silicon Snake Oil–Second Thoughts on the Information Highway*

Research & Development
Review: *Normal Accidents–Living with High-Risk Technologies*
Review: *R & D Collaboration on Trial–The Microelectronics and Computer Technology Corporation*
Review: *The Digital Economy–Promise and Peril in the Age of Networked Intelligence*
Review: *The Future of the Internet–And How to Stop It*
Review: *The Politics of Information Management–Policy Guidelines*

War on Science
Review: *The Republican War on Science*

Natural-Geographic

Climate Change
Review DVD: *National Geographic: Six Degrees Could Change the World*
Review DVD: *National Geographic–Human Footprint*
Review DVD: *The 11th Hour*
Review: *An Inconvenient Truth–The Planetary Emergency of Global Warming and What We Can Do About It* (Paperback)

Review: *COOL IT–The Skeptical Environmentalist's Guide to Global Warming*
Review: *Global Warming False Alarm–The Bad Science Behind the United Nations'*
Assertion that Man-made CO2 Causes Global Warming
Review: *The Real Global Warming Disaster*
Review: *The Skeptical Environmentalist–Measuring the Real State of the World*

Disease
Review: *The Health of Nations–Infectious Disease, Environmental Change, and Their*
Effects on National Security and Development

Environmental Degradation (Other than Emissions)
Review: *Acts of God–The Unnatural History of Natural Disaster in America*
Review: *Catastrophe–An Investigation into the Origins of Modern Civilization*
Review: *Environment, Scarcity, and Violence*
Review: *Environment, Scarcity, and Violence.*
Review: *Floods, Famines, And Emperors–El Nino And The Fate Of Civilizations*
Review: *Nature's Extremes–Inside the Great Natural Disasters That Shape Life on Earth*
(Time Magazine Hardcover)
Review: *Plows, Plagues, and Petroleum–How Humans Took Control of Climate*
(Hardcover)
Review: *The Biodiversity Crisis–Losing What Counts*
Review: *The Vanishing of a Species? A Look at Modern Man's Predicament by a*
Geologist (Hardcover)

Nature
Review: *Catastrophe–An Investigation into the Origins of Modern Civilization*
Review: *The Weather Makers –How Man Is Changing the Climate and What It Means*
for Life on Earth (Hardcover)
Review: *The Winds of Change–Climate, Weather, and the Destruction of Civilizations*
(Hardcover)

Peak Oil
Review: *Crossing the Rubicon–The Decline of the American Empire at the End of the*
Age of Oil (Paperback)
Review: *Resource Wars–The New Landscape of Global Conflict*
Review: *The Party's Over–Oil, War and the Fate of Industrial Societies* (Paperback)

Water
Review: *The Blue Death–Disease, Disaster, and the Water We Drink*
Review: *The Outlaw Sea–A World of Freedom, Chaos, and Crime*
Review: *Water–The Fate of Our Most Precious Resource*
Review: *When the Rivers Run Dry–Water–The Defining Crisis of the Twenty-First Century* (Hardcover)

America the Beautiful is still beautiful deep down, but she has been scarred by fifty years of Cold War Empire that has taken a toll on the public not previously tallied. A partial purpose of this book is to help every nation evaluate its wounds, and consider how to use The New Craft of Intelligence and Information Operations (IO) to reconnect humanity among humans, with the Earth, and with the intermediate institutions that have broken down in the face of increased complexity and the increased speed of multi-dimensional changes across all of the above categories.

Chapter 21
Conclusions & Recommendations

Conclusions

The global community lacks a Strategic Analytic Model with attendant open standards that will allow for multinational multifunctional information-sharing and sense-making, especially in real-time and near-real-time situations.

There are eight "tribes of intelligence" that do not share information or intelligence sources and methods nor do they share the burden of global collection, processing, and analysis. This leads to duplicate costs and lost chances.

Capitalism is focused on the one billion rich who have an annual aggregate income of one trillion dollars, while virtually no one is focused on the special needs of the five billion poor who in the aggregate have an annual income of four trillion dollars.

Recommendations

In combination, the Expeditionary Environment Analytic Model, and the World Brain Analytic Model should be integrated and enhanced so as to provide a standard web-based Strategic Analytic Model for all.

The poor should be the "center of gravity" for two reasons: 1. They represent the mass of humanity that will implode absent global reform of capitalism; and 2. Their human minds, if given cell phones and access to information, can create infinite wealth for all.

A World Brain Institute and standardized Centers for Public Intelligence, as well regional initiatives to create national hubs with reach to one another and some sort of multinational global hub, are all urgently needed.

Existing nations and organizations have a very constrained understanding of the art and science of intelligence (decision-support) and are making decisions that are often uninformed and/or based on ideological or other partisan preferences. A global appreciation for the new craft of intelligence is needed.

The human brain, not technology, is the one infinite resource we have in the face of a rapidly-changing earth, complexities such as climate change that we do not understand well, and imminent threats of catastrophe that will require adaptability in real time.

"We have met the enemy and he is us." Pogo (the cartoon character) said this in the 1950's and it remains true today. National budgets, national governments, and national publics are not healthy. There is too much waste (50% in US health and defense) and we are producing too many toxins while consuming too much of the Earth's non-renewable resources.

A Strategic Analytic Model with a global standard for Analytic Tradecraft, and a universal understanding of the need for holistic analysis (all ten threats in relation to all twelve policies all the time), combined with 360 degree "all stakeholder" thinking, is needed, along with incentives and methods for information sharing.

Regions, and eventually all nations and organizations, must agree on creating core forces for education, intelligence, and emergency response that enable the combined harnessing of all human minds all the time but connecting them with all information in all languages.

Using the Framework for the Analysis of Revolution presented in Chapter 15, we must evaluate ourselves using public intelligence that the public can appreciate, and then develop a range of tools, techniques, and protocols for achieving M4IS2 (Multinational, Multiagency, Multidisciplinary, Multidomain Information-Sharing and Sense-Making) in the public interest.

206

Part IV

Technical Intelligence—Clarity

Open Everything,
Global-to-Local Needs Table

Part IV consists of seven chapters addressing the practical technical aspects of creating a World Brain that can create accurate timely intelligence (decision-support) in every clime and place generally without new fixed cost, in other words, leveraging the distributed capabilities of nations, corporations, non-profit organizations, and individuals as they exist.

The heart of this approach is "Open Everything" beginning with Information and Communication Technologies (ICT) but expanding rapidly to embrace other open concepts and practices that create wealth for all while reducing waste as well as violence as scarcity is eliminated.

Chapter 22. Technical Intelligence Enablers. The success of the Free/Open Source Software (F/OSS) movement must be radically extended across all boundaries so as to permit no-cost to low-cost multinational information-sharing and sense-making. This will enable the harnessing of the distributed intelligence of all citizens, "Intelligence Minutemen," in the production of free, ethical Open Source Intelligence (OSINT) that makes possible M4IS2 (Multinational, Multiagency, Multidisciplinary, Multidomain Information-Sharing and Sense-Making). Open Spectrum completes the foundation—we must abandon assigned frequencies and move to smart devices that can share spectrum and consequently increase bandwidth and diversity of use, a necessity if we are to "connect" and assimilate the five billion poor.

Chapter 23. Participatory Budget Transparency & Panarchic Outreach. Brazil has led the way with both Participatory Budgeting and the Pedagogy of Freedom. Leveraging the digital freedom enabled by F/OSS, OSINT, and Open Spectrum, we must move to the next level in which all stakeholders have full voice in all decisions affecting them, and simultaneously can be active members of multiple networks without sacrificing loyalty or integrity.

Chapter 24. Earth Intelligence Network Concepts & Possibilities. The concepts and possibilities of the Earth Intelligence Network are briefly presented, including the World Brain Institute, the Center(s) for Public Intelligence, and the Global Game in which every person has the right to play themselves in relation to everyone else and real-world real-time information.

Chapter 25. "True Costs," Ecological Economics, and Moral Capitalism. Pioneers in this area, and their publications, are briefly presented to support the conclusion that environmental intelligence—public knowledge of the "true costs" of any product or service—is vastly more important to achieving a sustainable prosperous world at peace, than government regulation. The morality of capitalism can be restored as the business world discovers that the only sustainable business is the one that is both moral and green.

Chapter 26. Conscious Non-Zero Evolution & Global to Local Needs Tables. The world is finally rediscovering the wisdom of our ancestors, and realizing that humans are inherently empathetic and good, and that the height of evolutionary consciousness is the achievement of "non-zero" evolution in which everyone wins, no one loses. The practical means of arriving at this condition is the Global to Local Needs Table.

Chapter 27. Open Everything. The "Open" meme can be applied to many things including money. This chapter explores some of the possibilities.

Chapter 28. Conclusions and Recommendations. I conclude that there is nothing standing in our way except ourselves.

Chapter 22
Technical Intelligence Enablers

This is not a chapter that seeks to specify technical solutions, or even technical standards, only the over-arching environment—the only technical environment that in my judgment is infinitely scalable, adaptable, resilient, and affordable—the Open Environment.

This is not to say that commercial software, both legacy and emergent, does not have a place, only that commercial software will never scale to be free for the five billion poor, nor transparent for all to understand, and there are problems with both commercial offerings and government acquisitions.

These four problems persist:

1. Commercial mis-representation, fraud, and failure to deliver

2. Commercial mis-directions of contracts through undue influence

3. Government ignorance so profound as to be beyond belief

4. Government mismanagement (which is to say, no management)

I have followed with interest the sporadic efforts of the Office of Management and Budget (OMB) as well as the General Services Administration (GSA) and various other entities such as the Joint Forces Command (JFCOM), the Defense Advanced Research Projects Agency (DARPA) and its secret intelligence counterpart, and I have to be blunt: they are all so fragmented, so lacking in strategic coherence, and so unable to achieve consensus and then results that they might as well not exist. The top-down search for "common solutions" is not working and will probably never work for the simple reason that top-down "command & control" cannot keep pace with the rate of change in society.

In the USA today cyber-security is dead in the water because the US Government ignored my 1994 appeal, in partnership with several well-informed others, to both embrace the Hackers on Planet Earth (HOPE) and others with self-taught genius; and invest $1 billion a year [roughly comparable to $12 billion a year today, but back then we would have gotten ten times the value for our investment] in creating open standards and open software that would not be constantly displaying the infamous "blue screen of death," the poster child for second-rate software with first-rate marketing.

More recently, in an Op-Ed in *Homeland Security Today*, entitled America's Cyber-Scam, I contrasted the $12 billion per year we are about to spend on vaporware, with the 63 people actually qualified to work deep code issues in the USA.

Along with the extraordinary efforts of Diane Webb and Andy Shepard, I was one of the three people in the 1980's that got down to the specifics of what we need in a generic analytic workstation. The three references that bear on this, and also apply to collectors of information and to end-users of a mix of information on demand and intelligence on demand, are these:

1. 1988 Generic Intelligence Center Production Requirements

2. 1989 CATALYST: Computer-Aided Tools for the Analysis of Science & Technology

3. 1989 Committee on The Analyst and Technology 2000 Functional and Associated Technological Requirements for the Intelligence Analyst's Workplace to Optimize Data Processing

It is important to note that CATALYST was actually conceived in 1985 by Diane Webb with Dennis McCormick under the leadership of Gordon Oehler, then directing the Office of Scientific and Weapons Research (OSWR) at CIA; and that the generic needs were determined through a 70-person functional requirements analysis in 1986 across all CIA Directorates, all mission areas, done by the Office of Information Technology (OIT), Project GEORGE (Smiley).

There was also a Marine Corps Intelligence Center (MCIC) proposal to the Joint National Intelligence Development Staff (JNIDS) that we learned over a year later we had won, but our win was overturned by as Admiral who insisted against all established inter-agency agreements, on an anti-submarine project.

Below is an illustration of the analytic toolkit defined in 1986 by Diane Web, the best available depiction of general consensus, and still not available today.

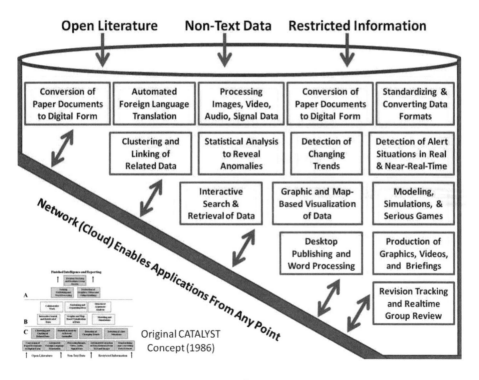

Figure 55. Needed F/OSS Functionalities

We still do not have these capabilities clearly and explicitly identified in 1989 for one simple reason: a lack of integrated management within government on the one hand, and a lack of broad societal dialog on the importance of achieving an Open Society with Open Everything.

As a founding member of the IC-wide Advanced Information Processing and Analysis Steering Group (AIPASG) I recollect that we found no fewer than twenty different "all source fusion" workstation projects, each spending roughly $10 million a year, each on a separate contract between a separate element of an agency (within agencies multiple competing contracts existed) and a single "special partner" in the private sector. Extend that finding across all the less wasteful nations and all the corporations and non-governmental organizations that have similar needs, and the opportunity cost is staggering.

With that as a preamble, I conclude there are three essential legs for achieving a World Brain—the harnessing of the distributed intelligence of all humans all the time for the shared benefit of humanity—that can provide human intelligence for Earth:

1. Free/Open Source Software (F/OSS)

2. Open Source Intelligence (OSINT)

3. Open Spectrum

Free/Open Source Software (F/OSS)

"Free" does not mean free of cost, but rather is about free (open) access to source code that permits anyone to study, change or improve the code. LINUX is F/OSS, and a global grid of volunteer experts that have over time learned to trust each other validates changes to the code in a manner that would shame any large corporation.

212

HOWEVER, "free" also comes into play in governments are increasingly realizing that government information funded by the taxpayers should be made available to the public without requiring that they buy proprietary (and costly) software. A global movement to use Ubuntu Linux is growing, Ubuntu is an operating system built by a worldwide team of expert developers and containing all the standard applications: a web browser, office suite, media apps, instant messaging and much more.

F/OSS is also gaining respect as both individuals and organizations begin to see that openly-developed software is stronger than software developed by narrow teams. As the Linux developers like to say, "Put enough eyeballs on it, no bug is invisible." Some quote this as "...all bugs are shallow." F/OSS epitomizes the strength of "peer-to-peer" distributed development. Wikipedia is an excellent source for additional information about the history, adoption, and other aspects of F/OSS, but Wikipedia is not a complete source.

Unfortunately, F/OSS has not moved beyond the standard applications.

We are now in the second phase of mis-management, where instead of trying to create in-house solutions for the all-source fusion workstation, the US Government has bought into a wide variety of commercial offerings, generally not easily inter-operable, certainly not sharing a coherent security architecture, and always creating obstacles to information-sharing across all boundaries.

The National Counterterrorism Center (NCTC) is known to have close to 80 different databases, and the analysts there—despite its being America's highest priority—not only do not have the suite of tools defined in 1989, but they are still "fat-fingering" data from multiple databases into their rather pedestrian personal workstations.

Despite the best efforts of OMB and GSA in their search for "common solutions," despite the best efforts of specific Chief Information Officers (CIO) such as Paul Strassmann during his tenure helping Sean O'Keefe rescue the National Aeronautics and Space Administration (NASA), the raw reality is that the US Government is not trained, equipped, nor organized to be a "smart government,"

213

and the commercial sector likes it that way—a fragmented ignorant marketplace is the most profitable marketplace.

Here is what the marketplace looked like in 2001 when Claudia Porter of Austin Info Systems briefed the international conference on open source solutions:

2001: Analytic Tools With a Long Way to Go

** Previously reviewed in the Fuld & Co. Software Report

Figure 56: State of the Analytic Tool Marketplace in 2001

Most of these products occupied tiny niches and did not provide for machine-speed data entry or multi-lingual data management or even multi-media and geospatial visualization. The hodge-podge that existed in 2001 still exists today,

214

in 2010, industry consolidation notwithstanding. Below is a list of the softwares used by the US Special Operations Command J-23 (Open Source Intelligence) Branch, shared with permission. I list them to make two points: 1) they are not integrated; and 2) they have not been displaced by newer offerings as of 2009 listed at the end of this section.

Collection
Copernic Pro (Internet search and download engine)
Teleport Pro (Internet spider)
Convera Spider (Spider — downloads all or selected parts of a website)
Inxight StarTree (Crawler (Internet web site relationship mapper)

Process
Copernic Summarizer (Summarizes individual files)
SummIT! (Specialty summarizer embedded within Retrievalware and Semio)
Convera Retrievalware (Data indexing and free text search engine)
Inxight ThingFinder (Categorizing entity extractor to identify relationships)
Semio Taxonomy (Puts data into pre-determined taxonomies)
Apptek Machine Translation
Database (Ibase / Ibridge) ((database for analyst notebook))
Inxight Categorizer (Smart categorizer)

Analyze
Convera Retrievalware (Data indexing and free text search engine)
Inxight ThingFinder (Categorizing entity extractor to identify relationships)
Semio Taxonomy (Puts data into pre-determined taxonomies)

Visualize
Webtas (Data into a timeline with corresponding map information)
Analyst Notebook (De-facto standard product for link product development)
Spire (Visualization application with "terrain" map view of data
MapInfo (Mapping package)
ARCView / ArcIMS (Mapping package)
Propeller (data linages (primarily communications focused)
Intranet Brain (Web site mapping)
EnFish Onespace (Indexing engine for analyst pc's)

215

These capabilities are NOT integrated and most of them are not "free."

The most successful *free* shared analytic suite of tools to date is the one created by Dr. Dr. Dave Warner (PhD, MD) for STRONG ANGEL, one of the most exciting and productive initiatives of the DARPA, and specifically focused on information-sharing and sense-making across all boundaries. He calls it The One Ounce Laptop (TOOZL), fitting on a flash drive, free online.

Software: Apache (Open Source foundation and community); APRS (Automatic Position Reporting System); FindU.com (database archiving weather, position, telemetry, and message data); FundU.com CGIs (advanced tools); GeoFusion (3D planetary visualization); Groove (now owned by Microsoft and no longer free); MapLab (MapTools now retired, the recommend 1) Quantum GIS or 2) MapStorer; Plone (Open Source Content Management); Python (Really Simple Programming Language); Skype (Free download, free calls and Internet calls); Squid (Internet Object Cache); UNM Mapserver (OpenSource Internet GIS system); Vonage (Free unlimited global calls for a monthly fee); VSee (free low-bandwidth video-teleconferencing); ZMapServer (Map Publishing Open Source Tools); Zope (Z Object Publishing Environment); ZWiki (Zope-based wiki that offers Email-integration, built-in bug tracking, and WebDAV. Extensions, documentation, and a user forum for discussion of the software).

Hardware: DVC-80 (Video Capture); SignalLink (USB interface); TigerTrack (GPS Tracking); Vonage.

Sites: Ham Radio Software; Ham Radio Store; Kantronics Supply.

This is the tip of the iceberg. As corporations and governments seek to "own" cyberspace, the public must inevitably do a repeat of Ham Radio and retake the airwaves. Infrastructure independence (e.g. Haggle) is essential if the public is to remain free of corporate and government fascism and excess.

Today, in 2010, three currents are converging but not harmonizing:

1. F/OSS is coming into its own. If corporations do not move in this direction by making their proprietary offerings F/OSS, then the public will create a F/OSS alternative. This applies not only to the software but to the content management and meta-tagging, moving away from proprietary data coding that does not lend itself to automated machine-speed fusion and sense-making.

2. Google is on the verge of a digital Blitzkrieg. Some of us have known this was coming but the various industries we have tried to warn (computing, database management, entertainment, online sales, publishing, telecommunications, to name just a few) have refused to pay heed. Google is a form of digital totalitarianism far worse than any political dictatorship for the simple reason that with Google there is not only zero privacy, but zero ownership. Google has the power to make a company, such as BMW, "disappear"—and China may not yet appreciate the implications of a Google counter-attack that dilutes China's Internet visibility outside of China.

3. Cloud Computing is emergent, with multiple parties competing for dominance including Google, IBM, CISCO, Amazon, and earnestly enough, a bottom-up "infrastructure independent" movement seeking to make all devices independent of any carrier or infrastructure able to charge toll fees. Ham Radio was the first "hacker" environment in modern history, and we look at that more closely in the third section here, on Open Spectrum.

In this context, the various business (data mining) or commercial (pattern detection) softwares recently reviewed by Fuld & Co. (Autonomy Inc., Brimstone, Cipher, ClearForest, Coemergence, Comintell, Cymfony, FirstRain Inc., Netro City, Nielsen BuzzMetrics (formerly Intelliseek), QL2 Software, Rocketinfo, Strategy Software Inc., TEMIS, Traction Software, and Wincite Systems) along with the 75 search engines reviewed by Stephen Arnold in Search panacea or ploy: Can collective intelligence improve findability?, are more or less toast. Proprietary

217

systems for desktop and back office analytics are caught between Goggle [and its Brazilian, Chinese, Indian, and Russian anti-Googles] on the one hand, and F/OSS combined with infrastructure independent capabilities that seek to avoid ownership of the digital commons. At the same time, the middle wares have many flaws and are not multi-lingual.

There are so many companies out there that seek to be single-point technology solutions there is no profit in attempting to list them. However, simply to illustrate both the existing state of the marketplace and the lack of integration among all these products and services, here are few that are not listed above that relate to Figure 55 on page 211.

INGEST Automated extraction of data (documents). CVision
INGEST Automated extraction of data (web). Knowlesys
INGEST Automated foreign language translation. Language Weaver
INGEST Conversion of analog to digital. Advanced Computer Innovations, Inc.
INGEST Image, signal, audio processing. STAR Analytic Services
FILTER Clustering & linking of related data. Pentaho
FILTER Detection of alert situations. Tsunami, flood, disease
FILTER Detection of change (fraud). Progress Software
FILTER Detection of change (geospatial). Overwatch Geospatial
FILTER Detection of change (online data). Copernic Tracker
FILTER Standardizing & converting data formats. CIS
FILTER Statistical analysis to reveal anomalies. StatSoft STATISTICA
ASSIST Graphic-based visualization of data. Flowing Data
ASSIST Interactive search & retrieval of data (images). SnapFind
ASSIST Interactive search & retrieval of data (text). DeepWeb
ASSIST Map-based visualization of data. Information Mapping GeoChat
ASSIST Modeling & simulation. Simulation modeling, RTI International
ASSIST Serious games. BigPictureSmallWorld
SHARE Collaborative work and analytic outreach. Mind-Alliance
SHARE Desktop publishing and word processing. OpenOffice
SHARE Production of graphics, videos, & briefings. Corel DRAW
SHARE Revision tracking and real-time group review. WikiMedia

The original three requirements documents from 1989 are still valid, and the US Government has failed—twenty years after the fact—to get it right, despite hundreds of billions of dollars spent by hundreds of largely "out of control" agencies and bureaus and divisions and services and commands.

F/OSS must be nurtured by public demand and wise public policy and coherent public acquisition. However, without content—and the freedom to share that content across all boundaries, we cannot build the World Brain.

Open Source Intelligence (OSINT)

This is where I have spent the past 21 years, since helping lead the creation of the Marine Corps Intelligence Center (MCIC) from 1988-1992.

Wikipedia's page on OSINT has been completely corrupted by vendors and Central Intelligence Agency (CIA) nay-sayers who have explicitly removed from the page all of the references to the actual pioneers of modern OSINT, thereby demonstrating their complete lack of integrity. Jimmy Wales was told about this and chose not to restore the integrity of the page.

Phi Beta Iota, the Public Intelligence Blog, is the front end for the 30,000 pages of original OSINT source material from over 750 world-class speakers at over 20 international conferences that is in permanent digital storage at OSS.Net.

Open Source Intelligence (OSINT) as a term applies to both the discipline that focuses on collecting, processing, and exploiting sources that are open (legally and ethically available) and the specific outcome of that process, which renders decision-support to a specific decision-maker or decision-making body with respect to a specific decision that must be made, such as "What should the mandate be for this peacekeeping force?"

The following definition comes from WordIQ.com: **Open source intelligence** or "OSINT" refers to an intelligence discipline based on information collected from open sources, i.e. information available to the general public. This includes newspapers, the internet, books, phone books, scientific journals, radio broadcasts, television, and others. Gray Literature is the term used for legally and openly available materials not easily known to exist outside of local or narrow networks. It *also* includes every bit of human knowledge that can be elicited in face-to-face interaction or in ICT-assisted interaction—every bit of oral history, cultural understanding, every bit of subject-matter expertise, and direct observations at any given point in time or space (see Chapter 19).

Collection of information in OSINT is a very different problem from collection in other intelligence disciplines because, by definition, the information sources are publicly available. In other intelligence disciplines, a major difficultly is extracting information from non-cooperative targets. In OSINT, the chief difficulty is identifying relevant, reliable sources from the vast abundance of publicly available information. Obtaining the needed information once a source is identified is a comparatively minor problem. Below is a single schematic of how I see the relevance of OSINT to both all functional mission areas and to each of the classified disciplines.

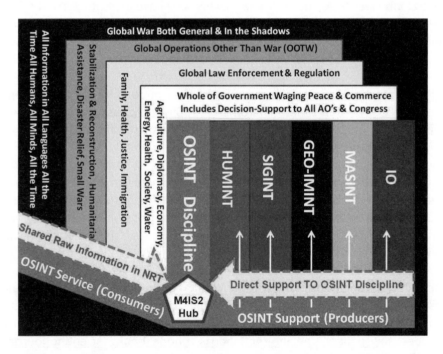

Figure 57. OSINT as a Hybrid Discipline Relevant to ALL Mission Areas

OSINT is deeply relevant to every aspect of the Intelligence Cycle, and this is one reason why I have been very concerned to see two different erroneous treatments of OSINT. The first treats OSINT as a sub-set of each classified discipline, such that all OSINT is classified secret on receipt and not shared. The second treats OSINT as an analytic outreach function in isolation from all other stakeholders, with similar consequences. Without its own coherent program, OSINT will not provide the "common view of reality" that is essential for both Whole of Government and Multinational Engagement operations.

In Figure 57, OSINT plays its strongest role in front (Whole of Government Waging Peace & Commerce), and lesser but still vital roles in relation to Law Enforcement, Stabilization & Reconstruction, and General War.

The core references on OSINT are easily accessible online, and include the latest published chapters on Open Source Intelligence (Strategic), Open Source Intelligence (Operational), the DoD OSINT Leadership and Staff Briefings, and three compilations of references, The Future of OSINT [is M4IS2-Multinational] and 1988-2009 OSINT-M4IS2 TECHINT Chronology.

Within the US Government, should it choose to fulfill its potential as a leader for global OSINT and M4IS2 an essential first task is to inventory both requirements and capabilities, and then agree on a coherent OSINT/M4IS2 strategy and program for the Republic (all eight tribes of intelligence); for each regional union of nations and organizations, and for the world as a whole.

Open Spectrum

We are—we must—return to the era of ham radio and stop the fencing in of spectrum. America's top commentator on this topic is David Weinberger, whose seminal work, *Why open spectrum matters: the end of the broadcast nation* Is complemented by Jock Gill's 2004 presentation, Open Wireless Spectrum and Democracy that very adroitly hits the high points:

- Open Spectrum maximizes connectivity and participation

- We must not fence the cyber-commons or favor incumbents and old science—new science makes licensing an inhibitor

- If we demand and enjoy Open Spectrum, this will stimulate creatively, innovation, entrepreneurship, and open new paths to creating wealth.

I agree with David Weinberger and Jock Gill. Open Spectrum is the third leg.

There is one negative associated with spectrum that I hope Open Everything will help to address.

For decades the US military and US corporations responsible for creating capabilities that use assigned spectrums have been both lazy about creating best in class capabilities that optimize spectrum use without collateral damage, and deliberately misrepresentative to the public of the safety of all of these devices.

Cellular telephones and cellular telephone towers are the latest in a series of ubiquitous channels for spectrum and electromagnetic pulses that we as a public are only now, in 2010, beginning to realize as a public come with severe hazards including brain tumors.

In broader terms, our military in Afghanistan is finding that on the one hand anyone can download the drone images and signals because no one bothered to protect those channels over the years; and on the other, that the drones and other operations are creating so many conflicting electromagnetic emissions that we are jamming ourselves.

Open Spectrum, as beneficial as it will be for the public, demands a great deal more study, and this is something that OSINT—public intelligence in the public interest, can provide.

Chapter 23
Participatory Budget Transparency & Panarchic Outreach

The Porto Alegre Alternative–Direct Democracy in Action and *Participatory Budgeting (Public Sector Governance)* are two extraordinary books about an extraordinary public initiative that the government of Brazil may yet revive.

Here is the best available online overview of Participatory Budgeting:

What is Participatory Budgeting?

Participatory Budgeting (PB) is a mechanism of public bodies which allows citizens to directly make decisions on a public budget. There is much debate around a clear and concise definition of PB which encompasses all that PB offers without being too prescriptive. The debate isn't resolved yet, however here are some options. Our definition is:

> *Participatory budgeting directly involves local people in making decisions on the spending and priorities for a defined public budget. PB processes can be defined by geographical area (whether that's neighbourhood or larger) or by theme. This means engaging residents and community groups representative of all parts of the community to discuss and vote on spending priorities, make spending proposals, and vote on them, as well giving local people a role in the scrutiny and monitoring of the process and results to inform subsequent PB decisions on an annual or repeatable basis.*

Wikipedia has defined PB like this:

Participatory budgeting is a process of democratic deliberation and decision-making, in which ordinary city residents decide how to allocate part of a municipal or public budget. Participatory budgeting is usually characterized by several basic design features: identification of spending priorities by community members, election of budget delegates to represent different communities, facilitation and technical assistance by public employees, local and higher level assemblies to deliberate and vote on spending priorities, and the implementation of local direct-impact community projects. Various studies have suggested that participatory budgeting results in more equitable public spending, higher quality of life, increased satisfaction of basic needs, greater government transparency and accountability, increased levels of public participation (especially by marginalized residents), and democratic and citizenship learning.

The World Bank says this about PB:

Participatory budgeting represents a direct-democracy approach to budgeting. It offers citizens at large an opportunity to learn about government operations and to deliberate, debate, and influence the allocation of public resources. It is a tool for educating, engaging, and empowering citizens and strengthening demand for good governance.

The department for international development describes PB as:

Participatory budgeting is an approach through which an entire community, or particular elements of a community, can participate in the budget process. The level of participation can range from the consultative to the design and execution of budgets.

Where did participatory budgeting originate?

Participatory budgeting has been most frequently identified as developing in the Brazilian City of Porto Alegre in the early 1980's. Porto Alegre has received much international praise for the way it has used PB to improve its administration of the city, and it has been the centre of much research into citizen engagement around public spending. PB was also developed in other Latin American cities at around the same time, and has spread to many other cities. As it has moved from city to city PB has always been adapted to the local situation, and so there is no one pure model of PB. Many other parts of the world have also been recognised as innovators in citizen participation. Developing, from different starting positions, similar experiences and principles of PB as those used in Porto Alegre. For example in India local people have been trained to read and question public budgets, and this has enabled citizens to have greater influence over public spending. In the 1980's New Zealand developed models of city administration that some have describe as forms of participatory budgeting.

Which countries are using participatory budgeting now?

From its early development in Brazil PB has been adopted worldwide. Across the globe, from Fiji to Canada, and from Finland to South Africa there have been many local government programmes that have acknowledged the influence of Porto Alegre in the way they are now engaging with citizens. Estimates vary but there are probably well over 500 different experiences worldwide, operating on every continent. Most frequently reported are those in Latin America such as Porto Alegre, but PB is being promoted by international bodies such as the World Bank, the UK Department for International Development and the Asian Development Bank in countries as diverse as Turkey, Spain, Pakistan, Poland, the United States and now also in the UK.

What are the benefits of participatory budgeting?

Each model of PB is different and will have different effects but there are three main ways that PB is regarded as offering benefits.

- *It can improve the democratic process, widening participation and re-invigorating the role of local authorities, local councilors and civil society, and increasing trust in public institutions.*

- *It can improve the effectiveness of public spending by improving the way money is invested, how service provision is monitored, and by increasing the knowledge available to the local authority and public bodies when undertaking service planning.*

- *Finally it strengthens the community and voluntary sector by investing in services essential to poorer communities, so enabling their development, by increasing the number of people taking part in local democratic processes, and it builds social capital by creating forums for local groups to meet, negotiate and take decisions together.*

Participatory budgeting is completely different from consultative budgeting, and should eventually be joined by participatory planning.

The critical difference is that participatory budgeting is transparent, bottom-up, and inclusive while consultative budgeting is top-down, selective, and subject to "behind closed doors" override.

Participative budgeting harnesses the distributed intelligence of the collective, and the aggregate grasp of nuance and detail that is the essential foundation for adapting to complexity—for resilience in the face of constant change.

Here we focus on the possibilities that emerge when the diversity of human minds can be brought to bear with clarity and integrity.   In one word: sustainability.   There are several "threads" that can be presented here, each deeply rooted in a broad emergent literature and real-life example of success: collective intelligence; wealth of knowledge, and panarchy. In my view panarchy is the opposite of anarchy in that it means the ability to be an effective member of multiple groups without disloyalty—with full integrity.

The figure below was inspired by the Epoch B concept attributed to Jonas Salk and furthered by Kirkpatrick Sale.

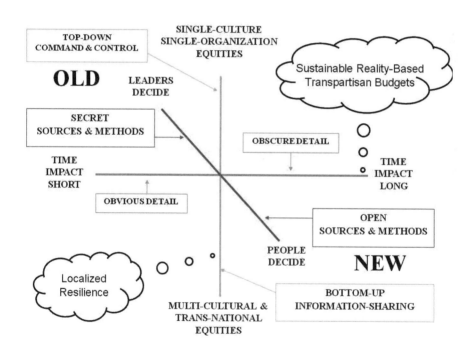

Figure 58: Infinite Possibilities in Bottom-Up Consensus

227

The reason this book is subtitled *Clarity, Diversity, Integrity, & Sustainability* is because the new paradigm sets aside "rule by secrecy" as well as "command & control," substituting instead the kind of clarity that can only come from transparency, a clarity that in appreciating diversity and in honoring integrity, allows not just for the development of sustainable decisions on one issue, but on all issues at all levels (neighborhood to global).

Panarchy, in other words, makes it possible for citizens to self-govern across all issues at all levels without being disloyal to any one community.

Collective Intelligence is the subject of a book, *COLLECTIVE INTELLIGENCE: Creating a Prosperous World at Peace* (EIN, 2008) from which the following by Tom Atlee, one of the 55 contributing authors, is drawn, in People's Preface:

Human systems in which we can observe and nurture collective intelligence:

- INDIVIDUAL collective intelligence (collective intelligence among our own internal subjective parts and voices)
- INTERPERSONAL or RELATIONAL collective intelligence
- GROUP collective intelligence
- ACTIVITY collective intelligence
- ORGANIZATIONAL collective intelligence
- NETWORK collective intelligence
- NEIGHBORHOOD collective intelligence
- COMMUNITY collective intelligence
- CITY collective intelligence
- COUNTY/SHIRE collective intelligence
- STATE/PROVINCE collective intelligence
- REGIONAL collective intelligence
- NATIONAL / WHOLE SOCIETY collective intelligence
- INTERNATIONAL GROUP/NETWORK/ORGANIZATION collective intelligence
- GLOBAL HUMANITY collective intelligence

Tom goes on to provide a paragraph of description for each of the following forms of Collective Intelligence:

- REFLECTIVE (dialogic) CI
- STRUCTURAL (systemic) CI
- EVOLUTIONARY (learning-based) CI
- INFORMATIONAL (communication-based) CI
- NOETIC (spiritual or consciousness-based) CI
- FLOW (mutual attunement-based) CI
- STATISTICAL (crowd-oriented) CI
- RELEVATIONAL (emergence-based) CI

The problem or the challenge facing both policy-making generally and participatory budgeting specifically is that most policy discussions tend to be too general to be real. Platitudes, general objectives, not grounded in reality, and not really helpful in focusing on where different stakeholders really have points of agreement and points of disagreement—that needs to be addressed.

"It isn't policy until it is in the budget." This was taught to me by Mr. Don Gessaman, the top civil servant at OMB responsible for all national security money from the Reagan era to the late 1990's.

The purpose of this book is to take us all away from simulations and false assumptions, and put every human in touch with all information such that panarchy is possible at every level on every issue.

Real-world budgets (easy to capture), combined with public intelligence about every issue (less easy but rapidly emergent), can and should inspire policy discussions about specifics, serve as a magnet for attracting real-world expertise from the citizen ranks (including top authorities from academia, business, media, etcetera), and (very important) when discussed or visualized online, can highlight the *specific* points of agreement and differences between constituencies for each of the *discretionary* elements of the budget.

In brief, citizens should never again take a back seat to, or be fooled by, corporations or governments. By being virtually present at all public meetings (see conference function), by applying the proven methods of intelligence (requirements definition, collection management, source discovery and validation, multi-source fusion, compelling presentation) to legal and ethical *open* sources and methods, we can create a Public Intelligence Network (PIN) that "breaks the code" and breaks the back of the special interests. Armed with intelligence, linked by the Internet, able to spend very modest sums of money as individuals who in the aggregate represent true democratic power, over time we get to the point where no policy-maker dares to ignore the open power of the people. Below is an illustration of how this could be implemented.

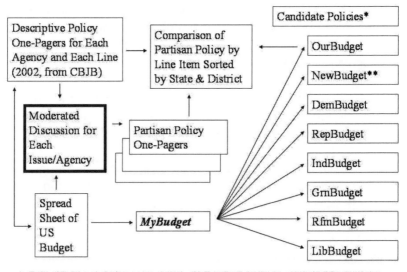

* Only official campaigns can enter. ** Sandbox for new or unaffiliated voters.

Figure 59: Concept for Broad Online Participatory Budgeting

Below are the functional requirements for implementation of this system. Our concept extends to the five billion poor who should be able to vote on publicly promulgated options using text messages.

#	Title	Description
01	Registration	Establishes name, party affiliation, zip code, age, income range, and race. Only data from real names is integrated into aggregate budgets. Party and zip code are used to establish aggregate budgets by party and state. Age, income range, and race are used to establish aggregate sub-sets. NOTE: we have anticipated both foreigners and "false flag" registrations (e.g. Republican extremists seeking to skew the numbers). Registration should provide incentives to foreigners to declare their nationality and "tell us what you think" while also informing them that the software is available as freeware for adaptation to their own budget and their own community. We should consider how to authenticate participants by IP address against zip code and the known demography of the zip code. Amazon has means of detecting anomalous trends and we should think about having something equivalent.
02	Core Budget	The core budget is "hard-wired" as the baseline for all other budget calculations. A second hard-wired budget converts all numbers into percentages of the total budget. In all budgets at all times, the mandatory line items will be "fixed" and not adjustable by the user. Only the discretionary line items, perhaps light green in background, will permit adjustment.
03	MyBudget	New registrants are asked to specify their interest—they can either work with the entire budget or one segment at a time. Whatever they choose, they may save it and return to other segments of the budget later. Segments they choose not to work with remain unchanged within their new budget. Within MyBudget, they can raise or

		lower percentages for any discretionary item. Ideally, the budget should remain "balanced" in that if they raise one item, they must find a corresponding decrease for another item. They should be allowed to save unbalanced budgets, but encouraged to balance.
04	Policy Baseline	From any agency title line or from any line item within the discretionary budgets of the 30 agencies having discretionary funds, the user can see a one-page policy paper (need upload management privileges for person entering policy papers). This is their educational baseline, a description of what the past year money actually paid for. Any page can be printed, and all of the one-pagers should also be available in a Policy Directory from which anyone can jump to the aggregate budgets, discussion groups, or their own MyBudget section.
05	Discussion Group	From any agency title line or from any line item within the discretionary budgets of the 30 agencies having discretionary funds, the user can jump to the related discussion group, carrying their identifying information with them (all discussants appear as name party state.
06	Aggregate Budgets	Once a user has completed and saved a section of MyBudget, it should be automatically aggregated into the corresponding party, state, and sub-set budgets, which should at all times show the number of original budgets. Aggregate budgets should be visible in two ways: as multi-year budgets for a single party, or as side by side columns for a single selected year, with all parties showing on a single budget for that year.
07	Focus on Priorities	Both within MyBudget and within any party budget and within any side by side budget the user should have the option of sorting all discretionary line items and mandatory line items

08	Focus on Differences	Ideal would be some means of color coding differences among the parties by line item. In a single line item, for example, differences that are more than 30% from the average have a red background, 20-29% an orange background, 10-19% a yellow background.
09	Focus on the Deficit	A separate policy paper is available on the deficit. It would be helpful to have a means of enabling users to both examine the assumptions that the various Administrations have or are using to justify its extraordinary deficit, and to see the impact on future discretionary income of reductions in the deficit.
10	Focus on Revenue	A separate policy paper will be made available on the assumptions behind revenue, and on future options for increasing revenue without increasing individual taxes. For example, $50 billion a year in tax avoidance has been found in corporations that manipulate import and export prices to launder money ($100 rocket engines going out, $3000 toothbrushes coming in). There are also billions in corporate taxes that go uncollected for a wide variety of reasons, all of which can be itemized.
11	Focus on How Others See Us	This feature could be both a means of engaging foreigners while keeping them from toying with what is intended to be a US citizen only simulator, and also a means of drawing foreigners out (and in the process educating our American participants) on how they see our spending. Many foreigners, for example, and very upset with the US for exporting weapons to the Middle East through its military assistance program, while contributing less than one half of one percent to foreign economic, medical, agricultural, and educational assistance that could help stabilize many areas in Africa. If this really takes off, it could be a citizen's "United Nations Forum", but using real world budgets (eventually, national budgets compared side by side through some sort of conversation process.

12	Library	As the site matures, there should be a free "Add A Link" and free "Add a Document" capability that permits anyone to add a link or document to the library associated with each agency or line item.
13	Rolodex	A national directory should allow anyone to upload a concise 1 page bio that can be indexed, and contact information, and allow them to self-identify by level of expertise and level of interest for any and all policy lines items or at the agency level. Some form of "karma point" system might be considered, based on votes in favor of comments made in the forums, or other factors.
14	Conferences	A global calendar of hearings, conferences, stakeholder meetings, etcetera could be created in which volunteers enter any and all events coded to both the line item they apply to, and the zip code where they are occurring. Some form of voluntary matching function could allow individuals to volunteer to cover the event and provide a one-page summary with links. Eventually this could result in "global coverage" and a "virtual presence" by Deaniacs at all policy and decision-making events open to the public, at the federal, state, and local levels.
15	Weekly Intelligence	Volunteers can "adopt a line item" and then do weekly searches that allow them to separate the wheat from the chaff and pick out the top seven stories only, and then create a word document with story title, lead paragraph, source information, and hot link, together with an analytical paragraph about "What's New" as the first element. This would be done at the federal level, but there is no reason why other volunteers could not do the same at the state and county levels, and citizens would select what they want to read based on line item and federal, state, or country (or all three) relevant to their zip code.

Chapter 24
Earth Intelligence Network
& The Global Game

This book is an earnest attempt to place before the public—all publics of all nationalities, religions, races, and levels of education—an implementable concept for creating the World Brain so as to connect—and empower—all humans and their minds to all information in all languages all the time.

This is how we create infinite wealth, revolutionary wealth, the wealth of knowledge, the wealth of networks. Human ingenuity is the one inexhaustible and infinitely variable resource we have on Earth, and I earnestly believe that a human transformation—a restoration of Humanity as our indigenous forbearers understood it, is both the only way to save Humanity and perhaps also one day to contribute to a larger Cosmos.

Humans are arrogant and ill-informed when they equate the demise of humanity with the demise of Earth. Earth is resilient. Humanity, unless it transforms, is *not* resilient.

What follows in this chapter is the original concept for Earth Intelligence Network (EIN), the 501c3 that is publishing this book and that seeks to help anyone and everyone create public intelligence in the public interest.

The goal is to harness the potential of shared information on a global scale that transcends individual nations' narrow interests or corporate special interests in favor of both local and global Whole-Earth interests. This would allow bottom-up consensus, the only consensus sustainable in time and space.

EIN is an enabling concept—a meme if you will—that nurtures the emergence of a confederation with infinite possibilities rooted in a global to local commitment to share information and share the burden and the privilege of sense-making with clarity, diversity, and integrity. Thus do we create sustainable self-governance at all levels across all domains in all languages.

EIN and this concept would not have been possible without the United Nations High-Level Panel on Threats, Challenges, and Change, and their report that prioritized the ten high-level threats to humanity as discussed in Chapter 1.

That cogent sensible list in turn made possible the selection of twelve "core" policies as discussed in Chapter 8.

As this chapter is written, a popular article is circulating in Washington, D.C. entitled *The Contested Commons*. Such a title is representative of an imperialist mind-set, and sadly out of touch with reality—in contrast, EIN seeks to help humanity as a whole with three long-term objectives:

1. Expanding the Commons. To facilitate information-sharing treaties and agreements as well as open standards among trans-governmental, governmental, and private sector information producers and consumers, such that all information in all languages can be easily accessed and exploited by every person everywhere using open source software or a cell phone connection to a live on-demand volunteer teacher.

2. Saving the Commons. To create compelling decision-support on costs versus benefits of early and precise investments aimed at eradicating the ten high-level threats to humanity through harmonized funding of the twelve policy action areas and—as quickly as possible—the creation of a Global Game that presents compelling actionable investment strategies to the eight major demographic players whose policies today will determine the future of the Earth and Humanity. This will be a service of common concern to Foundations, International Organizations, and Non-Governmental Organizations as well as Corporations and Governments.

3. Sharing the Commons. To harness over 100 million volunteers who speak one of the 183 languages still important, and have access to the Internet, organized so as to be able to educate the five billion poor "one cell phone call at a time" on any topic from stopping a plant disease to fixing a tractor to healing with natural or alternative cures.

In Chapter 8 I also illustrated and briefly discussed our concept for using information to harmonize investments, something I have called "information peacekeeping."

Our intent is to enable a global voluntary "grid" to leverage shared information and multi-cultural sense-making so as to harmonize up to five trillion dollars a year in spending by the following four communities:

1. Foundation Investment. One trillion dollars a year is directed toward alleviating poverty, eradicating disease, ameliorating environmental degradation, and so on down the list of the high-level threats. By enabling consensus on prioritized investment packages, decision-support can accelerate and increase the impact of targeted donations.

2. Corporate Investment. The pioneering work of Herman Daly, Paul Hawkin and others has finally yielded deep corporate interest in Natural Capitalism and Ecological Economics. By creating decision-support specific to individual corporations and their global presence, we hope to accelerate the "green to gold" trend, while also providing "true cost" information (water content, fuel content, unfair labor content, tax avoidance) to the consumer at the point of sale via cell phone.

3. Government Investment. National, state, and local budgets are becoming more transparent and also available online prior to legislative passage, by using the Global Game with embedded budgets to show trade-offs and consequences, over time we hope to inspire public demands for less spending on war, more on peace. We spend $1.3 trillion a year on war now, when redirection of one third of that amount could easily fund both infinite wealth and a sustainable peace.

4. Individual Investment. This could well be much greater than the other three forms of investment combined, in part because roughly 80% of the one billion rich do not give to charities and do not trust charities because of negative reputations having to do with excessive overheads and limited success in both deliverables and outcomes. In Chapter 26 I discuss the means by which we connect the one billion rich with the five billion poor.

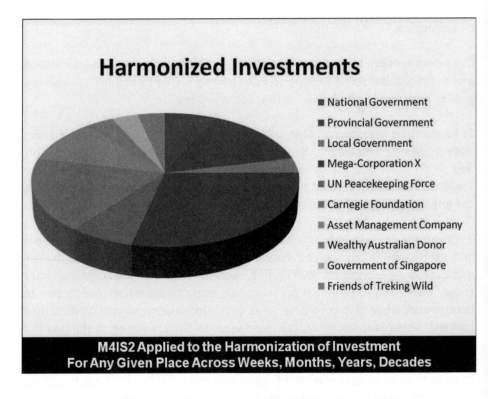

Figure 60: Public Intelligence & Budget Harmonization

In East Timor, for example, a stretch of waterfront property of considerable size could be donated by the government and people in return for harmonized commitments along the following lines, with the village governments specifically assuring peace and stability and the safety of all tourists:

- AUSTRALIA: timber hauling trucks
- CHINA: road construction
- FRANCE: airport construction
- GREECE: new shipping pier, one ship
- INDIA: local call center
- INDONESIA: open access
- KOREA: free Internet
- MALAYSIA: teachers
- NORWAY: free cell phones
- USA: timber processing technology
- VIET-NAM: hotel development

There is a fifth form of investment, the **negative criminal investment** that today comprises $2 trillion a year, of which fully one half, $1 trillion a year, is in the form of bribes to government officials.

I do not include white collar crime, revolving doors and post-retirement *quid pro quos* in this figure, but the reality is that if all forms of corporate-government fraud, waste, and abuse were calculated, it would equal half the total legal economy of $9 trillion a year—in the USA for example, it is now documented that half of every dollar spent on health is pure waste.

I believe that the profit can be taken out of crime in three ways: by providing tens of millions of volunteers with an easy means of anonymously sharing information about criminal activities they observe; by providing the poor with on-demand education that allows them to increase their legally-derived revenue; and by creating truly transparent "true cost" budgets on everything.

Obstacles

The primary obstacles to our goal are:

- Lack of open standards in the digital world
- Lack of western fluency in 183 languages in the developed world
- Amount of historical and current information in analog form
- Emphasis by nations and corporations on secret or proprietary sources
- Concerns over privacy and security when information is shared indiscriminately

Enablers

Fortunately, there are also multiple enablers supportive of our goal:

- Massive amounts of substantive information in all languages is readily available, and especially so from within the many elements of the United Nations and the varied Non-Governmental Organizations (NGO), educational institutions, and centers for public advocacy.

- A Global Game can be built for no more than $2 million a year that will scale very rapidly and ultimately allow every person to play themselves at every level with all needed information.

- Public intelligence based on open sources of information in all mediums, all languages, now makes it possible for decision-support to be provided to any person on any issue at relatively low cost, if not free.

- Transparency of budgets at all levels is accelerating, and this finally will allow all concerned citizens to judge budgetary trade-offs from an informed perspective, while using the Global Game and public participatory budgeting and deliberative open dialog to evaluate trade-offs.

- Open source software and free Voice Over the Internet is now available, allowing tens of millions fluent in various languages, many of them in impoverished straits, to earn micro-cash for micro-translation, or for teaching "one answer at a time."

- Individual routers that allow individual owners of information to control who can access their information and how it is shared, are coming on the market at the same time that Data at Rest encryption is becoming both routine and robust, generally free of charge.

- Finally, infrastructure-independent capabilities are coming into being, such as Haggle, possibly eliminating the threat of corporate toll-booths in cyberspace.

Our Strategy

Our larger strategy, for creating a prosperous world at peace, is discussed at length in the book, _COLLECTIVE INTELLIGENCE: Creating a Prosperous World at Peace_, and briefly in Chapter 1.

On a day to day basis, we will adapt the proven process of decision-support to open source information in all languages. That process consists of the following elements:

- Requirements Definition
- Collection Management (Know Who Knows)
- Source Discovery & Validation
- Multi-Source Integration and Evaluation
- Human Analysis (Historically & Culturally Grounded)
- Compelling Presentation
- Timely Helpful Dissemination

I call this Information Arbitrage—the conversion of information into intelligence and intelligence into wealth for all—and Information Peacekeeping—the use of shared information and free education "by the call" to create stabilizing wealth at the Bottom of the Pyramid, while nurturing a permanent peace for all. Chapters 17 and 18 discussed the New Craft of Intelligence in detail.

241

One Man, One Cell Phone, One Game, One World

With the cell phone, there is NO degree of separation. It's the wireless version of "hard wired." Ohm's law reminds us that a "perfect amplification circuit" is "straight wire, with gain" and no resistors in the circuit. According to Ohm's law, as voltage increases, resistance drops. Ultimate voltage equals zero resistance.

In Auric terms, and as we are human beings infused with electro-magnetism ourselves, this is denoted as a white, clear or golden aura, which is exactly what you see depicted in every religion's pictures of "holy ones", the "ones" with the "straightest wire" and least "resistance" to "the ultimate voltage". The halo is never colored, always clear and bright.

Our concept of "one man, one cell phone, one game, one world" has scientific underpinning, and will amplify the aura of the world. If we add universal translation, and social networking without borders, we get closer to heaven on earth, or at least "straight wire(less) with GAIN".

Global Game—the Most Serious of Serious Games

Inspired by Medard Gabel, one of the co-founders of EIN, we advocate the creation of a generic Global Game as a foundation for all serious games to follow. The following words were provided to me by Medard Gabel, they apply equally to his concept of an EarthGame™ and to our non-competitive identical concept of a Global Game.

The Global Game would be an online global problem-solving tool accessible to anyone in the world with Internet access where sustainable and affordable solutions to real world problems are envisioned, developed, costed out in all respects, and tested so they can be implemented as soon as possible.

It would be an online tool and game that provides "ordinary" people the opportunity and challenge of addressing real world problems in a way that builds knowledge, competency, and options for real world implementation.

It would be an experiential, interactive, and fun way of learning about the world, its resources, problems, and options that builds global capacity and alternatives

242

for sustainable prosperity, connecting real people with real-world "true cost" information in near-real time across any issue at all levels.

Adopting the Vision of Buckminster Fuller

To make the world work for 100% of humanity, in the shortest possible time, with present day resources and technology, through spontaneous cooperation, without ecological harm or the disadvantage of anyone.

—Buckminster Fuller

The world needs to see itself, across threats, opportunities, policies, and budgets, at all levels. It is especially vital, as Robert Ackoff has stressed, to see the Whole and all of the parts and to not focus on any one part to the detriment of other parts—what is good for one may not be good for the Whole—that is why holistic analysis and decision-making is necessary.

As a planetary species, humanity needs a tool for seeing the whole, for connecting the dots, seeing patterns and large scale trends, and most importantly, recognizing, defining and solving its most pressing problems in a global context. Nearly all of the world's most critical problems are global in scope and have been made increasingly dangerous by a piecemeal local approach that ignores interconnections and its resultant synergy.

The Global Game would be a tool that allows humanity to see the whole world in a problem-solving context will generate insight and solutions to problems that heretofore have seemed unsolvable.

Drawing on existing knowledge bases including the Millennium Project of the World Federation of UN Associations that has produced eleven annual State of the Future reports, the Global Game could serve as the decision-support tool of choice for individuals, organizations, corporations, and governments.

243

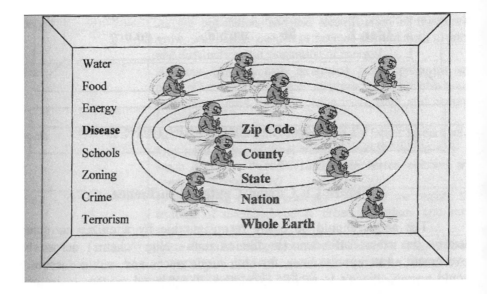

Water
Food
Energy
Disease
Schools
Zoning
Crime
Terrorism

Zip Code
County
State
Nation
Whole Earth

Figure 61: Citizen-Centered Self-Reorientation

Purpose

The purposes of the Global Game include:

- Aiding in the development of viable and affordable solutions to global and local problems
- Making accessible to growing numbers of people the information and information processing and visualization tools that aid in the development of solutions to global and local problems
- Increasing the amount of intelligence, creativity, imagination, and problem solving attention focused on global and local problems.

244

Users/Audience

The intended user community of the Global Game includes government, corporate, and NGO leaders, academics, researchers, policy analysts, the media, students from high school age up, game players, and concerned citizens. It is *not* a tool aimed at an elite few, but rather at a massive, society wide level of participation, useful to a growing variety of social networks addressing innumerable challenges.

Possible Uses/Users

- Activists— issue exploration, documentation, alternatives development
- Business—product development, market assessment, testing, "from green to gold"
- Foundations—optimize investment/giving, both direct and in alliances
- Gamers—fun, recreation, competition, recognition, rewards
- Government—policy exploration, development, testing, costing of tradeoffs
- Public—for lifelong free education online, creation of informed social networks

Plant and Animal Inputs

It is now possible for sensors in soil or embedded in plants and animals to "trigger" text messages that enter status data including warning to the game.

Budget and Timing

A detailed budget is available. It boils down to $2 million a year, placed in escrow in advance of hiring and project commencement, with three one-year cycles from zero to pilot, pilot to beta, and beta to release.

245

Staffing

6 Researchers/Designers
5 Coders/Designers
1 Graphic Designer
1 Administrator/COO
1 Marketer/Government and Corporate Liaison/Development
1 Designer/Executive Director

Note: Existing "serious games" cannot be integrated into one meta game—that would be akin to integrating baseball, soccer, basketball, jai ali, kickboxing, chess, skeet and 20 other sports and games into one game. One cannot mix purposes, scales, aggregate levels, rules of operation, conditions for winning, playing fields, props, etc. and expect a meaningful whole. However, you *can* create an open architecture others can expand upon.

The Global Game would be designed to be infinitely scalable as Free/Open Source Software (F/OSS).

EIN and the Global Game are intended to make possible the creation of the World Brain such that all humans and all information are "in relation" at all times regardless of the language of origin of any element of information.

Chapter 25
"True Costs,"
Ecological Economics, & Moral Capitalism

Rachael Carson's _Silent Spring_, published in 1962, is widely recognized as the first modern push-back against what John Ralston Saul calls _Voltaire's Bastards–The Dictatorship of Reason in the West_. We went awry, first in being dominated by corporations, then in the selling out of the universities, and finally in the politicization of science. While Carson's views have been validated by subsequent work such as _The Biodiversity Crisis–Losing What Counts_, the purpose of this chapter is to explore the vital need for establishing the "true cost" of every product and service at every level, so as to permit what Herman Daly calls _Ecological Economics_ and I and others call _Moral Capitalism_.

I cannot do Herman Daly justice—he has won every prize except the Nobel Prize and I personally feel that he is overdue for that recognition. Another of his books captures the gist of his vision perfectly: _For the Common Good–Redirecting the Economy toward Community, the Environment, and a Sustainable Future_. While I credit Donella and Dennis Meadows and oft-forgotten co-author Jorgen Randers with first establishing a simple formula and a simple public understanding of how the big pieces are connected, in their 1970's book _The Limits to Growth_, it was Daly who did the heavy lifting that leads us now to the non-negotiable need to establish "true cost" for every product and service as a means of enabling "360 degree" evaluation of the "net loss" or "net gain" to Earth and Humanity for each element. In my view, the literatures on Sustainable Design, _Cradle to Cradle_, and _Green to Gold_ concepts stem his work; he is Buckminster Fuller's alter ego.

"True Costs" are a public intelligence antidote to *Rule by Secrecy*, the practice of concealing and externalizing to the public expense many of the actual near and long-term costs of creating products and services such as pollution of the earth, toxins into the body, electromagnetic emissions into the brain, and so on. Here are just a few books representative of what can be known about corporate mis-behavior that goes unchecked by government regulation:

- *A Consumer's Dictionary of Household, Yard and Office Chemicals: Complete Information About Harmful and Desirable Chemicals Found in Everyday Home Products, Yard Poisons, and Office Polluters*

- *Blue Frontier–Dispatches from America's Ocean Wilderness*

- *High Tech Trash–Digital Devices, Hidden Toxics, and Human Health*

- *Made to Break–Technology and Obsolescence in America*

- *Pandora's Poison–Chlorine, Health, and a New Environmental Strategy*

- *The Blue Death–Disease, Disaster, and the Water We Drink*

- *The Next Catastrophe–Reducing Our Vulnerabilities to Natural, Industrial, and Terrorist Disasters*

- *The Unhealthy Truth: How Our Food Is Making Us Sick – And What We Can Do About It*

These are a small sample from my larger categories where many other books are available for review at Phi Beta Iota, for example in Banks, Fed, Money, & Concentrated Wealth (40); Capitalism (Good & Bad) (130); Complexity & Catastrophe (60); and Environment (Problems) (60).

Separate from the direct externalization of costs to the public commons by corporations is the larger matter of corporations co-opting and corrupting all other organizations including government, universities, and even religions.

That is not the primary focus of this book for the simple reason that once empowered by full knowledge of "true costs," there is no power on Earth greater than that of the public exercising its informed free will. However, for the sake of perspective, below are a few books that address the pernicious pathological effect of corporations run amok when government fails to serve the public interest.

- *Acts of God–The Unnatural History of Natural Disaster in America*

- *Confessions of an Economic Hit Man*

- *Dunces of Doomsday–10 Blunders That Gave Rise to Radical Islam, Terrorist Regimes, And the Threat of an American Hiroshima*

- *Killing Hope–US Military and C.I.A. Interventions Since World War II-Updated Through 2003*

- *Legacy of Ashes–The History of the CIA*

- *Overthrow–America's Century of Regime Change from Hawaii to Iraq*

- *Shake Hands With The Devil–The Failure Of Humanity In Rwanda*

- *The Global Class War –How America's Bipartisan Elite Lost Our Future – and What It Will Take to Win it Back*

- *The Globalization of Poverty and the New World Order*

- *The Naked Capitalist*

- *The Sorrows of Empire–Militarism, Secrecy, and the End of the Republic*

- *The True Cost of Conflict/Seven Recent Wars and Their Effects on Society*

- *Weapons of Mass Instruction*

Below is reprinted with permission.

"TRUE COST" OF ONE COTTON T-SHIRT

(non-organic, foreign-made, 200 gm/7 oz/0.44 lbs)
Details of calculations at http://true-cost.re-configure.org

Water Use: 570.6 gallons, 45% irrigation water consumed (evaporated) by the cotton plant; 41% rainwater evaporated from the cotton field during the growing period; 14% required to dilute the waste water flows that result from the use of fertilizers in the field and the use of chemicals in the textile industry. Add: washing machine use after shirt purchase.

Energy Use: (kWh=kiloWatt-hours) Cotton production on irrigated land=1.42kWh, Ginning=.046kWh, Spinning=.5kWh (new machine) 1.42kWh (old machine) Weaving=1.66kWh, Finishing=4.13kWh, Making-up=.05kWh (total of 7.8 to 8kWh) 11 to 29 grams of diesel. 11g=Xinjiang to Shanghai (China rail) to L.A. Xinjiang is Chinas major cotton producing region. 29g=Tx to N. Carolina to Miami to Honduras to Miami to NYC. N. Carolina is the major thread producing region, Honduras the major shirt-knitting region, Miami the major port to ship to and from Honduras. Add: cranes, importation of pesticides & fertilizers, forklift propane, washing and drying machine use after shirt purchase (60-80% energy use in shirt life cycle is in "consumer care"). Also consider energy that went into tilling soil, planting crops, producing fuel, fertilizers, pesticides, dyes, packaging, making and repairing machines.

Emissions: (cotton can be considered carbon neutral due to absorbing more than is emitted from harvesting equipment + cotton produces oxygen), Diesel exhaust=carbon/soot, carbon monoxide, nitrous oxide, nitrogen dioxide, sulfur dioxide, carbon dioxide, volatile organic compounds=ethylene, formaldehyde, methane, benzene, phenol, acrolein, and polynuclear aromatic hydrocarbons. 90,000 cargo ships travel the ocean, and it's been stated by a UK Guardian study that 15 of the largest ships now emit as much sulfur dioxides as the world's 760 million cars.

Import & Export: $0.60-$1.05 per imported shirt (low=white, high=color), $0.57-$0.66/ lb/raw cotton/world price, $0.44-$0.55/lb US price ($0.50/lb subsidies for top US farmers, remove subsidies and world price of cotton increases 6-14%) Add: some fertilizers & pesticides are imported. US exports more cotton than any country. 3M tons exported in 2007/08, approx 40% of the world total.

Travel: (miles/est) TX to N. Carolina to Cent America to NYC=5,554 Train from Xinjiang to Shanghai, ship from Shanghai to Korea to Los Angeles=9,417 (Lubbock/CaryNC/Miami=2,400 Miami/Honduras/Miami=1876 Miami/NYC=1,278) There is a chance some cotton from TX is shipped to China, then returns to L.A. (in this case, Lubbock/L.A.=1,207 and L.A. to China to L.A.=13,038 for a total of 14,245) Add: some pesticides & fertilizers are imported

Hazards: Machinery, electricity, occupational lung disease/Byssinosis (from cotton dust), carpal tunnel syndrome (sewing), pesticide poisoning/contamination/death. 1-5M poisonings per year/20,000 deaths, Water/River contamination=USA, China, India, Pakistan, Uzbekistan, Brazil, Australia, Greece and West Africa. Mishaps during cargo transport by land and sea.

Chemicals/Toxins: (US pesticide use may have declined 77% from 1997-2007 due to biotech) Fertilizers=Nitrogen, phosphate, potash, sulfur, (insecticides most harmful to health outside of US=aldicarb, parathion, methamidophos), dicrotophos (most used) endosulfan (most used organochloride), monocrotophos, deltamethrin, herbicide, nematicide, microbicide, growth regulator, algaecide, fungicide, Fabric Process=hydrogen peroxide, detergents, dyes, urea-formaldehyde to cross-link molecules to reduce shrinkage and wrinkling/or mechanical compacting. Dyeing and printing often use compounds of iron, tin, inks containing heavy metals that require large quantities of water to wash out the dye residues. USDA 2007: 55.3M lbs of herbicide (27.7M), insecticide (8.4M), fungicide (0.1M), other (19.1M) applied to produce over 9 billion lbs of cotton=1.1g per 200g shirt. British study claims over 3 grams per shirt. China=6x more fertilizer & pesticide than growers in sub-Saharan Africa. As China's textile industry has doubled, so has the waste-water (1 in 4 of China's 1.3 billion people drink contaminated water). Global cotton production may use approx 1/3 of global pesticides.

Human Labor & Equipment: Biotech, soil prep, seeding, fertilizing, irrigation, soil testing, applying pesticide/herbicide/fungicide, harvesting (global competition ranges from handpicking, plow & oxen, vs. $250,000 picking machine), ginning/separations for foods/ oil, fiber-testing, combing, spinning, dyeing, weaving/knitting, inspection, cutting, sewing, printing, mechanics, transport, packaging, warehousing, machinery distributors, consultants, crop processors, other support services, insurance, finance/banking, standard testing, sales/ merchandising. China, India, US and Pakistan lead in cotton production.

Child cotton labor 2007-2009: Argentina, Azerbaijan, Benin, Brazil, Burkina Faso, China, Egypt, India, Kazakhstan, Kyrgyzstan, Mali, Pakistan, Paraguay, Tajikistan, Turkey, Turkmenistan, Uzbekistan, West Africa. Child wages range from zero (family debt) to 5-13 cents/kg, 50 cents/day, $1-2/12-15 hr day, $3.30-10/month

Sources: Waterfootprint.org, Textileworld.com, Reiter Machine Works, JOCsailings.com, Cotton Inc, National Cotton Council, National Institute for Occupational Safety and Health,

International Cotton Advisory Committee, National Council of Textile Organizations, Anvil, Fruit of the Loom, Pesticide Action Network, US Dept. of Agriculture, US Dept. of Labor, US International Trade Commission, Containership Register, SustainableCotton.org, Apparel Graphics Institute, Environmental Justice Foundation, Peterbuilt, Oxfam, Mississippi State Univ, International Institute for Sustainable Development, Chemical Industry Information Centre, Made-In-China.com, China Statistical Yearbook of the National Railway, China National Textile & Apparel Council, OceanAir Logistics, Books: The Travels of a T-Shirt in the Global Economy, Maritime Economics

US currency consists of 75% cotton
Concept and research produced by the non-profit/501c3 **Earth Intelligence Network**
www.earth-intelligence.net | www.phibetaiota.net |

true-cost.re-configure.org | earthintelnet@gmail.com

Ecological Economics and Moral Capitalism come together in being centered on the duality of a sustainable Earth and a sustainable Humanity. Kirkpatrick Sale offers an inspiring vision in his book _Human Scale_ but I must emphasize that the survival of Humanity is not in any way connected to the survival of what one author calls _The Resilient Earth_.

This chapter has focused on "true costs" while the next chapter focuses on human consciousness and a means for connecting every human to every other human. Then in the final chapter on "Open Everything," I wrap the book up with the big picture exploration of how we displace money and scarcity by substituting the open meme, restoring the commons as a commonwealth.

I must stress that all of these ideas that I have strung together are not mine in isolation, but rather from the minds of many others, crafted by myself into a single story, however crude, that I offer as a roadmap to our shared future.

Chapter 26

Conscious Non-Zero Evolution & Global to Local Needs Table

Common sense and communal consciousness appear to have been very well developed among the indigenous peoples of the past (Chapter 16) and within the close-knit communities of the agrarian era.

The industrial era and the commoditization of humanity destroyed kinship and the ethics of kinship. Lionel Tiger's book, *The Manufacture of Evil–Ethics, Evolution and the Industrial System*, is an early exploration of this theme. A more recent book, *The Marketing of Evil–How Radicals, Elitists, and Pseudo-Experts Sell Us Corruption Disguised As Freedom*, pursues the theme.

Now that we are beginning to understand the "true costs" of government and corporate and other organizational misbehaviors—I address this in the chapter on "Paradigms of Failure" in *ELECTION 2008: Lipstick on the Pig*—human consciousness—or cognition—is re-emergent.

There are many variations of consciousness and cognition, the best forms characterized by balance between individual fulfillment as envisioned by the Founding Fathers and communal achievement of peace and prosperity.

In this chapter, after first listing a number of books that are representative of the integrative nature of the consciousness that is emerging, I will discuss how the emergence of consciousness completely overturns the existing paradigms of secrecy, scarcity, and security as profiteering by the few at the expense of the many.

Let's begin with a listing of key books directly relevant to this discussion.

- *Conscious Evolution: Awakening Our Social Potential*
- *Evolutionary Activism by Tom Atlee*
- *Global Mind*
- *Holistic Darwinism: Synergy, Cybernetics, and the Bioeconomics of Evolution*
- *Integral Consciousness and the Future of Evolution*
- *New World New Mind—Moving Toward Conscious Evolution*
- *Nonzero—The Logic of Human Destiny*
- *Not by Genes Alone: How Culture Transformed Human Evolution*
- *The Compassionate Instinct—The Science of Human Goodness*

Most interestingly, the rise in human consciousness is directly related to the broadening of interest in civilization-building.

- *Beyond Civilization—Humanity's Next Great Adventure*
- *Rethinking Civilization: Resolving Conflict in the Human Family*
- *The Empathetic Civilization—the Race to Global Consciousness in a World of Crisis*
- *The leadership of civilization building—Administrative and civilization theory, symbolic dialogue, and citizen skills for the 21st century*

There are naturally many other relevant books. Here I do not critique a single policy of any government or corporation, nor do I summarize the above stellar contributions. This is all converging now. Revolutionary activism is here now.

Intelligence for Earth demands a mature appreciation of both the nature of intelligence as decision-support, and of the costs to the Earth and Humanity of failing to leverage intelligence (decision-support) so as to optimize outcomes for everyone. Below is a depiction of how intelligence as decision-support must mature if we are to achieve our full potential.

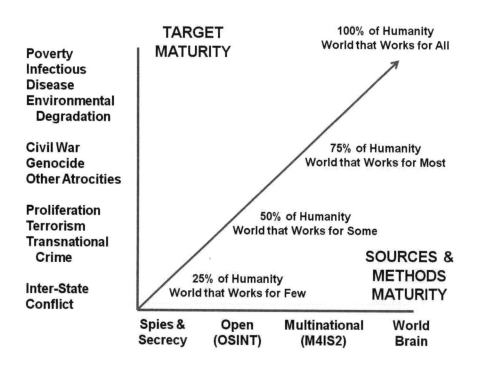

Figure 62. Intelligence Maturity Scale

The intelligence communities of the world, by virtue of being primarily focused on secrets for the top leaders of governments, have focused on armed threats rather than on humanitarian threats and related opportunities for creating a prosperous world at peace, a win-win or "non-zero" outcome beneficial to all.

The first two eras of what is traditionally known as "national intelligence" were in the first era known generally as "Secret War" or war by other means, means not attributable to the antagonist; and in the second era, the era of Sherman Kent, as "Strategic Analysis," a deliberate attempt to arrive at "best truth" using all available sources and methods including open sources of information.

The second era did not last very long—it was corrupted by the politicization of intelligence, over-whelmed by the military-industrial-congressional complex (MIC), now the military-industrial-intelligence-congressional complex (MIIC). Sherman Kent might cringe, but his righteous intent ultimately was summed up in his asking Sam Adams, upon accepting the Pentagon's demand that the Viet Cong not be counted in a guerrilla war, "have we gone beyond the bounds of reasonable dishonesty?"

"Reasonable dishonesty" sums up everything that is wrong with corrupt practices in government and in business and in foundations and other ostensibly non-profit organizations that cheat the public by consuming 50% or more of all contributions as "overhead."

The third era is one that others have thought about, but I may reasonably lay claim to with my two articles, E3i: Ethics, Ecology, Evolution, & intelligence (An Alternative Paradigm) in Whole Earth Review (Fall 1992), and Creating a Smart Nation: Strategy, Policy, Intelligence, and Information (Government Information Quarterly, 13/2, 1995). Other articles and chapters followed over time, all generally focused on reconnecting humanity with reality for constructive ends.

I call this the era of the Smart Nation in which the eight tribes of intelligence (decision-support)—Academia, Civil Society, Commercial, Government, Law Enforcement, Media, Military, and Non-Governmental Organizations—can all share information and come together to do sense-making in an open manner that achieves sustainable consensus.

Ultimately consensus leads to a rejection of the war paradigm and a general acceptance of the non-zero peace paradigm, particularly as the relative cost of war versus peace becomes obvious, as illustrated in figure 63.

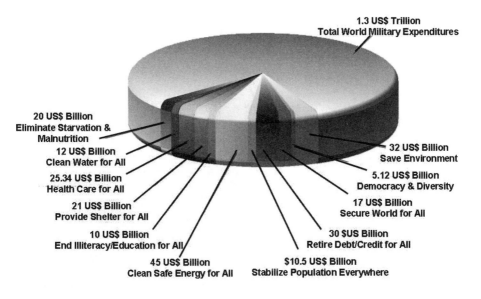

1.3 $ Trillion for War, When $227.96 Could Buy BOTH Peace AND Prosperity

Figure 63: Relative Cost of War versus Peace and Prosperity for All

I am indebted—we are all indebted, to Professor Medard Gabel, founder of BigPictureSmallWorld, inventor of the Earth Dashboard, and pioneer with Buckminster Fuller in creating the analog World Game and the concept for a digital EarthGame™ for permission to use the above illustration, forthcoming in his book, *Seven Billion Billionaires*.

On the next page, to drive this point home with respect to the United States of America (USA), I illustrate the true cost of the military to the public purse.

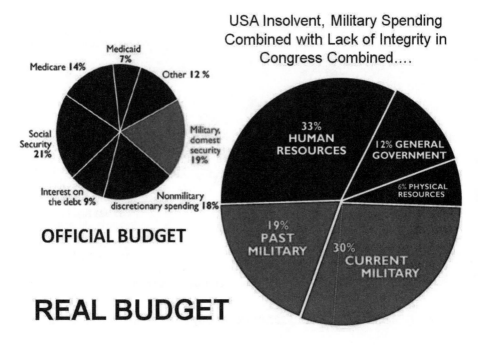

USA Insolvent, Military Spending Combined with Lack of Integrity in Congress Combined....

OFFICIAL BUDGET

REAL BUDGET

**Figure 64: The False Official Military Budget
Share versus the Real Share**

The above depiction comes from the Center for Defense Information (CDI) with the pie chart on the right focusing on actual share of disposable or non-entitlement annual expenditures by the federal government. This impeachable but consistently over-looked fraud by both the Congress and the Executive in perpetuating the myth of a "low share" military combined with the abdication of our citizens from their responsibility to hold their elected representatives accountable for clarity and integrity, have allowed the bankruptcy of the Republic, even before the twin debacles of an elective war on Iraq and an elective bail-out of Wall Street at taxpayer expense.

Taken together, Figures 63 and 64 demonstrate the impact on the public of excessive spending on military procurement and personnel and the attendant elective wars, in sharp contrast to modern needs for more responsible spending to stabilize and reconstruct the Whole Earth.

As human consciousness is expanded by a combination of more humans being connected directly to one another, something the Internet and the almost negligible cost of wireless communications are making possible, with access to more and more information as well as more and more sense-making in the public domain, I believe that there will be a sharp rejection of the war paradigm in favor of the peace paradigm. War is win-lose, peace is win-win.

OLD WAR PARADIGM   NEW PEACE PARADIGM

Obsession with Current "Intelligence" Driven By Fear & Partisan Ideology	Unilateral Aggression Without Real Diplomacy	Respect for History & Indigenous Cultural Heritage	Multinational Diversity as Primary Approach to All Challenges
Emphasis on Secrecy & Inner Circle Decisions Ignoring Congress	Spend More Making War Than Waging Peace	Open Dialog, with Clarity, that Respects All Parties	Create Infinite Stabilizing Wealth by Sharing Free Education "One Cell Call at a Time"

Bottom Line: In the 21ˢᵗ Century, Thinkers, Not Shooters, Must Predominate

Figure 65: Rejecting the War Paradigm in Favor of the Peace Paradigm

It will not be easy and it will not happen without deliberate efforts by all concerned. The final step in achieving a prosperous world at peace is that of harmonization, not just of investments as discussed in Chapters 23 and 24, but in assuring every human being their "daily bread" as found in the Lord's Prayer. We do that with a Global to Local Needs Table as illustrated below.

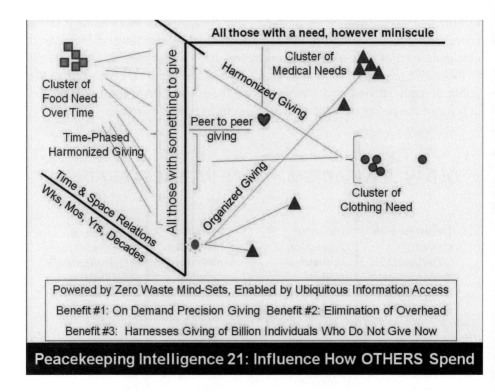

Figure 66: Global to Local Need Table Online

This table, combined with millions of volunteers online connecting the five billion poor with the one billion rich via call centers and related networks competent in 183 languages not only permits the meeting of individual needs at the item within household level, and the combination of individuals to meet a need by sharing costs of acquisition, transport, and installation, as well as the aggregation of needs for fulfillment in low-cost bulk, but it also eliminates the current fraud that diverts 50% (or more) of charity to "overhead."

Chapter 27
Open Everything

The depiction below sums up my personal view that there is a power to openness that no other force can consistently over-whelm.

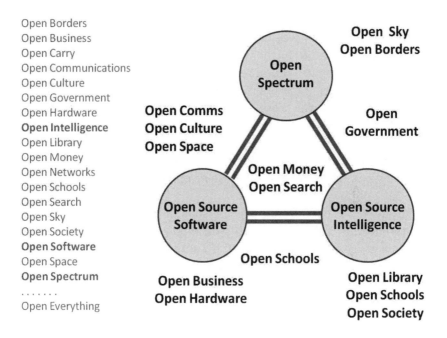

Open Borders
Open Business
Open Carry
Open Communications
Open Culture
Open Government
Open Hardware
Open Intelligence
Open Library
Open Money
Open Networks
Open Schools
Open Search
Open Sky
Open Society
Open Software
Open Space
Open Spectrum
. . . .
Open Everything

Figure 67: Open Everything

I was inspired by <u>Chris Prillo</u> and <u>Gnomedex</u>, when invited to be the opening speaker, and entitled my presentation "<u>Open Everything</u>."

The big three, the trifecta, are Free/Open Source Software (F/OSS), Open Source Intelligence (OSINT), and Open Spectrum. On the latter, I will always be indebted to both Jock Gill for his 2004 contribution Open Wireless Spectrum and Democracy that introduced me to the work of David Weinberger, and of course to David Weinberger himself, the long-time champion of Open Spectrum who contributed **Why open spectrum matters: the end of the broadcast nation** to the first book in this series, *COLLECTIVE INTELLIGENCE: Creating a Prosperous World at Peace*, and more recently, his own book, Everything Is Miscellaneous– The Power of the New Digital Disorder

In the balance of this chapter, just a few words (and a link) for each of the other Opens (there are more, these are just the ones I have focused on).

Open Borders. The only way to stop illegal immigration is to stop the global class war that continues to further impoverish the southern hemisphere while simultaneously looting its natural resources. In my view, Open Borders are a means of acknowledging the reality that we are all one humanity within one earth, and we must take those measures to stabilize and reconstruct the impoverished nations as if they were—because they are—our neighbors. Not only must we make unnecessary the "Berlin Wall" mentality that has characterized the Department of Homeland Security (DHS), but in doing so, we must make it possible to redirect all those resources to more peaceful effect.

Open Business. An open business is transparent in its accounting; respectful of all stakeholders both formal and incidentally affected; adheres to open standards and by definition, applies the earned benefits and profits for all, rather than redirecting profits created by the many toward the benefit of a few. Open businesses optimize social production with or without financial measures of merit.

Open Carry. Open carry is shorthand terminology for "openly carrying a firearm in public", as distinguished from concealed carry, where firearms cannot be seen by the casual observer. It is also called "open display". It is an inherent Constitutional right of US citizens that cannot be curtailed by local and state or federal authorities, and is the signal mark of a sovereign public.

Open Communications. I use the term to refer to both equal and open access to all forms of communication across the planet, and to the presence of clarity and integrity in all forms of communication between and among individuals and groups.

Open Culture. This concept is still under development. I use it to refer to a culture of openness that reveres diversity, rather than those fundamentalist exclusive cultures that are more cult than culture. By extension, an open culture would embrace an atmosphere of open multi-cultural information-sharing and sense-making.

Open Government. Open government is the political doctrine which holds that the business of government and state administration should be opened at all levels to effective public scrutiny and oversight. I specifically take this to mean that state secrecy must be sharply limited, and that "national security" priorities and decisions must be public in nature rather than arrived at by a small elite with its own agenda that profits from war.

Open Hardware. More commonly known as Open-Source Hardware, this refers to hardware—both physical and the code embedded therein, that is openly shared. Generative devices allow end-users to experiment and enhance, while closed devices are treated as lock boxes and not part of this open culture.

Open Library. Open Library is a project designed to create a comprehensive online database of books. It is a project of the Internet Archive. As with Open Culture, I consider this term to be under development, particularly since so much original work is now by-passing the Library of Congress cataloguing system and being shared directly. As strongly as I feel about knowledge as the commons of the era, it must be said that organizations such as Google that seek to copyright that which they digitize, and particularly the work of "dead souls," are not to be trusted nor rewarded—I hold Google in disdain for its lack of ethics and the manner in which is does great evil while pretending otherwise.

Open Money. This term has been ably pioneered by <u>Michael Linton, Eric Harris-Braun, Jean-François Noubel</u>, among others, and it has extraordinary potential as a tool for restoring commonwealth. Below is the illustration created by the pioneers to substantially expand what some might call intangible wealth.

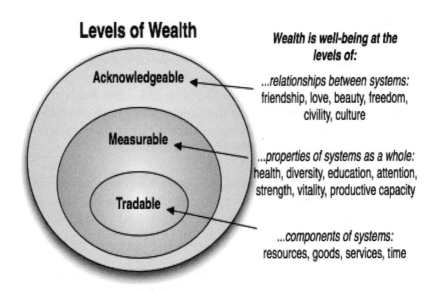

Figure 68: Open Money Wealth-Acknowledgement System

The pioneers have been careful in stating that their wealth-acknowledgement system in an information system. While various forms of software and hardware and metrics are under development, the most common practical application is one that is community-based. <u>Interra</u>, a credit card that by common consent returns a percentage to the specific community that adopts it, is one example.

Open Networks. This also is a term in its infancy. I put forth as a proposed definition infrastructure independence, such as Haggle and FreeNet. In the ideal, as with ham radio operators of the past, point to point without a hub.

Open Schools. Not to be confused with any particular program or technology, I offer this term to describe a future in which anyone can learn anything free, and knowledge rather than credentialing is the measure of a person. I particularly believe that education, intelligence (decision-support), and research must be understood, managed, and appreciated as a whole, and that Open Schools, the Open Library, and all the other Opens come together to create the World Brain.

Open Search. I recognize with the link the open-search initiative, proposes to build a distributed, peer-to-peer, search-engine. By combining the already existing technologies of peer-to-peer file storage, distributed crawling and peer-to-peer searching, the imitative hopes to solve the problems inherent to a centralized search-engine: manipulation, censorship and profiling. I acknowledge Grub as such an effort, and I specifically repudiate Google for its programmable search engines that produce what someone else has paid to place before the searcher rather than the best available response on merit. In the ideal, every individual should own and control their content from the point of creation, and that point should also be the participating entity in globally distributed search or Open Search.

Open Sky. More commonly known as Open Skies, the treaty entered into force on January 1, 2002, and currently has 34 States Parties. It establishes a program of unarmed aerial surveillance flights over the entire territory of its participants. The treaty is designed to enhance mutual understanding and confidence by giving all participants, regardless of size, a direct role in gathering information about military forces and activities of concern to them. Open Skies is one of the most wide-ranging international efforts to date promoting openness and transparency of military forces and activities. I believe that Google Earth has been a positive contribution, but that Google's willingness to conspire with governments to conceal specifics on command has been a form of harm to the public that should be condemned. As micro-UAVs (Unmanned Aerial Vehicles) become commodities, I anticipate that the public will gain access to all skies, and this will be liberating in the same way that cell phone videos of abusive law enforcement and other persons can be.

Open Society. The open society is a concept originally developed by philosopher Henri Bergson. In open societies, government is responsive and tolerant, and political mechanisms are transparent and flexible. The state keeps no secrets from itself in the public sense; it is a non-authoritarian society in which all are trusted with the knowledge of all. Political freedoms and human rights are the foundation of an open society. In Karl Popper's definition, found in his two-volume book *The Open Society and Its Enemies*, he defines an "open society" as one which ensures that political leaders can be overthrown without the need for bloodshed, as opposed to a "closed society", in which a bloody revolution or coup d'état is needed to change the leaders.

Open Space. Open Space Technology (OST) as devised by Harrison Owen is an approach for hosting meetings, conferences, corporate-style retreats and community summit events, focused on a specific and important purpose or task — but *beginning* without any formal agenda, beyond the overall purpose or theme. Highly scalable and adaptable, OST has been used in meetings of 5 to 2,100 people. The approach is characterized by five basic mechanisms: (1) a broad, open invitation that articulates the purpose of the meeting; (2) participant chairs arranged in a circle; (3) a "bulletin board" of issues and opportunities posted by participants; (4) a "marketplace" with many breakout spaces that participants move freely between, learning and contributing as they "shop" for information and ideas; and (5) a "breathing" or "pulsation" pattern of flow, between plenary and small-group breakout sessions.

The possibilities are infinite.

Chapter 28
Conclusions & Recommendations

Conclusions

Recommendations

The complexity of the Earth and Humanity cannot be addressed with a constellation of closed systems that fail in ways that cannot be diagnosed nor corrected.

F/OSS, OSINT, and Open Spectrum allow for the creation of an infinitely scalable constellation of "open" solutions that can be enhanced and shared by any and all.

The "elite" cannot comprehend the reality of local needs and possibilities in the same way that the engaged public can—only the public can prioritize its own needs.

Participatory Budgeting, when combined with the pedagogy of freedom, enables the harnessing of all stakeholders and their knowledge for the good of all.

Humanity has but one Commons— the Earth, and must rapidly transform itself so as to expand, save, and share the Commons. It can do this by harmonizing investments using shared information to eliminate waste.

The great demographic powers— Brazil, China, India, and Indonesia, must join with others such as the USA and Russia, Malaysia and Turkey, the Congo and South Africa, to create the World Brain and the Global Game.

Ecological intelligence—the awareness by each individual or organization of the "true cost" of any given product or service or supply ingredient, is the only means of reducing global waste patterns.

The public, not the government, must take the lead and use its powers, including Twitter, to discover and disseminate the "true cost" of every product and service so as to inform all stakeholders.

The only inexhaustible resource we have is the human brain and the vision and imagination that can be brought to bear by humans as individuals and in the aggregate.

The cost of war is three times the cost of peace and prosperity. The cost of the military within the budget of the USA is easily five to ten times greater than is normally acknowledged.

No amount of confiscated wealth can meet the needs of the five billion poor. At the same time, 80% of the billion rich do not give to charity or directly to the poor. In evaluating the needs of the poor and the means to eradicate poverty, the number one high-level threat to humanity, we conclude that providing the poor with connectivity—a cell phone— and access to information "one cell call at a time," is the means we seek.

Education, Intelligence, and Research must be re-directed to optimize the global to local challenges and benefits of sharing information among all parties.

The informed public—a Nation's best defense according to Thomas Jefferson—must demand that government cease spending that is inconsistent with the public interest.

A Global Range of Needs Table that is online and infinitely scalable from nano-needs at the house- hold level to regional needs for water purification and desalination plants, can enable the harnessing of all possible contributions by both individuals and organizations in new ways that combine a giver, a transporter, a deliverer, and a verifier. The priority should be free cell phones to the five billion poor, backed up with call centers.

Epilogue

If I had to name a handful of leaders who in my estimation have done more than all others to prepare civil society for a future of peace and prosperity, emphasizing two who are alive today and who I consider the "matched pair" that has defined my worldview as an adult, I would have no difficulty naming names: Nelson Mandela of the Republic of South Africa, and Lee Kuan Yew of the Republic of Singapore.

Truth & Reconciliation, in my view, is co-equal to Mahatma Gandhi's concept for non-violent resistance as embodied by Martin Luther King and his followers. It shames me to know that Martin Luther King was murdered by the government he sought to uplift by reconnecting it to the principles of life, liberty, and the pursuit of happiness for all its citizens. From Nelson Mandela I learned that no amount of reconciliation can be achieved without the truth to make it an *authentic reconciliation*. The truth at any cost reduces all other costs, and helps end the cycle of violence among humans who have more in common regardless of race than any living species.

Demography not Democracy, is my lesson from Minister-Mentor Lee Kuan Yew. I graduated from the Singapore American High School, and it says a great deal that our two class heroes were John Wayne and Lee Kuan Yew—one cannot invent such a perfect pairing. Demography is reality, democracy is inherently corrupt as it is practiced now. This in no way yields the future to those who dictate and loot the fortunes of their publics, but rather it acknowledges the intellectual and ethical primacy of demography over democracy—it is more important to assure the integrity of the public body—its education, its ethics, its evolution—than it is to play the theatrical farce of a White House sleeping with Saudi despots and cravenly begging from Wall Street financiers, while betraying the public trust. *Authentic democracy* must respect the demography of Brazil, China, India, and Indonesia, particularly. *St.*

Glossary

24/7	24 hours a day, 7 days a week	CBRN	Chemical, Biological, Radiological, Nuclear
9/11	September 11	CCASG	Cooperation Council for
AF	Arria Formula		the Arab States of the
AID	Agency for International		Gulf
	Development (US)	CCC	Coalition Coordination
AIDS	Acquired		Center (USCENTCOM)
	Immunodeficiency	CDI	Center for Defense
	Syndrome		Information
AO	Action Officer	CE	Combat Engineers
AO	Aerial Observer	CE	Conscious Evolution
Arab League	League of Arab States	CEN SAD	Community of Sahel-
ASEAN	Association of Southeast		Saharan States (AU)
	Asian Nations	CEO	Chief Executive Officer
ASG-DS	Assistant Secretary	CI	Collective Intelligence
	General for Decision-	CI	Counterintelligence
	Support (UN)	CIA	Central Intelligence
AU	African Union		Agency
B	Billion	CINC	Commander-in-Chief
BENELUX	Belgium, Netherlands,	CINCCENT	Commander-in-Chief
	Luxembourg		USCENTCOM
BMW	Bayerische Motoren	CIO	Chief Information Officer
	Werke	CIS	Commonwealth of
C&SC	Command & Staff College		Independent States
C/O	Case Officer (Clandestine	CMOC	Civil-Military Operations
	Service)		Center
C3I3H3	Command,	CO2	Carbon Monoxide
	Communications,	COG	Continuity of Government
	Computing; Interagency,	COMESA	Common Market for
	Interdisciplinary, Inter-		Eastern and Southern
	Operability, Heuristics		Africa (AU)
	(Cube) of the Community	CPI	Center for Public
	Intelligence Cycle		Intelligence
CA	Civil Affairs	CRS	Coordinate Reference
CATALYST	Computer Aided Tools for		System
	the Analysis of Science &	CS	Cognitive Science
	Technology	CSTO	Collective Security Treaty
			Organization

CTBTO	Preparatory Commission for the Nuclear-Test-Ban Treaty Organization
DARPA	US Defense Advanced Research Projects Agency
DefAtt	Defense Attaché
DESA	Department of Economic and Social Affairs
DFS	Department of Field Support
D-GA	Democrat-Georgia
DGACM	Department for General Assembly and Conference Management
DIA	Defense Intelligence Agency
DIOSC	Defense Intelligence Open Source Center
DM	Department of Management
DocEx	Document Exploitation
DoD	US Department of Defense
DPA	Department of Political Affairs (UN)
DPI	Department of Public Information
DPKO	Department of Peacekeeping Operations
DSS	Department of Safety and Security
DTG	Date Time Group
E3i	Ethics, Ecology, Evolution, and intelligence (not secret)
EAC	East African Community (AU)
ECA	Economic Commission for Africa
ECCAS	Economic Community of Central African States (AU)
ECE	Economic Commission for Europe

ECLAC	Economic Commission for Latin America and the Caribbean
ECOWAS	Economic Community of West African States (AU)
EEI	Essential Elements of Information
EIN	Earth Intelligence Network
EISAS	
EOSG	Executive Office of the Secretary General (UN)
ERC	Emergency Relief Coordinator
ESCAP	Economic and Social Commission for Asia and the Pacific
ESCWA	Economic and Social Commission for Western Asia
EU	European Union
EWCP	Early Warning and Contingency Planning Units
F/OSS	Free/Open Source Software
FAC	Forward Air Controller
FAO	Food and Agriculture Organization of the United Nations
FIU	Field Information Unit
G	Gram
GA	General Assembly
GAO	US Government Accountability Office
GDP	Gross Domestic Product
GIS	Geographic Information System
GPI	Genuine Progress Indicator
GPS	Geographic Position System
GSA	US General Services Administration

GV2TN	Global Volunteer Virtual Translation Network	IJIC	International Journal of Intelligence and Counterintelligence
HAARP	High-Frequency Active Auroral Research Program	ILO	International Labour Organization
HABITAT	UN Human Settlements Programme	IMF	International Monetary Fund
HEWS	Humanitarian Early Warning System	IMINT	Imagery Intelligence
HIC	Humanitarians Information Capability	IMO	International Maritime Organization
HIV	Human Immuno Deficiency Virus	IMTF	Integrated Mission Task Force (UN)
HOPE	Hackers on Planet Earth	INSTRAW	UN International Research and Training Institute for the Advancement of Women
Hr	Hour		
HTT	Human Terrain Team		
HUMINT	Human Intelligence		
I&W	Indications & Warning	INT	Intelligence
IAEA	International Atomic Energy Agency	IO	Information Operations
		IOU	I Owe You
IBRD	International Bank for Reconstruction and Development	IR	Infra-Red
		ISI	Inter-Services Intelligence (Pakistan)
ICAO	International Civil Aviation Organization	ITC	International Trade Centre
ICC	International Computing Centre (UN)	ITSD	Information Technology Services Division (UN)
		ITT	Interrogator-Translator Team
ICRC	International Committee of the Red Cross	ITU	International Telecommunication Union (ITU);
ICSID	International Centre for Settlement of Investment Disputes		
		J-23	OSINT Branch, USSOCOM
ICT	Information and Communication Technologies	JFCOM	US Joint Forces Command
		JFK	John Fitzgerald Kennedy
		JMAC	Joint Military Analysis Centre
IDA	International Development Association	JOC	Joint Operations Centre
IFAD	International Fund for Agricultural Development	Kg	Kilogram
		kWh	Kilowatt Hours
IFC	International Finance Corporation	LA	Los Angeles
		lb	Pound (weight)
IGAD	Intergovernmental Authority on Development (AU)	LEA	Law Enforcement Agencies
		LNO	Liaison Officer

273

Ltgen	Lieutenant General	NGO	Non-Governmental
M	Million		Organization
M4IS2	Multinational Multiagency	NIO	National Intelligence
	Multidisciplinary		Officer
	Multidomain Information-	NL	Netherlands, The
	Sharing and Sense-	NORAD	Northern Air Defense
	Making		Command
MAG	US Military Advisory	NRBC	Nuclear, Radiological,
	Group		Biological, & Chemical
MB	Mega-byte	NSA	US National Security
MCIC	Marine Corps Intelligence		Agency
	Center (today a	NSC	National Security Council
	Command)	NSSM	National Security Study
MCU	Marine Corps University		Memorandum
MD	Medical Doctor	OAS	Organization of American
MDSC	Multinational Decision-		States
	Support Centre	OCHA	Office for the
ME	Multinational		Coordination of
	engagement		Humanitarian Affairs
MIC	Military-Industrial	ODA	Office for Disarmament
	Complex		Affairs (UN
MIGA	Multilateral Investment	OIT	Office of Information
	Guarantee Agency		Technology (CIA)
MIIC	Military-Industrial-	OMB	US Office of Management
	Intelligence Complex		and Budget
MINUSTAH	UN Stabilization Mission	OODA	Observe, Orient, Decide,
	in Haiti		Act
MLK	Martin Luther King	OOTW	Operations Other Than
MP	Military Police		War
MPS	Military Planning Service	OPCW	Organisation for the
	(DPKO)		Prohibition of Chemical
NAFTA	North American Free		Weapons
	Trade Agreement	ORCI	Office for Research
NASA	National Aeronautical and		and the Collection of
	Space Administration		Information (UN)
NATO	North Atlantic Treaty	OSA	Open Source Agency
	Organization	OSIF	Open Source Information
NBC	Nuclear, Biological,	OSINT	Open Source Intelligence
	Chemical	OSS	Open Source Solutions
NCTC	US National		Network, Inc.
	Counterterrorism Center	OST	Open Space Technology
NEO	Non-Combatant	OSWR	Office of Scientific and
	Evacuation Operation		Weapons Research (CIA)

PAP	Pan-African Parliament (AU)	SG	Secretary General
PB	Participatory Budgeting	SICA	Central American Integration System
PfP	Partnership for Peace (Eastern Europe, with NATO)	SIGINT	Signals Intelligence
		SIPR	Secure Internet Protocol Router
PhD	Doctor of Philosophy	SME	Subject-Matter Expert
PIF	Pacific Islands Forum	SMS	Short Message Service
PKO	Peacekeeping Operations	SOLIC	Special Operations and Low Intensity Conflict
PMC	Private Military Contractors	SPU	Strategic Planning Unit (SPU)
POE	Peace Operations Extranet	SRS	Spatial Reference System
POW	Prisoner of War	SSI	Strategic Studies Institute (US Army)
PSC	Peace and Security Council (PSC)	TCM	Traditional Chinese Medicine
R&D	Research & Development		
REC	Regional Economic Commission	TECHINT	Technical Intelligence
		TOOZL	One-Ounce Laptop (STRONG ANGEL)
REG	Regular (Budget)		
RMDSC	Regional Multinational Decision-Support Centre	TX	Texas
		UAV	Unmanned Aerial Vehicle
RN	Royal Navy	UK	United Kingdom
RSO	Regional Security Officer (US Department of State)	UMA	Arab Maghreb Union (AU)
		UN	United Nations
S&R	Stabilization & Reconstruction	UNAIDS	Joint United Nations Programme on HIV/AIDS
S&T	Science & Technology	UNASUL	Union of South American Countries (Portuguese)
SA (V)	Specialized Agencies (Voluntary Contributions)		
SA(A)	Specialized Agencies (Assessed)	UNASUR	Union of South American Countries
		UNCCD	United Nations Convention to Combat Desertification
SAARC	South Asian Association for Regional Cooperation		
SADC	Southern Africa Development Community (AU)	UNCDD	Convention on the Rights of Persons with Disabilities
SASC	Senate Armed Services Committee	UNCDF	UN Capital Development Fund
SCO	Shanghai Cooperation Organisation	UNCTAD	UN Conference on Trade and Development
SEATO	Southeast Asia Treaty Organization	UNDCP	UN Drug Control Programme

UNDEF	United Nations Democracy Fund	UNRWA	UN Relief and Works Agency for Palestine Refugees in the Near East
UNDP	UN Development Programme	UNSAS	United Nations Stand-by Arrangement System
UNEP	UN Environmental Programme	UNSSC	United Nations System Staff College
UNESCO	United Nations Educational, Scientific and Cultural Organization	UNU	United Nations University
		UNV	UN Volunteers
UNFCCC	United Nations Framework Convention on Climate Change	UNWTO	World Tourism Organization (UN)
		UPU	Universal Postal Union
UNFIP	United Nations Fund for International Partnerships	US IC	US Intelligence Community
UNFPA	UN Population Fund	USA	United States of America
UNHCR	Office of the United Nations High Commissioner for Refugees	USAF	US Air Force
		USB	Universal Serial Bus
		USCENTCOM	US Central Command
		USG	US Government
UNICEF	UN Children's Fund	USIA	US Information Agency
UNICRI	UN Interregional Crime and Justice Research Institute	USMC	US Marine Corps
		USMC	US Marine Corps
		USS	US Ship
UNIDIR	UN Institute for Disarmament Research	USSOCOM	US Special Operations Command
UNIDO	United Nations Industrial Development Organization	UZAN	Union of South American Countries (Dutch)
		WFP	UN Food Program
UNIFEM	UN Development Fund for Women	WHO	World Health Organization
UNITAR	UN Institute for Training and Research	WIPO	World Intellectual Property Organization
UNODIN	UN Open-Source Decision-Support Information Network	WMD	Weapons of Mass Destruction
		WMO	World Meteorological Organization
UNOPS	United Nations Office for Project Services	WOG	Whole of Government
UNPROFOR	United Nations Protection Force	WTO	World Trade Organization
UNRISD	UN Research Institute for Social Development		

Annotated Bibliography

I had intended to list the individual titles so each could be selected from the online version (and so readers of the hard-copy could understand the decade of thinking by others that contributed to this book), but it ran toward 30 pages and would have increased the book size and cost by 10%. So instead, I list here the categories and in parenthesis the number of books in each category. The lists below are the "good news" categories and do not repeat all the books listed in Chapter 20. The list of lists with all links active can be directly accessed at http://www.phibetaiota.net/?cat=2796 .

Africa (4)
Analysis & Problem-Solving (62)
Atlases (6)
Bio-Economics (32)
Capitalism Reincarnated (16)
China (7)
Civilization-Building (6)
Collective Intelligence (16)
Common Wealth (26)
Conscious, Evolutionary, Integral
    Activism & Goodness (33)
Dialog for Truth & Reconciliation (27)
Diversity of Voices & Values
    (Other than USA) (46)
Diversity of Voices & Values (USA) (46)
Education for Freedom
    & Innovation (19)

Evolutionary Dynamics (14)
Future (9)
Health (3)
History (10)
Innovation (28)
Leadership for Epoch B (29)
Peace (20)
Philosophy (6)
Priorities (11)
Self-Determination & Secession (7)
Stabilization & Reconstruction (17)
Strategy (23)
Technology & Web 2.0 to 4.0 (30)
Visualization (8)
World Brain and Mind (6)
Universe (5)